D0744511

CALGARY PUBLIC LIBRARY

OCT   2011

THE ESSENCE OF
BUDO

THE ESSENCE OF
BUDO

The Secret Teachings of the Grandmaster

Masaaki Hatsumi

TRANSLATED BY
Doug Wilson, Bruce Appleby,
Craig Olson, and Paul Masse

KODANSHA INTERNATIONAL
Tokyo · New York · London

神火変風順逆不動心吽

TENSHIN-SHINYO-RYU
天真真揚流

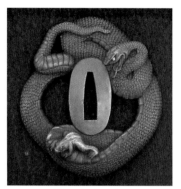

Picture by the author

鎬リ返シ

裏手返

鯉腹切

（図）直チニ（肉）ノ上段ニ
振上ケタルトキニ同
人ハ右鯉腹ヲ透キ
有主我左足ヲ右足ト
踏ミ出シ体ヲカワシテ
ト共ニ右ニ切ルナリ
（肉）ハ右足後ヘ下ゲ切
込ム長巻ヲ上段ヨリ
ヤート答ヘテハズシ
受止メ図ノ如クスル
ナリ

（図）ハ此ノ時直ニ太
刀ヲ正ニアテタル拳
故我ガ腰ヲ引右
足ヲ後ヘ引テ下腹ニ
カワシ又直チニ
長刀ノ刃ニテ
ノ右横直ニ図ノ如ク
切付ルナリ
（肉）ハ此ノトタンニ太
刀ノ右ヘヤート返シ
ラ又ヲ受止ルナリ
受止タル太刀ヲ右道
ニ右ヘヤート返シ

片手上段

（肉）ハ両足ヲ揃ヘテ
右ハ一流ガシ刀ヲ
図ノ如ク両手ニテ
シカト受止ルナリ
此ノ気ヲ能ク吞ヲ
ミ込ミ図ノ如クノ
スヘシ

（長）ハ（肉）ノ右ハ太刀ガ
流ルヽ透アルニニ
スグ両足ヲ揃ヘテ
長巻ヲ両手ニテ上段
ニ振リ上ゲ（図）ノ直句
ニ折リ下ストタンニ太
刀ノ直ニ下ス
足ヲ後ヘ引テ下タ
ト共ニ切ルヽハ第一図
腹ヲカワシエル
ノ如ク又第二図見
合スヘシ

此ハ圖ヨリ太刀ノ方ヘ
掛引有ルナリ
ノ態ト透ヲ見セテ元
ノ出ス所ヘ長巻
ノ切ヲ下向ニシテ敵
ノ顔ヲ見ナガラ
タチくヽト此ノ圖ヨリ
セシ因ノ圖ヨリ
真向ヲ直ニ向ヘヨリ切ル
一三足四足下ル軍圖
ニ随ヒ三足四足ヲ追
ヒ敵ヲ直ヘヨリ切ル
ル心組ナリ

此時圖ハ右ノ元ノ所ニ
立止リ右ノ手ニテ
長刀ヲ圖ノ如キ位ノ
所ヲ捕ミ敵ノ顔ヲ
見込ムナリ 又肉ハ
尺余ノ間ニテ
立止リタル時
我レニモ油断セス
直ニ圖ヲ右足ヲ
進ハ上段ヨリ切
リ勢ヒヲ見ヤセンナリ

長ハ肉ノ陰蓑ニミヱキ有
故ニ直ニ左ノ足ヲ一歩
踏出シ長巻ヲ真ニ
引返シ鑓ヲ明門
ト男太陰蓑一突タリ
圖ノ如クナス肉ハ突出ス
鑓ヲ打タヨリ右ヘ
打捕ヒシ此ト久君
足ヲ後一引クコト圖ノ
如クナリ

長ハ此時肉ノ足ニ透有
ル故ニ直ニ長刀ヲ車ノ如
クニ左ノ足ヲ進ナ踏ミ
出シ敵ノ右足ヲ切込
ム事圖ノ如クナリ
肉モ又直ニ右足ヲ後
一足引ヤ直ニ受止ル
ナリ 又モ二圖ヲ見ル
ベシ
圖ハ又右ノ足ヲ踏ミ
出シ長巻ノ柄ノ真
中程ニテ

圖ハ又ヲ因ノ左リ横
顔ニツキ有ルヨリ右
足ニ一歩ニ踏ミ込ミ
此トタンニ長刀ヲ
返シ長巻ノ又ノ
大ニテ因ノ左ノ横
面ヲヌイト共ニ切ノ
入ル因ハ此時両足
ヲ揃ヘテ前ノ半ヲ
上段ノ如クヤート
声ト共ニ受止メ
回ノ如クニナスベシ

廻リ返シ敵ノ左リ足ヲ
切込ハ又因ハ左リ足
ヲ一足後ヘ引キ
回ノ如ク後止ナリ
此所ハ一寸口伝ニ相
成ニ書ニモ認
回ニモ認

又因ハ第一回ノ如ク
廻リ庭シテ敵ノ左足
ヲ切込ム故ニ因ハ又
同ジク左足ヲ引テ受
止ルナリ即チ一回ト
三回ハ同ジ囲

昭和三十五年 二月五日 立春
天神真楊流 師範
初見良昭

此レ九手尾〆長巻之形ト云

二回ノ如ク圖ヨリ因ノ真向ヲ
塊ヲ割ル心持ニテ
ヌイト腰ヨリスヘニ
切込ムナリ
大刀ハ我体ヲカハシ
長巻ノ空ヲ切セ
太刀ニテ其功先ヲ
打チ押付ルヽセリ

圖ハ前ノ半半上段ノ
心モチニテ長刀ヲ振リ
上ケテ敵ノ直向ヘ平イ
ト打落ス此時左足
シ一足後ヘ引キ右手近
シ下腹ニ力ヲ入レナリ
因ハ軍切ニ三度足
ヲ切込ミタルヲ受止
シ大直ニ上段ニ振上ケ
左足ヲ少シ後ヘ引
キ敵ノ切先ヲ見
込ナガテニシテ
体力ル

CONTENTS

CHAPTER 4
Heart, Technique, and Body   161

NOTE FROM THE PUBLISHER

This book is presented only as a means of preserving a unique aspect of the heritage of the martial arts. Neither the publisher nor the author makes any representation, warranty, or guarantee that the techniques described or illustrated in it will be safe or effective in any self-defense situation or otherwise. Readers may be injured if they apply or train in the techniques illustrated. To minimize the risk of injury, nothing described in this book should be undertaken without personal and expert instruction. In addition, a physician should be consulted before deciding whether to attempt any of the techniques described. Federal, state, or local law may prohibit the use or the possession of any of the weapons described or illustrated in this book. Specific self-defense responses illustrated in these pages may not be justified in any particular situation or applicable under federal, state, or local law. Neither the publisher nor the author makes any representation or warranty regarding the legality or appropriateness of any weapon or technique mentioned in this book.

The names of modern and contemporary Japanese appear in the Western order, while those of historical figures (pre-1868) are written in the traditional order: surname preceding given name.

Edited in cooperation with Musashi Editorial Ltd., and Matt Cotterill.

Photos by Norio Tsuburaoka, Sheila Haddad, Paul Masse, Isabel Benchetrit, Justyn Olby, Naoto Suzuki, and Kyuzo Akashi.

Distributed in the United States by Kodansha America, LLC, and in the United Kingdom and continental Europe by Kodansha Europe Ltd.

Published by Kodansha International Ltd., 17–14 Otowa 1-chome, Bunkyo-ku, Tokyo 112–8652.

Copyright © 2011 by Masaaki Hatsumi.
Translation 2011 by Doug Wilson, Bruce Appleby, Craig Olson, and Paul Masse.
All rights reserved. Printed in Japan.
ISBN 978–4–7700–3107–5

First edition, 2011
20 19 18 17 16 15 14 13 12 11   10 9 8 7 6 5 4 3 2 1

www.kodansha-intl.com

CHAPTER 1

What Do We Mean by Essence?

What is the Essence?

There is an expression: "infinite changes, no surprise." How old is the universe? Recently it has been said to be 13.7 billion years old. I feel that things of tradition, things loaded with history, concepts that could be called life and death, light and darkness, the life force of a flash of DNA, should be closely studied precisely because they have survived.

But these things do not exceed an instant in the long years of human existence. Consider the image of flint striking stone to become fire. Through the connection between the flames (from a flint and stone), change (henka 変化), which can also be read as changing flames (henka 変火), evolved from the first flame to the second flame, the third, fourth, and fifth flame; and is like that which causes birth and death or change between wood, fire, earth, metal, and water. Through this we can glimpse part of the "change" which is contained within the essence. The crucial thing for humankind when handling fire is to know that fire is an apparition, a ghost, and we should pursue this image. The ghost of the essence appears in the writings of Sanyutei Encho (1839–1900).

As Takamatsu Sensei (1889–1972) once said: "Martial arts masters seem to make their strong points the essence of their art." The essence, or gokui, is not something specific; it is not something limited that is restricted to masters (meijin 名人) or experts (tatsujin 達人). Rather it is something that suddenly changes or mutates; it is the talent of the person who can change themselves into a dark or deep person (meijin 冥人) yet does not become a master (meijin 名人); one who drives themselves to the bone and becomes a firework (hanabi 花火) or a "hidden flower" (hanabi 花秘) (see the Japanese Noh actor and playwright Zeami).

Within the principles of the gokui there is the secret teaching of kyojitsu tenkan 虚実転換 (the interchange of truth and falsehood). However, this can also be written as Infinite falsehood, Greatness of truth (kyojitsu tenkan 虚実展観). The eyes that can penetrate the perfect wall of the azure sky, the unripe, blue-green sky, and see in the moment of divine sight are the eyes of life and death. Many who pursue the study of Budo believe the gokui, or essence, is victory—but this is not the case. Unless you can understand the essence within failure you will not reach the true essence within victory. If we say winning is a plus, then defeat is a minus; we might say that you must know where the light is made at the meeting point of plus and minus, and when winning and losing touch the light the duality of sounds is both sharp and flat.

As Mastered by the "Great Fool" Ryokan

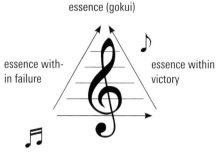

Essence (gokui 極意), has myriad interpretations and can also be written as the ultimate position (gokui 極会), the height of understanding (gokui 極異), and extreme change (igoku 異極). At the other extreme (igoku 異極) it is like a sparkling star of martial power. When people think that they have reached the ultimate goal, they can fall foul of being controlled by it. This is truly the meaning of hell (gokui! 獄意) and is to be lost on the path of the "six worlds" hell (jigoku 地獄), hungry demons (gaki 餓鬼), beasts (chikusho 畜生), fighting spirits (syura 修羅), humans (ningen 人間), and heaven (ten 天). So, change from being a great fool (taigu 大愚) to being the level of an unusual or excellent fool (myogu 妙愚). Those who attain this level, celebrated priests or humble priests, enter meditation and contemplate their situation in life.

So, let's look hard at the essence of Budo not from a different point of view but rather from our blind spot. Ryokan (1758–1831), the Zen priest renowned for his free and easy writing and his skill in waka and haiku, was said to have played with children every day, and, rejecting power and influence, called himself the great fool Ryokan. There is a saying: The soul of a three-year-old child remains the same even if you are a hundred years old. Fortune-telling also uses the law of three years. In Japan, something that is an important treasure is known as Tora no ko (虎の子); child of a tiger.

From long ago in Japan the concept of behaving foolishly was considered praiseworthy, accompanied by expressions such as "big fool," or "giant fool." Playing the big fool was not considered stupid or idiotic, but rather it demonstrated one's ability to hide words of witty escape, which were praised as clever. For example, there is the expression Gu no koccho, "the height of folly," but I would like you to understand this to mean having the "knack of foolishness." ("Gu" is also frequently used in Japanese to paraphrase the English word "Good.") Now then, even if you refer to the old books of strategy and tactics, in reality your chances in a modern battle would be low or close to nothing (kaimu 皆無) and your army might fight erratically (kaimu 皆武). However, old manga stories of heroism also play out in reality.

The reason that Ryokan called himself the "great fool" is that although he longed for the state of a great fool he could not reach this, and so he praised the the Zen-like dream vaguely (bakuzen 獏然), like the image of the mythological animal "baku," a supernatural being that devours our nightmares and dreams.

It is good to consider the subconscious truth (shinso shinri 深層心理) in the phrase

"If it won't sing let's wait for it to sing" as spoken by Ieyasu (1543–1616), who was known for his earnest way of life and diligent character, and in the phrase "Let's wait until they bite," spoken by the Chinese angler Jiang Ziya. Regarding "great foolishness," how about worn-out military men? Or those in their old age? When deeply impressed by martial arts or splendid art, a phrase is often used which goes: "That is a worn-out technique, the form is like worn-out silver." I think Takamatsu Sensei's adoption of the name Moroku came from that meaning. The warrior Musashi (1584–1645) was searching for, in Takamatsu's words, the "true spear" (shinso shinri 真鎗真理). As though to express this he drew a masterpiece portraying a shrike bird on a withered (worn-out) tree.

Essence and Tradition

There is no shortage of books written about the essence of Budo, but it is preferable to regard most of these as autobiographies of people with experience. We must not lose sight of the mystery zone of budo/bugei/strategy in which if there is too much knowledge (chishiki 知識) it becomes foolishness (chishiki 痴識).

Moreover, we must consider the fact that even the people who wrote about "essence" had experienced defeat in fighting matches. Nevertheless, these defeats became good transmissions. Indeed, it is when the defeated realize their mistakes and errors and transmit this understanding to future generations that the truth of Budo is inherited.

To go further, within the gokui, we can say that there is a way of seeing "between time" (time intervals). There are some, like Tokugawa Ieyasu, who came to rule the whole of Japan through understanding the "changing intervals" (makeru 間化る) of losing (makeru 負ける). In contrast to this, there are examples of people who work hard to always score victories, but become so intoxicated with their abilities they mistake the way of the samurai (shido 士道) and hurry to death (shido 死道).

Read the "ma" (負) of "makeru" as "fu" (the Chinese reading). "Fu" also means narrative or poetry. In other words, it is the "fu," or narrative, of a warrior (mononofu 武士). The soldier (fu 歩) in the game of Japanese chess (shogi) becomes a general. If you do not understand this transformation you have not attained manhood.

They say that a master of the martial arts once said, "Do not walk behind a horse," because there is a danger the horse will kick you. In nature there are many hidden reflex reactions, blind spots, and dead spaces. One way to avoid these is expressed by this saying about the kyojitsu of the horse's leg. We might say that this is an oral transmission regarding reflexive encounters. I keep two horses, Cookie and Tobi, and the point is to

know the nature of the horses and give them love. I have never been kicked by either of my horses.

If you read the Chinese characters "gokui" (極意) in reverse they become igoku (いごく). Yes, this is like movement "ugoku" (動く). Movement represents unlimited changes or transformations. When we are caught up by "common sense" or assumptions based on fixed, intractable thinking, the gokui is lost. On Earth are the North Pole and the South Pole. The essence of the art of war starts with North, South, East, West, and is all directions. Within the Kihon Happo is the essence of showing movement (doji igoku 動示意極), the essence of timely change in movement (doji igokui 動時移極), and also dignity manifesting the way (doji igoku 道似威極). Observe the movement in the rat, the first of the twelve signs of the Chinese Zodiac, and the igoku of the last signs. The rat is Daikokuten (the God of Wealth).

When you approach the ancient writings including those regarding Budo, if you read them with a fixed conception you will misunderstand the secrets between the type (katsuji 活字) or winning characters (katsuji 勝字) that change in multifarious ways. The writings regarding the essence are strange books (kihon 奇本) or basic books (kihon 基本); when you train by observing the teachings correctly you will naturally receive the essence in which lives the oneness of shingitai—where the basics (kihon 基本) are a living book (kihon 生本).

The Essence of the Four Heavenly Kings

I hear the distant transmission of my teacher saying, "The essence is the essence that different people make of their own strong points." In ancient times secret writings would be preserved by inscribing fragments in ancient Japanese characters. The essence of the martial ways of the schools I have inherited is blown by the winds of those times and, like Miyazawa Kenji's famous expression in the poem, "Don't be defeated by the wind or rain," these writings have continued to shine on. They continue to be conveyed after having been recorded throughout life's many hazardous situations.

If we were to liken these writings to the Four Heavenly Kings who defended the teachings of the essence we could say they are like the flow of blood of these kings. The phenomenon, or form, of this blood is like the four blood types A, B, AB, O. They are records written in blood that have continued to live by riding the four blood types. We could also liken these four types to the secret writings of Shinmei Shira. Again, let's liken them to the form of the Four Heavenly Kings. We can also say they are figures who have protected

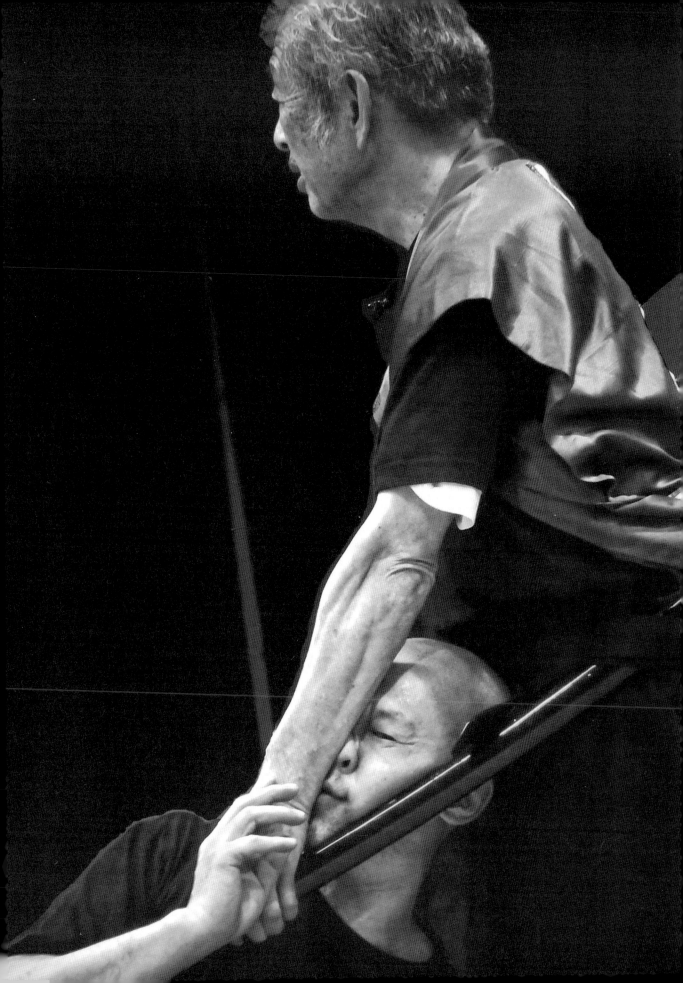

the four elements of civilization and narrators who impart the translation of the four elements of civilization.

In this book, I would like to express the essence like the greatness of the secret writings that were partially left long ago, as the radiance of a flickering light. This is because I don't believe the gokui is something that needs a long and wordy explanation. Therefore this book imparts the gokui through images and paintings rather than text.

There is No Gokui

I believe it would be right to say, "There is no gokui." Why is this? Because gokui is something which suddenly appears from the space (kukan 空間) of mindlessness (mushin 無心). The secret skill of thinking that something is there that isn't, or something is not there that is; that is the sound of zero. There are many people who say that the essence is the thickness of a piece of paper. However, the essence exists *within* the thickness of a piece of paper. You will no doubt agree with the teaching that says, "Don't talk about the gokui because you cannot fully express it." We might also say that the answer to the gokui is expressed by the gap within a sheet of paper. I will share teachings with the readers of this book by pouring my efforts into a kind of "picture book" to show those with a fresh mind (doshi 童視) or those with a kindred soul (doshi 同志).

Some scrolls enhance the explanation of the essence by adding illustrations. When writing this book on the essence I have used some "seasoned" expressions with a light or jocular feeling. We can think that the way (michi 道) or unknown terrain (michi 未地) of the gokui began at the moment we were born; no, before we were born—from the time the sperm began its long journey to find the egg. And this gives birth to the question of whether it was the egg that came first or the chicken (二羽鳥). The reason I wrote chicken with the characters for two birds is that without the male and female birds the chickens will not hatch.

Sutemi Waza ("sacrifice" techniques)

There is a word "takusu," which means "to entrust to." This concept of takusu applies to many techniques of sutemi waza. It is also similar in sound to the English word "tax." Tax is "zeikin" (税金) in Japanese. Zeikin here can also mean "wise words" (kin, 金) and "using reason to convey feelings or thoughts" (zei, 説). Zeikin is an expression of the essential element of protecting the environment, and of the "demand-guardian-economy."

Initiation into the essence comes from respect and honor of people, from person to person. It is important to be trusted and meet people that you can trust. When this idea spreads and develops into a gokui network of give and return, there will be less conflict and rivalry in the world. This idea of entrusting means to know that for us humans we do not live alone but we receive help through our connections with others. This is not limited to people but means an attitude of trusting and being trusted by living creatures and nature. Unless one has the self-awareness and the manners of a responsible person this attitude cannot be realized.

Ascetic monks visit the houses of many families begging and accepting food from those they meet (takuhatsu 托鉢). Meals in a Zen temple involve going with the bowl of compassion and charity. The monks in the Dominican order, Franciscan order, and Carmelite order advocate the path of helping people while living life by receiving alms.

What is "Truth and Falsehood"?

We often hear of Samurai (bushi 武士) or military men (bujin 武人), but what type of person is a Samurai? The 38th generation emperor Tenji Tenno (626–671), who reformed various institutions during his reign of Japan, selected healthy-bodied individuals from the peasant class with just and honorable hearts to become soldiers. The character "bu" 武 was originally written as "sei" 正, or truth, and a concept surely at the core of the military man is truth in body and mind. So we notice the fact that merely strong individuals who unjustly pursued conflict were not chosen to serve as soldiers.

There is a saying that those who have a just heart have no enemies. However, enemies do exist, and when faced by an approaching enemy one should avoid them in order not to injure them. If the situation is unavoidable, however, the true form is attained by raising one's courage to a level whereby one is prepared for death. That is to say, showing the attitude "come any time" while holding a sword in either hand is kyo (虚), illusion, and avoiding the situation is the jitsu (術), true form. Without this truth and illusion one has not mastered the martial ways of the warrior.

Here let me share an old story, a funny conversation with my teacher. When someone steps on your foot, looking for a fight, if you ask, "Is that your foot riding on mine?" the quarrel vanishes. But if by chance a quarrel should ensue, know the poem of the gokui that teaches one to bend one's back and feign disability, thus fending off a fight.

Likewise, in Taijutsu, if you show that you are about to pull, you should push, and if your opponent thinks you are going to push, then pull. Show left, and then throw right.

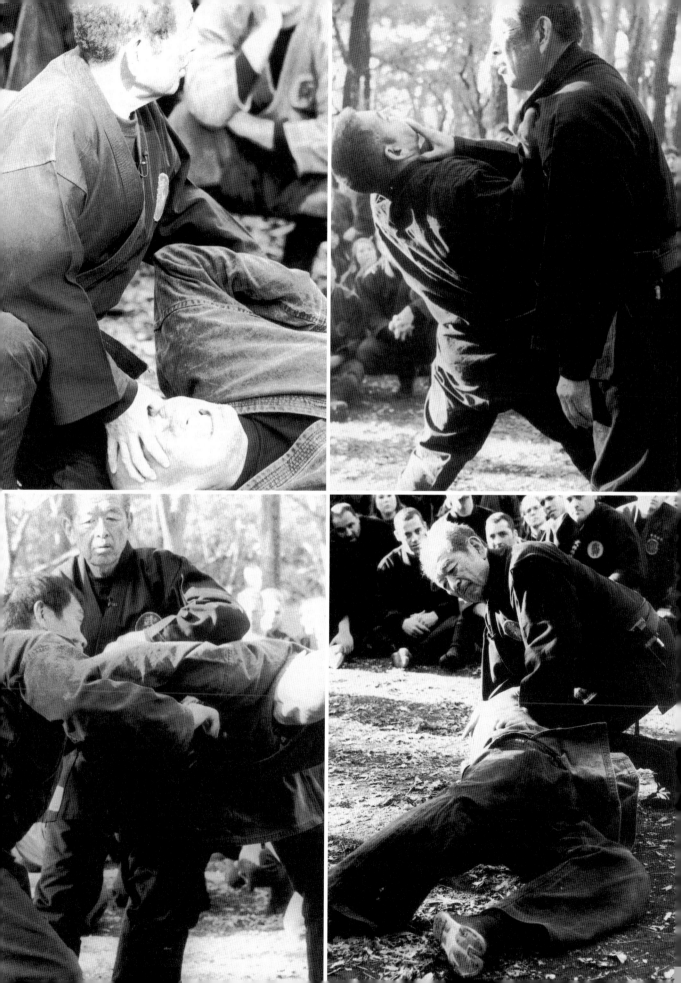

This resembles the tactics of the merchant who claims, "I would like to sell it, but at that price I won't make a profit so I cannot," and in this way negotiates a price with a good margin. This is what is meant by "the (interchange of) truth and falsehood." This kind of "deception" is allowed in the martial arts, but if you apply it too much your opponent will begin to read you. So, you should neither use it too much nor too little. Within this arise the martial ways of the essence and the ability to see through black magic and witchcraft; what appears as subtle and profound, what appears as occult. Furthermore, the ability to see the divine, supernatural, and unique or alien phenomena arises. In this way, I hope that you can grasp the gist of all the various forms and phenomena of the gokui.

And, when one encounters difficulty or danger or misfortune, consider the rotation of the cup in the tea ceremony (saji 茶事), and let us reverse that movement from clockwise to counterclockwise. In doing so, we can reverse fate and avoid danger, and we can find the essence contained in events and traditions from ancient times.

The Iron-ribbed Fan (tessen) of Martial Fortune

Around half a century has passed since I began to receive the teachings of Takamatsu Sensei. For seventy-seven years I have led an unconventional life and it seems as though I am ordained to live longer. And it feels as though I have escaped from the life in which "the way of bushido is to find death." I say this because even at this age, I have been asked by Kodansha International to write two more books!

One day, when I receive my posthumous Buddhist name, it will be declared "Hakuryu, the divine shinobi who lived eighty years!" A thankful day! The Buddha only entered Nirvana after living to the same age of eighty years. We might say this is why his teachings are still alive today. Zeami (the Japanese Noh playwright) also said that one returns to innocence at the age of eighty. The true form of the warrior is to persevere in the martial ways, and the meaning of bushido is not so much to find death (shinu 死ぬ) as to persevere as a samurai (shinu 士貫).

The famous philosophers Alain de Bottom, Carl Hilty, and Bertrand Russell, for example, wrote on the topic of happiness. However, I would like to touch on the truth and falsehood of happiness as seen by the Budoka. If, as the German philosopher Georg Wilhelm Hegel said, God is one's own consciousness, then happiness is one's own consciousness. Relish well the old martial poem, "My own heart hurts my own body, becalm the unrest in my heart."

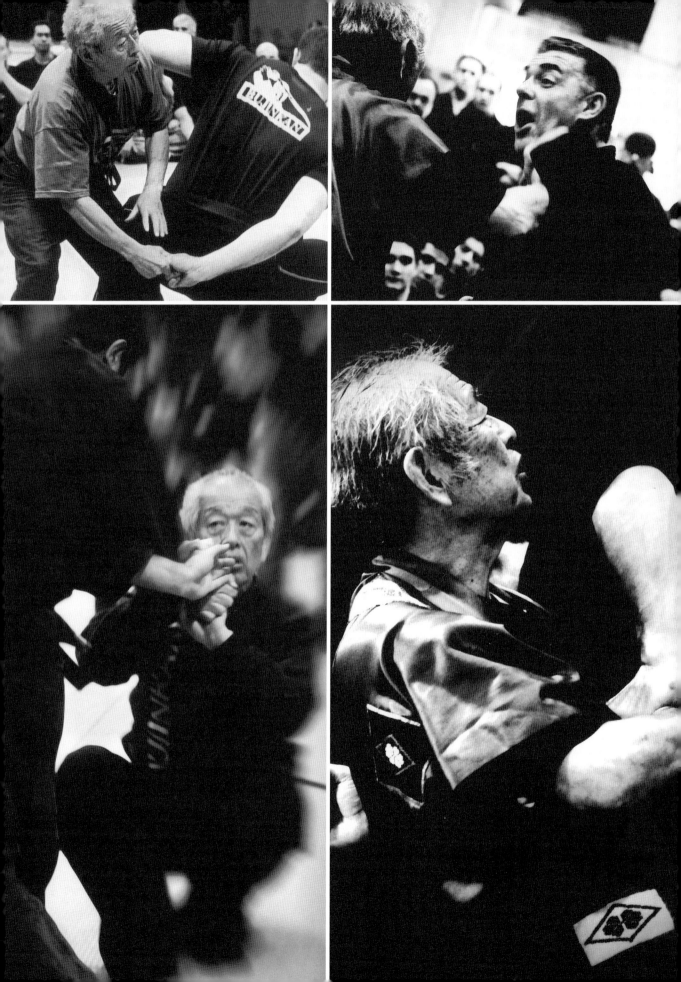

Teachings of the Way of the Warrior — The Writings of Takamatsu Sensei

Takamatsu Sensei was born the eldest son of the Takamatsu house and was raised by his stepmother as one of seven children. His stepmother also bore her own children. I have heard that Takamatsu Sensei took care of his aged stepmother to the end of her life. He explained that as her time of death drew near she clasped her hands together in thanks, saying, "I never expected that you would look after me in this way." This was where the drama of his life changed. He lived overseas in many places, including China during the Manchu reign at a time of great upheaval, enveloped in the atmosphere of the prewar days of Japan.

As for myself, I grew up with my mother and father and an elder sister. I am told I was very demanding of attention in my childhood; always wanting to be carried on my grandmother's back even when I was so big my feet almost touched the ground.

When he wasn't drinking, my father was literally a Buddha, a man with feeling who could sense the pathos of things. However, when he drank, he was a completely different man—he would swing a knife and break things in a drunken frenzy. And, in order to pin him down and get him to sleep I naturally felt the need to learn Budo. This was one of the reasons that I entered into the study of martial ways in my boyhood.

So from my childhood I was accomplished at hearing the footsteps of my drunken father coming home from a hundred paces away, hiding any dangerous objects, and taking the drawn blade that he would brandish and holding him down until he fell asleep. To this day I think of my intuitive sense that exceeds that of ordinary people as something imparted to me by my father during this time and I am grateful to him as one of my teachers in life.

In the same way, clasping my hands together and praying to the gods and Buddha also became a natural method of ascetic practice. The actor and theater director Stanislavski said, "Leave your daily existence behind"—this is something that also applies to the Bugeisha.

Immediately before and after the Second World War society changed completely. This society also made me walk the path of Budo. While walking the path of Budo I also learnt many things from the world of masterpieces. Speaking of "michi" 道—the way—there is a gesture of pathos and humor in the film *Gelsomina* played by Giulietta Masina, which I like very much. I used to gaze at the form of Marilyn Monroe that expresses the phrase of the famous kabuki actor of female roles Ayame Yoshizawa: "Hazy, dreamy . . . ." I also lost myself in the sound of Frank Sinatra's *My Way*.

My friend Shinji Soya, who is a doctor and author, has published a book called

Palpitation and Puppets. Making your road and walking it is life. Speaking of this, I am reminded of director John Huston's film noir *Asphalt Jungle.* When tobacco smoke dances in the light emitted by the projector in a movie theater immersed in that nostalgic atmosphere the theater can seem like a Noh stage. I also have the memory of quickly eating noodles walking along Fifth Avenue in New York with my friend Yoshiteru Otani. His parking ticket was only for fifteen minutes after which he would have to pay additional money, so we both ate them down in the blink of an eye. I still cannot remember what those noodles tasted of. Eating quickly is an important habit of the warrior.

Let's speak of a conversation about birds between Takamatsu Sensei and myself. Regarding birds (tori 鳥) there are the legends of the Blue Birds, the mythical Firebird Goddess, the Immortal Phoenix, and the Three-legged Crow, but there is also the "tori" or the last and most important performer who appears on the stage or in theater. This is a story of Takamatsu Sensei, my tori (training partner), and me at the age of forty-one. Takamatsu Sensei's "Guidebook to Happiness" begins with the following words:

> Everyone, let's throw away our sorrows and gain happiness. Happiness is life's greatest satisfaction. Happiness is to rethink or change one's mind by throwing away sadness and complaints. Foretelling misfortune and misery by changing our thoughts through enlightenment is also happiness.

I recall it was a cold spring day when Takamatsu Sensei handed down the transmission of Budo to me with this verse. The gokui is something that exists in all things /places and the guidebook to the gokui of Budo is also the same for all things. It is important to change one's heart when studying Budo in the correct direction.

Looking back, without the self-awareness to follow one's own compass (rashin 羅針) or one's naked heart (rashin 裸心) there would have been no gokui of Budo or gokui of happiness. In the next part I will share with you the words from a dialogue with Takamatsu Sensei.

The Heart of Justice

Firstly, how shall we think of the gods and Buddha? There are great men of history that are thought of as gods or buddhas after death, but people do not believe in them; rather they worship or admire them, and saying that they are the physical personification of a god is nothing more than a way to teach people of hundreds or thousands of years ago.

Gods (kami) and the Buddha should be entities who urge people to admonish natural

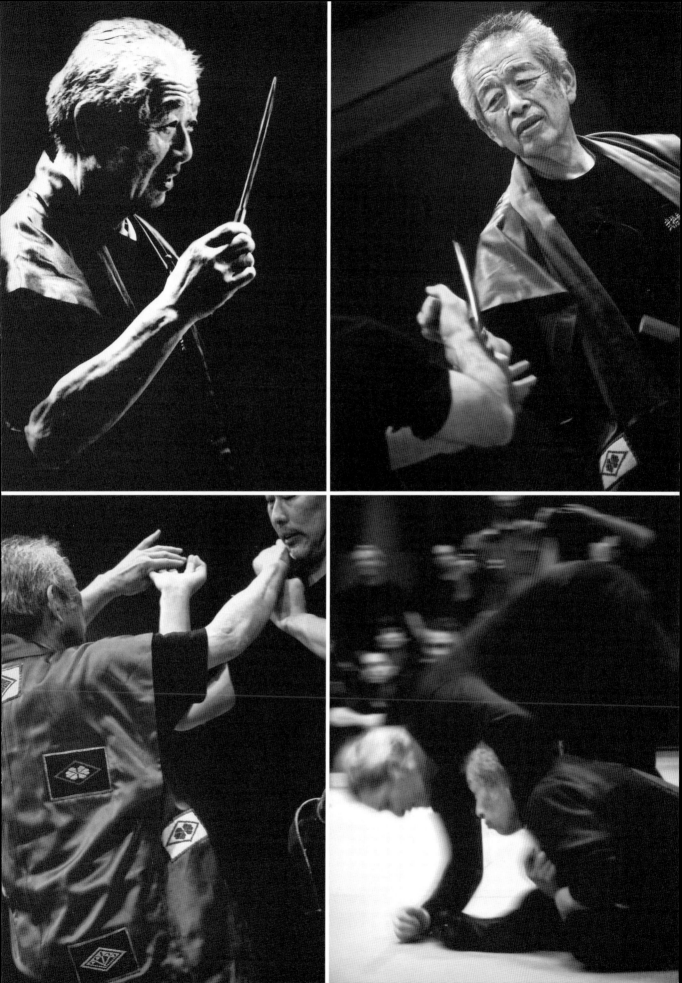

forms of life with the essence of truthful ideas and justice without making them scared or lost or afraid. Otherwise it is difficult to talk about gods or the Buddha.

If we talk of the saying "For the martial heart, 'wa' 和 (harmony) is the greatest of virtues," the Japanese spirit of justice (seigi 正義), of living justice (seigi 生義), and divine justice (seigi 聖義) can be described as the family crest or emblem of the samurai.

From this we can say the following: the heart of justice is divine. It is the divine spirit. This teaching is not emotional; it is just. It is not nationalistic but for the whole world; not for a single group but for humanity and for the good of all life. In other words, it is for all life of the natural world. Within this you can distinctly see the existence of the theory of the gokui. Judging from this point, we can say gods and the Buddha are like mighty "true spirits" to whom we offer natural justice.

AUTHOR'S NOTE: Justice and justice; justice and injustice; injustice and injustice. I have applied these three forms of justice to the Sanshin no Kata. When visiting America in 1982 I declared to my students without premeditation, "I am not Japan, I am no country, I am a UFO." Like this word, we are facing the time when we must look at the Earth from this kind of "universal" perspective, and we must protect the Earth at a global level.

The Path That Transforms Fate

"Mightiness" means something of unlimited size or excellence and something that we cannot currently fathom. We must therefore understand that the climatic changes and other natural disasters are a warning from the gods for our disregard for the laws of nature. We must understand that this is a just warning and to contest it would mean our own destruction. We see around us nature's counter-attack in regards to global warming and the disharmony of the world's delicate ecosystems from excessive use of the world's resources.

There are also those who say the earth has entered another ice age, but if we do not make ourselves aware of the changes in nature the time when we are judged by the gods will surely come. This is because if anything in life is in excess or deficiency there arises an imbalance. Unless we revise our ways the world is in a desperate situation.

Now, it seems that the world is turning as though in a cycle of death and rebirth from capitalism that flows to the abyss of liberalism, socialism, and communism to "universalism," or naturalism.

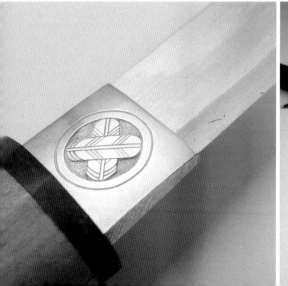

Author's note: To go further we might hope that this sign language of "isms" will change to the meaning of harmony, and the meaning of industry. One example of this is the European Community, which in its infancy looked as if it would set out on the path of "For the martial heart, wa (harmony) is the greatest of virtues." But the world has drifted and lost its way, and we must look hard at our direction in order to ride the tide of industry and survive. And by finally arriving at the island of living justice (seigi 生義) we can reach the utopia of true justice (seigi 正義). This means that by changing the meaning of belief (shinko 信仰) to that of an exchange with the gods (shinko 神交), doing god's work (shinko 神行) and progress (shinko 進行) one can find the way to live as a god. At present it seems that the god of justice is pronounced destroyed. By living with a correct heart, I would like to invert fate and reach the gokui of happiness.

Awake (Kakusei) and Be Happy in the Form of an Ancient Governor (kakusui)

Humans are able to discern good and evil. It is important to make judgments that are not incorrect, rectify faults, and change what should be changed. Because of one's special nature, which is a person's unique character or individuality, it may be difficult to make changes or transform oneself. By making a practice or habit of something, however, it is certainly possible to change. Doing this gives rise to vicissitudes or ups and downs.

The embodiments of this change are the countless former demons that are incarnated in the form of Buddha that protect people kindly like Hariti (goddess of children and childbirth), the Buddha who was a demon in a previous existence.

By our choosing to correct our ways and become just, and by working together so we can more quickly rehabilitate the natural environment, nature will be revived and we will become happy. Within this crisis we awake in the same way that families who have reached the height of adversity and have been pushed to the edge of collapse awaken and recover. To judge things as bad and to repent is the justice we need to survive.

All living things in the universe, having been born into this world, have the desire to live. Naturally all humans have desires and appetites. However, it is wrong to make mistakes through our desires. Because of this, below I want to answer questions regarding business, law, pathology, religion; further, construction, housing, and marriage—all things that are necessary in life.

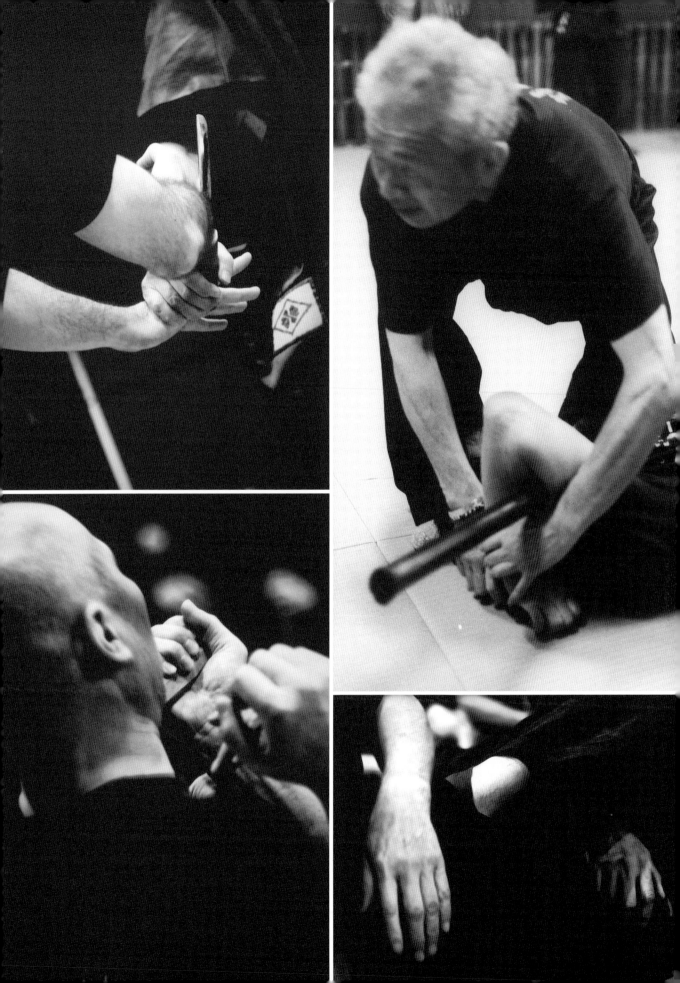

AUTHOR'S NOTE: I remember the figure of Takamatsu Sensei. He was holding tongs with both hands on the brazier when he said some very short words to encourage me, and soon after that he smiled. At the time of this dialogue I remember that there was a development plan to cut down the trees in front of Kashihara Jingu station which Takamatsu Sensei opposed and was instrumental in preventing from going ahead.

—Do humans have a desire to live from the moment they are born into this world?
Ordinarily humans are not conscious of their desire to live, but no one can deny we all experience hunger and the need to satisfy our appetites. The clearest evidence that people have such desire to live is the fact that when humans are confronted by their own death, at first even if only temporarily, a strong urge to survive and continue life arises. The history of conflict and the manner of death of soldiers described within it is handed down in various ways for the benefit of loved ones, family, and relatives. I think it is important to show respect towards these departed spirits.

AUTHOR'S NOTE: In the year of Heisei 21 (2009) I held a service in honor of the dead. The fact that I am alive and training is thanks to the people who have died before me, and so I erected a memorial tower to the nine Ryuha, a memorial tower to the Bujinkan dojo; a lighthouse to link the past and future, so that the words of my teachers will resonate through the ages.

Traditionally, humans have acted under the control of their spirits and because of this there are desires, joys and sorrows, pleasure and sadness. If you were a person whose normal state was to think of nothing much then you would be ruled by your desires and feel them to be important.

Your heart/mind is you; you are your heart/mind. There is no you separate from your heart/mind and no heart/mind separate from you. This is why the hearts/minds of those soldiers who in battle esteemed self-sacrifice over the desire to live were able to encounter a unity of mind and body. We might call this a desire for the pure or sacred (seiyoku 聖欲) rather than the desire to live (seiyoku 生欲).

—Well then, does this mean that a lunatic who has gone mad and who has lost his mind has no desire to live?
When the mind is in disorder the workings of intelligence and knowledge behave separately. Normally, the faculty of intelligence receives information and passes directions to

the body. But when the mind is in disorder, intelligence and knowledge are out of harmony and work separately, and even information that would normally invoke a desire to live is not transmitted to the body by intelligence. In other words, the "original universe spirit" and one's own spirit are acting separately. As evidence of this, "madmen" often ask a question to themselves, answer it, but then deny the answer. Therefore, for example, when they think they are hungry they ask themselves if they are going to get something to eat or not.

Even though their intelligence encourages them to eat, the information is interpreted as not to eat. There is no mental unity about this desire to eat and as a result they are unable to get sufficient nutrition, and come to harm in this way. When there is disorder (madness) in the brain, one's desire to live is not reflected truthfully.

—Well then, what is the purpose in trying to satisfy our mutual desire to live?
All living things naturally have a desire to live, but while we exist we aim to attain happiness in our lives. Happiness means satisfaction of the mind, but you should know within this there is also the satisfaction of misunderstanding blind spots and dead spaces or angles. You should also become aware of the line between happiness and illusion.

> **Author's note:** It is crucial to look hard at reality and know the importance of co-existence with others in our living space. And it is important to have the desire to correct our desire to live.

—Well then, if we train enthusiastically in order to make our minds satisfied, could there be any problems?
The perseverance to continue with one mind, without relying on anything, is to nourish one's heart, and to never cease developing one's technique. This is the true forbearance of the ninja; and because you walk this road you will be led to happiness and nothing bad will come. However, if you leave the path and, for example, lose your self-disposition and come to believe that the key to being saved is offering thanks to the gods and Buddha, to the extent that your livelihood suffers, and you offer your property until you have almost nothing—this only satisfies you, the giver, and means you would still be a long way from the gods. You should also know the difference between enthusiasm and wild zeal.

In general, because we want to live a happy existence in our everyday lives we try to satisfy our physical and spiritual desires at the same time, and end up overdoing things. But, because different people have different physical, financial, or "will power" limitations,

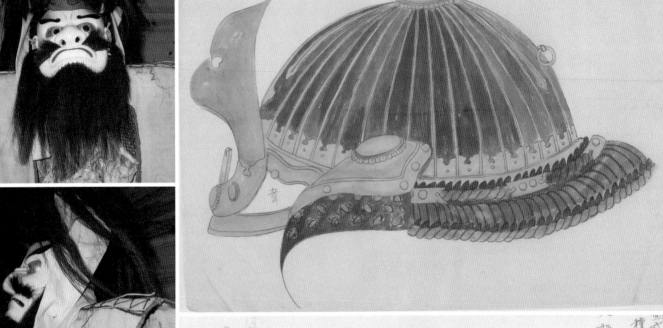

those who are not sufficiently endowed with all these abilities sometimes fall into unhappiness when the situation does not meet their intentions. When making a Japanese sword that sparkles with its beautiful hamon (the temper line of the Japanese sword where the metal of the cutting edge meets the body of the blade), an excellent sword is born only after the metal has been heated and beaten to remove all the impurities, and then plunged in pure water.

—How are Seirei (original spirit), Chino (intelligence) and Chishiki (knowledge) different?
Original spirit, intelligence, and knowledge are each different things but they are closely related. First, knowledge is the function of "natural consciousness." Intelligence, depending on the designated sense, is the function that acquires knowledge. Depending on the strength of the function of intelligence, cleverness or foolishness is judged. Knowledge, usually speaking, is limited to its own area of specialization and therefore has a narrow scope or range. That is to say, knowledge without experience is a poor thing. If intelligence works normally depending on the person's aims, effort, and education, knowledge can be gained regarding any topic, in any direction.

The original spirit of the universe is the power that makes use of intelligence, and it is by this that differences in intelligence emerge, whether they be wise intelligence or inferior intelligence, which cannot understand common sense or courtesy. Without the cooperation of the mighty power of the original spirit, mistakes are often made in judgment. Even though some people have studied the ways of the modern world, the circumstances in which some societies find their populations unable to find employment, or the destructive power of weapons that have been developed by "intelligence" that do nothing but kill people and devastate nature, which is greater than humans, gives us pause for thought.

—What is the relationship between intelligence, experience, and livelihood?
Depending on the function of intelligence, one can gather experience through trial or taking a risk of some sort. So there is a close relationship between intelligence and livelihood.

Also, because people try to live equally they live, grow old, and die—this is a law of all ages and nobody can avoid it. The reason people die is that there is a limit to the development of people—amongst the various organs, the heart is the slowest to develop, and furthermore, even though it continues to develop until old age, it too has a limit and this, I think, is why people die. The development of intelligence has no limits and the body is ruled by this intelligence, but intelligence weakens as we grow older.

The Budo that I call upon reveals that the merit of a person is the degree to which

PORTRAITS OF TAKAMATSU SENSEI

they preserve life, and it is not possible to preserve life with an incorrect lifestyle. In order to correctly protect life, the protection of the body and the protection of the spirit are necessary, but all people desire to live an easy life. In order to satisfy this desire, the body and mind become overexerted, and with the accumulation of overexertion we fall into unhappiness, and this affects even our descendants hereditarily. Therefore the correct path acts as a guide to the true path of happiness based on humanity.

When you look at the aftereffects of modern war I think you will nod in agreement to this. Unless we can measure where the bomb blast and bomb clouds will go through the martial ways of zanshin (a state of remaining aware), we are in an age in which the life of nature itself is threatened.

—*Within the secret writings of Amatsu Tatara, passed down within ancient Shinto that I was instructed in by Takamatsu Sensei, are the medical writings of shinshin shingan (divine heart, divine sight) and, based on these, martial and religious rituals from ancient times. However, I feel that medicine (igaku 医学) is the same as the study of intention or thought (igaku 意学). Consequently if medicine develops further, I wonder if this kind of caution or advice will become unnecessary.*

That would be a big mistake. Humans, from the beginning, have the powers of resistance and healing to naturally cure themselves. For example, a dog licks a wound with its own tongue and heals itself. When people first realize that they are sick and learn that their own power doesn't reach this far, they receive an examination by a doctor and request medication. However, there are illnesses of the heart/mind that cannot be cured by medication from doctors. When we are afflicted by such an illness it can invite unexpected misfortune that affects our family, relatives, and friends. I can say with conviction based on experience, however, that there are no enemies (should we say divine enemies), including disasters, on the true path.

AUTHOR'S NOTE: When I visited Africa we drove in a Land Rover through a danger zone in which many wild animals lived. The guide said, "Let's stop here and have some coffee because it's safe," but sensing danger, I said we should not. Nevertheless, he was convinced it was safe and the two Land Rovers stopped ominously. As we got out of the vehicles and were about to have some coffee, the local guide entered a nearby bush, then came frantically running back, having found a rhinoceros close by. Everyone seemed to think it very strange and commented, "Sensei, how did you know there was a dangerous rhinoceros even though the guide said it was safe?"

—*How is it possible to know about these things in advance through the study of bujutsu?* "Correct" people have the ability to transcend. And, in the same way that it is no wonder when water flows downhill, it is possible to know of these things through intuition or instinct if you have a right heart. If your heart is "correct" then your heart will be utterly truthful. The insight is direct and certain. There are many who, in big or small ways, have had the experience of the intuitive workings of the "original spirit."

AUTHOR'S NOTE: In the same way when I opened the seminar in Africa I spoke about how Ninpo can erase the world itself. That night, there was a lunar eclipse that greatly surprised the participants in the seminar!

—*I feel, however, that it is not necessary to encourage others to believe in your thinking about the heart of the martial ways or religion, which are a means to maintain your own unperturbed attitude.*

AUTHOR'S NOTE: This reminds me of the great erudition (unchiku 蘊蓄) or "building luck" (unchiku 運築) of the answer I received to a question during a conversation with a hundred-year-old high priest: "Enlightenment means you are you. I am me. That is enough."

When a person is endowed with character, they become someone who is gentle and sincere. And then naturally they develop benevolence and love for humanity. Whereupon that person shares with others what is good for themselves and, when they see other people suffering, they go to their rescue to the limits of their strength. They transcend their instincts: when they see an extremely rich person they don't flatter or court their favor, and if they become rich themselves they don't show off or brag.

AUTHOR'S NOTE: This is one aspect of heijoshin 平常心 (everyday mind). In Japan, there is the expression "eight million (innumerable) gods"; the metaphor of "eight hundred lies"; and the eight hundred and eight towns (the whole metropolitan area of old Edo).

CHARACTERS AND DRAWINGS ON YARI BY THE AUTHOR ▶
The characters are the ten-verse Kannon Sutra

Martial Religion (religion from a martial perspective)

Continuing the conversation with Takamatsu Sensei:

—Is the heart of the martial ways and religion one kind of courtesy or manners?

As a person, one must have manners. A person who has no manners is a person without merit. Of course, this is in regard to one's seniors, benefactors, and superiors; and one must not forget manners with regular people and juniors or subordinates. Indeed, because people are equal it is all the more necessary to have manners. If we were to take away manners from people there would be no difference between us and other animals. If this were to happen, society would fall into chaos and survival would become a battle of strength.

When I traveled the world, I viewed the "rei" 礼 of "reigi" 礼儀 (manners) as the "rei" 零 (zero) of a round heart. This is the attitude of Theta (the eighth letter of the Greek alphabet). Incidentally, Theta is also used within Settai in Zen.

To put it another way, religion and the martial ways are teachings about the correct heart. There are those who say they need not accept the teachings of religious people because they are the owner of a correct heart themselves. But it is necessary to investigate whether one's current thinking is correct or not. For example, if one's own child is facing death and does not respond to medicine, is that not the time when one's ability to behave as a person who shows the authority of the martial ways and who has transcended life and death in the form of benevolence becomes visible?

People always have desires. It is when you have that desire that you need to cleanse your heart. This "cleansing of the heart" is similar to having a bath to maintain hygiene; it is of course desirable but it is possible to live without it. Conversely, if you wash too many times every day this can cause harm. Sometimes people without piety mistakenly believe they lead a life of happiness, and as I mentioned previously, if you carry faith too far, you become fanatical; this too is harmful. The difference between instinct (honno 本能) and worldly desires (bonno 煩悩) is paper-thin. In the belief that I advocate, there is no fear of fanaticism because it is correct faith. There is no excess; the more enthusiastic one becomes, the higher the character rises.

Author's note: This enthusiasm (nesshin 熱心) is the root of the message (nesshin 根通心). It is the heart that leads to the root; one's true nature. Explaining enthusiasm and truth also resembles the making of a Japanese sword.

This faith transcends religious, ideological, or philosophical thinking; it is something

grasped within the friendship (shinko 信仰) or divine exchange (shinko 神交) between Budoka.

Author's note: Try changing the character divine (shin) with the eight characters: new, advance/go forward, happy, heart, deep, parent, center/core, and truth. 新・進・辛・心・深・親・芯・真.

You want to have the intuition to be able to read the "shu" character of shukyo 宗教 (religion) as "sou" and "mune." It is also interesting to try changing this to the 12 characters: principal/important, preeminent, find/pick up, practice, great number/the masses, accumulation, final, cultivate/master, boat/vessel, dedicate/offer up, capture/prisoner, smell/ hint. 主・秀・拾・習・衆・襲・終・修・舟・収・囚・臭.

—I know someone who says "I try to have faith, but sleep when I want to sleep, eat when I want to eat, and I want to live a wealthy lifestyle. Otherwise, I couldn't say that I have happiness." Shame on him!

It is easy to achieve that kind of living. However, before this it is necessary to know the substance of heaven, earth, and nature. In the same way that there is heaven and earth, there is the sun and moon and there is light and darkness. Without exception there is unhappiness on the reverse of happiness and happiness on the other side of unhappiness. By doubling your efforts and experiencing more hardships than others you will come to live a life that leads you to the true nature of prosperity (eiyoeiga 栄耀栄華). And you will be satisfied with your own life.

Author's note: Let's add "nourishment/nutrition leads to prosperity" (eiyoeiga 栄養栄我) and the essence of prosperity is self-reflection (eiyoeiga 栄要映我).

What is the Substance of That True Nature?

The substance is not at all something isolated or independent; rather its character is in its connectedness. It connects skillful with poor, it connects strong and weak things. Connected to ease is suffering; connected to love is hatred. If there is someone who becomes merry there is someone who becomes gloomy. Depression comes with anger; honesty comes with bias, cruelty with benevolence. Dissatisfaction comes with satisfaction. If someone wins, someone loses; happiness comes with sorrow. Pain is connected with life; it is like the defense mechanism of living things.

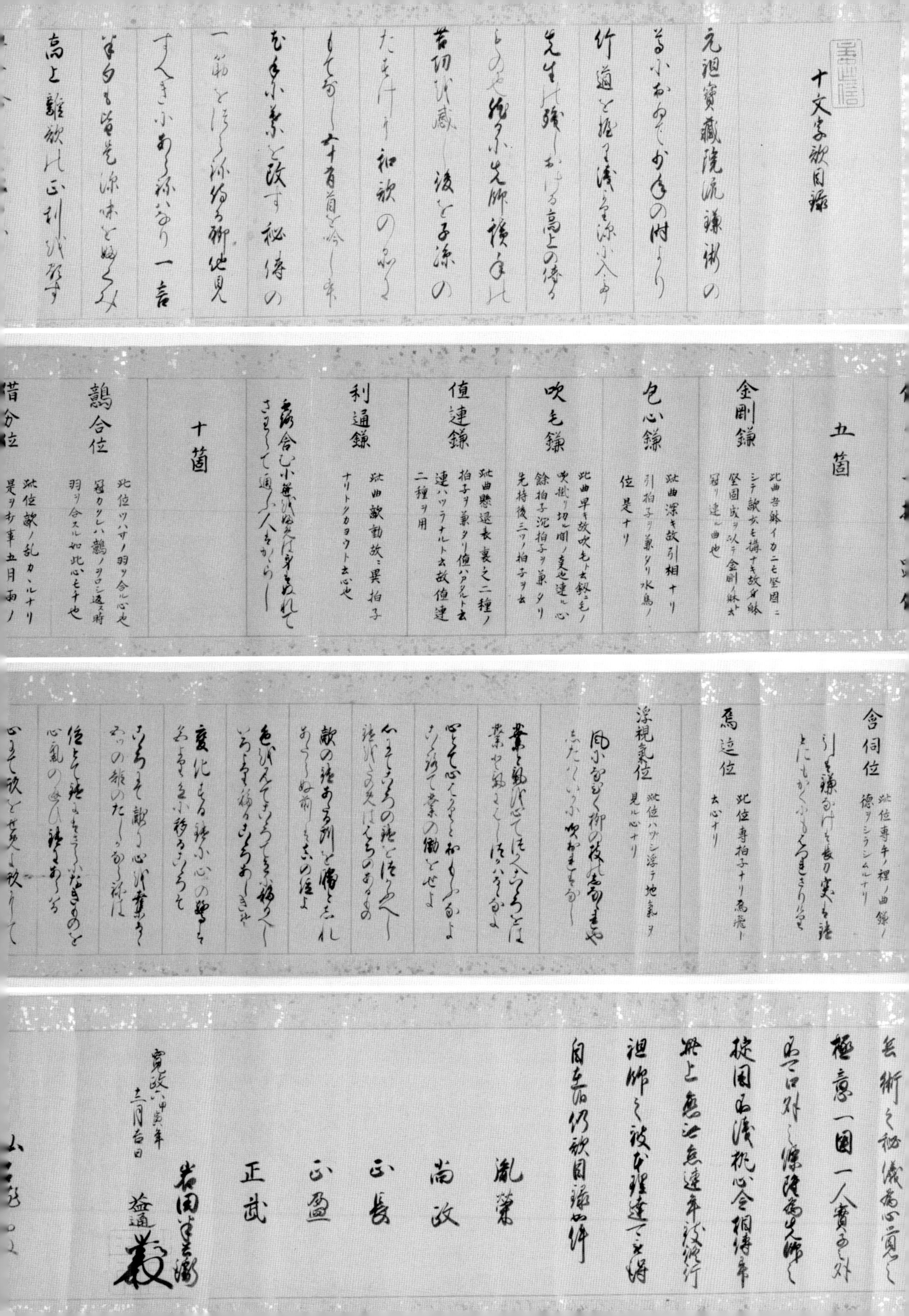

元祖宝藏院流鎌術の

竹道を極め淺さを源小入て
先生せ強しおける高上の傳へ
もろ人や組小先師預かれ
若切武藏し後と子源の
た者り秘傳の和歌の

もとも小業と改す秘傳の
一箭ともほう添ゆる御他見

すき小あら添なり一言
高上に雖歌此正利武藏す

五箇

金剛鎌
此曲昔鍊イカ二と堅固二
シテ歌以を搆き故ぞ鍊
堅固成ゆへて金剛と鍊也
冠り連曲也

包心鎌
位是ナリ
此曲深き故引相十ナリ
引拍子ゟ兼ク兼タリ水鳥ノ

吹毛鎌
此曲早き故火もト去鍊毛ノ
吹撥り切に聞ノ支毛連に心
餘り拍子沈拍子ゟ兼タリ
先持後三ツ拍子ヲ去

偃連鎌
此曲懸退表裏之二種ノ
拍子ヲ兼タリ偃ハツラと
連ハツラナルト去故偃連
二種ヲ用

利通鎌
此位歌動故ヽ異拍子
ナリトクョウト去ナリ

十箇

鵤合位
此位ツバサノ羽ツ合心也
冠り夕レハ鵤ノタロニ返リ時
羽リ合スル如此心七十也

借分位
此位歌ノ乱力ニルナリ
是ヲす力事五月雨ノ

含伺位
此位専チ理ノ曲鍊ノ
德ヲシラシムルナリ
引を兼るけを搆り實を諸
とにもかくふもくるまより心を

為造位
此位専拍子ナリ高飛ト
去心ナリ

深視気位
此位ハツシ浮ヲ地気ヲ
見ル心ナリ

寛政六申寅年
三月吉日
岩国住...
益通（印）

正武
正盈
尚政
亂策

In this way, it is a rule that within the character of people, to a greater or lesser extent is light and darkness—omote and ura. In the same way that sunny and gloomy days coexist, if satisfaction is carried to excess it creates harm—when there is excessive anger this leads to mental and physical change.

There is a connection between the substance of the martial and religious, and this cannot be cut. This is a truth the extent of which must be understood. It is the martial way that guides me to this comprehension, commonly referred to as religion; it is when fudoshin is understood that people are able to transcend. This is a substance that one can understand as the same as the interchange between unmoving mind (fudoshin 不動心) and "wealthy or fortunate moving heart" (fudoshin 富動心).

—Well then, does that mean that this substance (of martial arts and religion) is something that cannot be divided in two?
It is certainly not possible to divide. In the same way that living things on earth cannot be grown by the power of the sun alone or the power of the moon alone. It is the natural state to be aware that man is connected with the universe, and not realizing this opposes a principle of the universe.

This connection cannot be divided; in the same way, neither can that between the religious and the martial. In Buddhism there are "expedient means"; in the workday world there is "the law of convenience"; and in Budo there is kyojitsu.

AUTHOR'S NOTE: When talking of the true nature (shotai 正体) of things, look at the true nature (shotai 正体), read between the lines of the presented form (shotai 招体), and infer or sense the hidden form (shotai 消体). The mon 門 (gate), or shumon 宗門 (religion), and bumon 武門 (martial), are captured beautifully by the shutter of the famous cameraman Ken Domon (1909–90).

—If someone were to live a life of religion would there not be cases where they would have to quit their occupation as they are bound by the rules never to deceive or pretend, and never to be cruel?
There is also kyojitsu in a person's livelihood. In Buddhism this is called hoben (方便; skt. upaya), or expedient means. In Buddhism, regarding telling "lies," it is bad to do so for one's own benefit, but there is no guilt if you do so to benefit others as an expedient means. For example, there is no harm for a trader to tell a "lie" as tactics in negotiating business, but if this is taken to extremes they would lose trust and this would lead to bad

conduct coming back to them. In the martial ways, we also have the expressions "active means" (katsuben 活便), "shouting or exclamatory means" (katsuben 喝便), and "winning means" (katsuben 勝便).

Furthermore, working as a butcher who kills animals such as pigs in order to eat, for example, could not be said to be cruel. Taking the life of those kinds of animals is simply carrying out the purpose of them having been raised with care to become meat; this is therefore a deceit that cannot be helped.

The guidebook to happiness is something that connects with the path of the essence of Budo. I have seen this result (kekka 結果), or "connected flowers" (kekka 結花), as I have made a pilgrimage not of Japan's eighty-eight temples (a famous pilgrimage around Shikoku Island) but rather of the world's eighty-eight places!

Teacher and Apprentice

The transmission of an art (isshi soden 一子相伝) is a natural phenomenon in which all things are united into one. This also has the meaning of being "one in ten thousand." That is, it is divine will that there is one person among many who will walk in the path of his teacher.

Teacher and apprentice—I think sometimes it is good to train with the kind of connection as that between a director and performer. That performance (engeki 演劇) that should also be called an "extreme connection" (engeki 縁激) takes a different form or shape depending on the moment or period, and to know what kind of truth it is one must listen to it as a sonata.

The story told is full of apparitions and phantoms (yokai 妖怪); and is conveyed graphically by the methods of using pictures (yokai 用絵) or via the main points of enjoyment (yokai 要快). At the present time the period of early computerization has passed and we are in a period in which one must cultivate a mind and body that can scrutinize various types of information in which truth and error are intermingled like in a ghost story or a rakugo. We must cultivate a mindset of heijoshin.

This was said by my teacher Takamatsu Sensei: Perseverance (nintai 忍体) means cultivating the heart, continuously devoting oneself to technique; persistence (shinbo 辛棒) is the true ninja. The "shin" 辛 in this word leads to hearing divine will (shin'i 神意). Now that I am an old person (koreisha 高齢者) I think of these words as "a person of the bell of happiness" (koreisha 幸鈴者); I continue to ride to the hearts of the students who

visit from countries around the world, while ringing the bell and riding Santa Claus's sledge. All living things need to cultivate the body, cultivate the heart, and cultivate consciousness.

Win without Drawing — If You Must Draw Don't Cut

Religion (shukyo 宗教), is also "teaching the masses" (shukyo 衆教). When you look at religion globally, there are many different gods that are worshipped. In Japanese religion (Shinto) we find the idea of eight million kami (divinities). This is the same as the eight fundamental techniques of the Kihon Happo and shows a universal, inclusive worldview that surely has great meaning for the modern world. It is likely that in Japan from ancient times there was a kind of earth within the earth. Due to changes occurring globally, I have the feeling that now, more and more people are gaining an awareness of the "United Countries of Earth."

Since the Warring States Period in Japan (from the 15th to the 17th centuries), the leading samurai who held power, namely the daimyo, built castles in each district, and towns sprang up as vassals and merchants gathered to live close by. This was known as a castle town (jokamachi 城下町), however, I expect they also played a role as a "town which purified" (jokamachi 浄化町) by cleaning up the people and natural environment and maintaining peace. A scene in which there was no wall built around such towns is something that was commonly seen only in Japan.

To the extent that the person who held power was usually righteous and just, it does not seem that the feudal system (hokensei 封建制) that protected people and the environment was an entirely vicious one. Many people regard the feudal system as a relic of the past and do not think it a good thing, but in the case of a society of samurai, the language is comprehensively that of the sword (hokensei 包剣制). Indeed, this is why when the samurai would form a procession they would cover the handle of their sword and tie it with string. This was the spirit of not drawing their swords and was a stance taken to show that they did not like fighting. I think you will agree with the words, "Firearms and other projectile weapons are cowardly." This is why the following poem, one teaching of the essence of the martial ways, has been passed down through the ages:

"Win without drawing; if you draw don't cut.
Just forebear. Know that to take life is a serious matter."

The words, "The way of the samurai is to find death," found within the book *Hagakure*

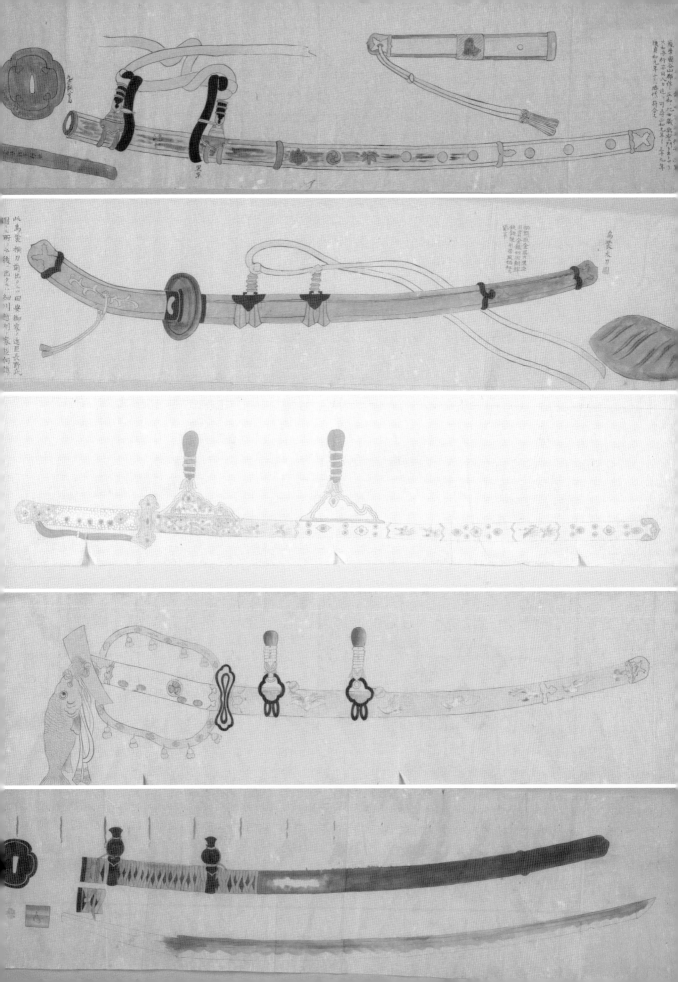

薩摩國谷山郷住正國 己世歳数 文政五年ヨリ
太平行 二月八日 □ 可 □ 嘉永元年 二 丁未九年

此烏箕擱刀前比ヘ 白安御家ノ遠臣長野氏
關ス所ナ後 馬ヲ 如川 御刊 家臣 何椎

烏箕太刀圖

written by Yamamoto Tsunetomo (1659–1719), are well known, but the original form was not shinu 死ぬ (death), but shinu 士貫 (to maintain oneself as a samurai); to continue with bushido. This is why I tell my students—don't read "Haga" kure, but rather read the hidden scrolls of "Toga" kure.

This is the means to discard one's impure heart and at the same time live life correctly while purifying the unclean world. In order to do this, it is important to look at the world forgivingly. I would like to say this is not rokkonshojo 六根清浄 (purification of the six roots of perception), but rokkonshojo 禄魂笑浄 (happy soul, purification by laughter). While it is important to get along in unity within a group, has not the time in which it is also required to grow as an individual, responsible adult not arrived ?

Gokui Is The Wisdom in Order to Live

Martial artists must dedicate themselves to pursuing the way of the warrior; this is the saying "I alone am honored in heaven and on earth," as asserted by Buddha. It is likely that the samurai, aware of their existence between life and death in frequent conflict, naturally developed a "hygienic reaction to life" in order to survive in those days. This is why if they had needed to live in the mountains I think they would have chosen a place where they could live comfortably by collecting fruits and edible plants. Nature is ghost-like. Entering the mountains is also the beginning of the training to subjugate or exterminate ghosts.

In order to acquire knowledge of extrasensory perception, the master of martial arts would leave the workday world and enter the mountains to do training such as conditioning the hands or practicing to move freely even in places where no footing could be found. Training in nature, where there is not only a lack of footing but one is attacked by the wind and rain, is greatly different from training in a dojo with wooden floors or mats, and with air conditioning installed. The sensibility which could adapt to these kinds of extremes in nature would have endowed the martial artists with the wisdom to produce "something from nothing" when required in battle.

There were also times when they would train by making opponents of the birds and beasts. Birds and beasts are agile, have strong powers of sense, and possess extrasensory perception of their own which makes it difficult to see how to catch them. Discern and catch the extreme.

The gokui means the wisdom not to submit even in encounters with ghosts in the real world, and to survive by being able to make a reaction fitting the occasion. Nowadays,

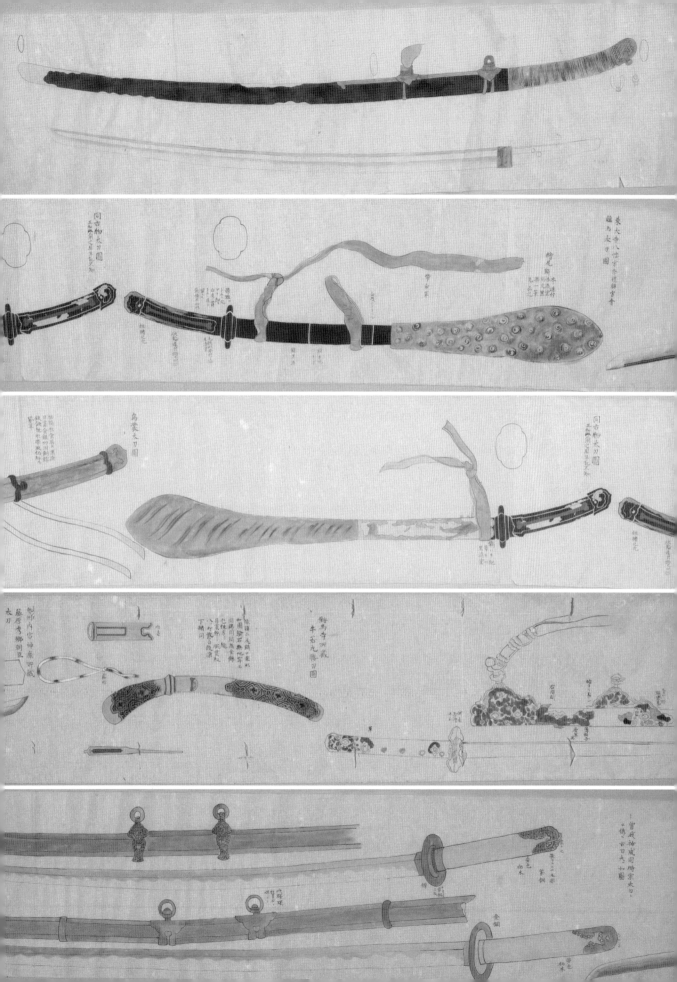

even when you sit watching an image projected in the TV you must be able to see the reality beyond the mere TV screen. This is the kind of age in which we live. A high priest of the Edo period, Tosui, threw away his splendid temple and chose to live his life as a "natural person" selling straw sandals in the form of a beggar. He rose above preaching and left human habitation. Naturally, in his choosing not to live by Buddhist teachings or follow the ways of ordinary people, this behavior became an example to lead the people. This gives some kind of food for thought to modern people who have simply thrown away teaching and studying.

In any case, what I am writing here about shumon and bumon is not my view of martial arts or religion. It is not teaching, it is a mon or gate. It is the sound of Ken Domon's camera shutter.

In and Yo

Takamatsu Sensei would often say, "Don't cut relations," and "Connections are important." Recently I have started to understand this much more deeply. In and Yo are connected. Men and women are connected. Life and death are connected. Heaven and earth are connected. Light and dark are connected. Omote and ura are connected. Soke and generation after generation of teachers and students are also connected.

From here is born love, happiness, life. If one did not know of these connections, it would not be possible to discover or bring forth the gokui. The next generation would not be born.

In this connection, in the fifth-dan test in the Bujinkan, the ability of the person sitting in front to sense the killing intent of the "enemy" behind is tested. I believe the connection between the person in front and behind is the hara 腹 (lower abdomen) which is also the connection of the umbilical cord. Through this is born the growth of the life of the warrior. I think you will nod in appreciation when you hear that "kami" 神 can also be read as "himo" (cord or string). In ancient times they called life a "bead cord."

In my own case I have reached this point simply through my connections with Takamatsu Sensei and the connection with my family. In the modern world, differences in people's consciousness, religion, and thinking are causing much disorder, and the disorder is increasing. I believe the path to resolving this situation is "connection." The gokui is something connecting all ages and thus all kinds of societies. It is gokui; meaning "everlasting enlightenment" (gokui 悟久意). However, I wonder whether people are in danger of losing sight or missing that connection.

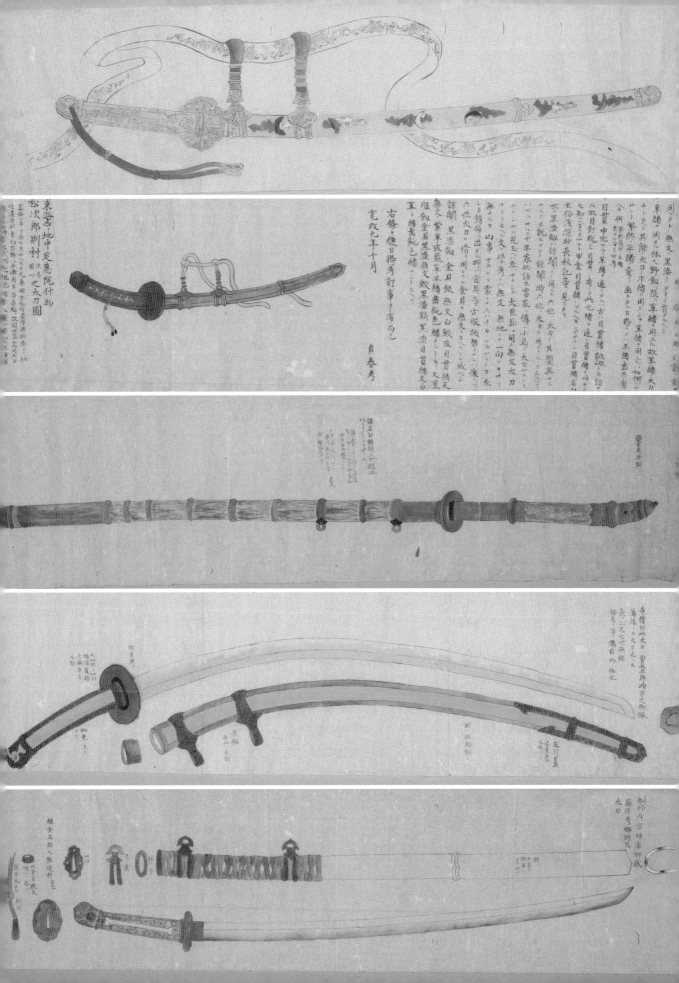

東海寺地中定惠院什物
松次郎則村
圖名之太刀圖

右條々後日得考訂事ニ有而已

寛政九年十月

自春考

諸名公補欹入極秘

蕨真作刻

寺僧曰此太刀曾祖次郎時宗之所佩
薩後五太刀長也
長三尺七寸有餘
幅廣考物劒是備前物也

總金具的大銀造作品

舶州內宮神庫所載
藤厚考物劒是
太刀

Thereupon, rather than In and Yo, this becomes an unraveling of the "string." We can find the world of common sense (joshiki 常識) through the "consciousness of the string" (joshiki 縄識) that connects in the space. In 2009 I was teaching people how to find for themselves that Budo taijutsu is also connected like a string or rope. This means that the real form of Budo is like the moment a piece of string returns to the normal or universal movement (jodo 常動) or the way of the string (jodo 縄道). In the martial arts, we also talk about "common sense" (joshiki 常識) taijutsu or the "rope sense" of taijutsu.

Around the world, throughout history, the sense of those fighting played out like a drama of that particular period. It was weathered and changed by the times. This "sense" was just like a wind-pollinated flower, and by chance Bushido flourished in Japan. As one continues in training, however, Bushido becomes like a one-way ticket that can be cruel and can lead to mistakes in judgments about life. Depending on the period, there is also the danger of being swallowed by a wave, a type of surge about which nothing can be done. In this situation, I experienced how to live truthfully through the kyojitsu of Budo and Bugei. Unless you have the kyojitsu of two ways—transforming the literary (academic) and martial (Bunburyodo 文武両道) into the artistic and martial (Bugeiryodo 武芸両道)—you will not attain the meaning of the gokui. Two ways (nido 二道) are a heavy road (nido 荷道). Amongst Tokugawa Ieyasu's famous wise words were these: "The life of a person is like traveling a distant road carrying a heavy load. Do not hurry." These words should be a warning to those who drive recklessly.

Fighting and Provisions

There is the expression "to cut through a dilemma." As stated by Takamatsu Sensei— "People, if they can eat, can beat illness," and "Countries that have food will go on fighting indefinitely."

And on a later day, "If that country has an abundance of food, they will not lose the war." And it was indeed so. I eat my own combination, mainly brown rice, black soy beans (kuromame), azuki beans, and shiitake mushrooms. Furthermore, I try to cut down on flavorings and eat a diet of food that is natural. Food, sex, and consumption— these are the cycle of creation where the "next one" is born.

Songs of the Gokui

I shall have you listen to some songs of the gokui. That sound and rhythm—is it enka? Or is it chanson? Is it jazz? Is it a canzone? Is it a Russian folk song? Or the sounds of people all over the world? It is rhyming phrases. First, I would like you to listen to these songs as things that echo in your heart. Then I would like you to look at them not as sacred songs (seika 聖歌) but living songs (seika 生歌). Observing (mikiki 見聞き) or "looking at the feeling" (mikiki 見気き) of the world—we live now in a time in which missiles of great destruction can be sent remotely. Let's listen to these songs of light eternally, so that we ourselves don't vanish in a flash of light.

There is no strong or weak, strong or soft. Therefore I detach from my mind, comprehend the character "ku" 空, and regard the body as empty. (Toda Shinryuken)

People say that it is with their own strength that they perform techniques, without knowing that their body is led by the gods.

Don't make an opponent of an approaching enemy. If they rise against you, trust your feelings; finally know sutemi.

Win without drawing; if you must draw, don't cut. Just forebear. Know that it is a grave thing to take a life.

It is the very mind itself that leads the mind astray; of the mind, do not be mindless. (Takuan, Zen Master)

There is no country on which moonlight does not shine, but it lives in the heart of people that look at it.

Riding ahead of the flood, the chestnut shell floats because it has entrusted itself.

Amongst the soldiers that have prepared themselves and will show their bravery, the true gokui is in the heart.

The secret to fighting is to use the strength of the opponent, and to have a heart like a willow tree in the wind.

Thrusting into the space with the tip of the bo staff, if you feel a response with your hands; this is the gokui.

If you are impatient to win a battle, you will yield an opening and are bound to lose.

The teachings of god; correct heart; eternally protect me.

Bottomless waves that reflect on the water's surface, it is humiliating for my mind to be known.

Some people will forebear themselves in the future, as people have tendencies of remembering their past.

If you possess a heart like clear water, the opponent is reflected as though in a mirror.

Jujutsu means to both use the force of the opponent and have a heart like a willow in the wind.

Know that the gokui of Taijutsu is the foundation of peace. To learn this is the road to fudoshin.

The two guardian gods take the form of In and Yo. The movement of their fists, and also the breath.

The body of the ninja (nintai 忍体) or perseverance (nintai 忍耐) means to nourish one's heart and be assiduous in technique; eternally patient the true ninja forebears.

Water flows down, but this is the beginning of its ascent.

Everything for you, day and night I continue to refine, correct technique.

With no thought of one's self, float in the torrent by throwing oneself in.

The gokui is found in the depths of your heart. It is found only with single-minded devotion. (Note: Depths of the heart = limits of one's consciousness)

Under the raised sword is hell indeed. Just step in; ahead is paradise.

Our art fells those that oppose. Just pray. That is the art of not fighting.

Know that the essence of jujutsu is the basis of peace. If you can endure, it is the true essence.

Practice is kamae of the heart, kamae of the mind, both demon and Buddha are in the techniques (waza 技) sitting peacefully (waza 和座).

Everyone, anything, and everything; if it is for the sake of nature, spend day and night refining your knowledge of it.

If your heart is good, without wetting your hands, you will get victory (kachi) or value (merit).

If you hold a sword, or even a spear, it is one path. Correct technique is true technique.

Clear water, raging waves, trust yourself to them, obey. You will float in the current.

Know that the essence of jujutsu is the basis of peace. It will calm wild spirits.

If you think serenely; that which is hit and that which hits, both are just a playful dream . . .

Ninjutsu. It is from the true warrior, the master, that Ninjutsu arises.

The child of the letter "a," the beginning and end of all things, the sound of "un" is born, it grows and returns back to the birth place of "a."

These lyrics (kashi) 歌詞 are like flower poems (kashi) 花詩; traditions of the samurai harmonize well with the sound of existence. And the day that all the martial arts have finally been transmitted from the East has arrived. That is to say, as I was living in Kanto in the east of Japan, Takamatsu Sensei would sing that his pupil comes from the East. From ancient times, weapons were never to be used for evil ends, but only to defend one-self when necessary with the understanding that they have been received from the shrine.

CHAPTER 2

Secrets of the Art of the Spear

The Spear and Christ

In order to better understand the importance of the spear, let us turn its tip and our attention back to the dawning of the ages. It was during this mystical time of legends that in the heavenly realms the original and most mighty group of kami (gods), called Koto-Amatsu-Kami, summoned into existence two divine beings named Izanagi-no-mikoto and Izanami-no-mikoto. They were given the heavenly spear known as Ame-no-Nuboko that was infused with divine power, and sent to create land. These two divine beings used the heavenly spear to churn the ocean below, and upon removing the spear tip from the water, an island formed called Onokoro-jima. As water droplets continued to fall from the tip of the spear, landing back in the ocean, they formed Oyashima, the eight great islands of the archipelago of Japan.

Incidentally, the rich traditions of the Maori tribes were formed on another chain of auspicious islands and they also pay special reverence to the spear. I have heard that the shafts of the spears of the Maori tribes are only created using lumber harvested from trees that have been cultivated in sacred ground. Without doubt many other world cultures place great reverence and traditional importance on the spear, as in India where the spears are of course Carmunger (iron carbide and bamboo crafted from the Munger district of Bihar State in Eastern India). They are made by cutting a sixty-year-old shaft of bamboo in the summer, striking it against water to create the desired shape, leaving it out in the sun to dry until its outer layers become yellow, and then, without removing the joints, infusing it with character through a smoking process.

Next the bamboo is submerged in the Ganges River overnight, and the following day it is removed from the water, stood upright, and a bottle of peacock oil is turned upside down and placed on the top end of the bamboo. Pray to the Peacock King! That phase lasts for approximately six months and then wisps of appeasing incense from the Buddhist rite of cedar-stick burning waft up to the heavens. The radiance of the jet-black Carmunger shines through together with the crescent moon.

Transform into a most divine entity. Become the symbol of the indestructible truth, foster the immeasurable mercy and compassion of the most revered heavenly Kannon, and truly open your eyes with the sacred spear of "Longinus."

As we follow the shaft of the legendary spear of Longinus back in time, it brings us to a most gruesome scene. Positioned near the feet of Christ being crucified on the cross is

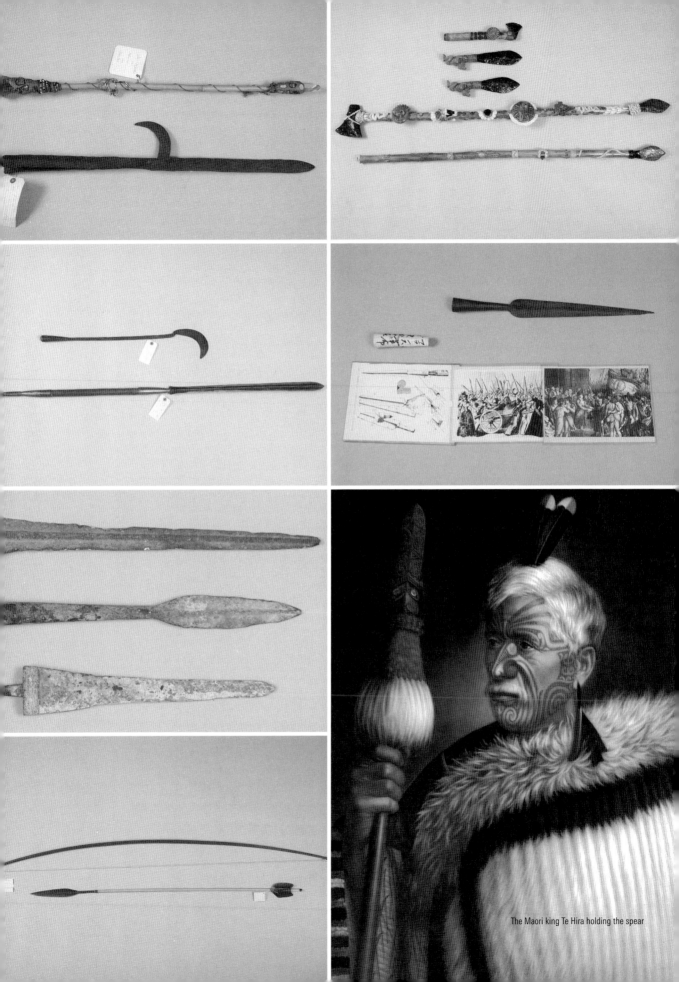

The Maori king Te Hira holding the spear

a nearly blind Roman soldier named Longinus. He has been given a spear, and ordered to thrust it into the side of the man on the cross. Not knowing that it is Christ he must spear, Longinus thrusts when given the order. Some of Christ's blood pours out over the spearhead and flows down into the eyes of the virtually blind man. At that moment, the eyes of the soldier are opened and from then on Longinus is bestowed with sight. Guided by the love of the almighty Christ, it is said that Longinus was then converted and began to learn the teachings of Christ.

Written Transmissions of The Art of the Spear

If you were to write Sojutsu, the art of the spear, with the Japanese characters for "wooden spear" 木片の鎗 and "wooden tip" 木製の穂先 it would become a hilt 柄. Then if you were to write "spear" with the character for "iron" 鉄の柄の鎗, it would make it an iron-shafted spear. If you were to write this art of the spear, or Sojutsu (槍術), as Sojutsu (争術), meaning fighting techniques, you would see a dramatic change in the concept of the spectacle of fighting with spears on the battlefield.

And now it is through this chapter that I will share the written transmissions of the art of the spear that I inherited from the true master of the spear, Sojutsu Soke Taka-matsu Sensei. Rather than fixating on these photos as practical instructions on form, I would like for you the reader to feel the weight of the tip of the spear, see the forms as if they are a pantomime, and listen to the long history of infinite fighting.

Sojutsu 鎗術—The Art of the Spear

When talking about the various kinds of spears that have been created over the different eras, it is necessary to look back to the very foundation of the natural world—that is of course land and the materials on the land. The most prevalent natural materials in use during the age of the spear were those such as wood, stone, bone, bronze, and iron, and as a matter of course, these different materials are what contributed to the creation of different kinds of spears.

Another important influence on the development of specific kinds of spears was of course the preference of the person wielding the spear. As a result of these preferences, particular types of spears came to include Teyari, Takeyari, Nagayari, Tanyari, Tetsuyari,

Kamayari, Jujiyari, and many more. In Kukishin-ryu they favored the Tanyari. The techniques of the spear include these nine methods: Kanpo, Shihogi, Hicho-Nage, Hito-Tsuki-Ai-Ho, Icchu-Santo, Hassai, Hiso, Tenchi-kaku, Happo-yaku.

Those methods of the spear consist of nine tracks. It is this all-out, do-or-die spirit: "GoKoKyoHenSeiShinFuDo." This power of nine methods becomes the secret technique that thrives in the faces of a hundred enemies.

Whether using the very long shaft of an iron-forged spear or the severed shaft of a wooden one, realize the long and the short of it (i.e., the advantages and disadvantages) and thrust into the very depths of the opponent's soul.

Kanpo 扞法

Draw the right leg back one step and thrust the tip of the spear towards the opponent's eyes. Lower the hips a little, so the back end of the spear ends up lower than the tip of the spear. Thrust from there with the body, draw back, raise the right hand to the right shoulder, and thrust repeatedly into the opponent's chest. Make sure to pull back quickly and thrust repeatedly. This keeps the opponent from entering in. Draw the left leg back and with the right hand bring the back end of the spear to sweep the opponent's left leg and knock him down.

Shihogi 四方技

Direct the tip of the spear so that it is facing down; the right hand is above the head. Widen the stance so that the legs are spread two shaku (1 shaku = 30.3 cm) wider than normal, and press forward one step with the left leg. Thrust the spear quickly and repeatedly, aiming for the chest of the opponent. Pull back quickly, open up to the right, thrust repeatedly, pull back, and at the same time hit into the left side of the opponent's face with the back end of the spear. While doing this, release with the left hand and spin the spear one revolution, grip it behind the right hand, and thrust in with the left. Pull back and use the back end of the spear to strike up into the opponent's groin.

Hicho-nage 飛鳥抛

This technique is with the spear aimed at the opponent's chest from Chudan no Kamae. Thrust in, and when pulling the spear back leap out to the right side. At the same time release with the left hand and smash the head of the spear into the temple area of the opponent's head. Pull back and thrust in quickly and repeatedly. Then once again leap out to the right side, release with the left hand, and smash into the temple area. Pull back and posture as if ready to thrust in. Assume Zanshin.

Ittotsuai 一突挨 / Hito-Tsuki-Ai-Ho 一突挨法

Developing a little from the left side, Hito-tsuki-ai-ho begins with the posture of holding both ends of the spear menacingly overhead and ready to impale. When setting to throw the spear take a step forward with the right leg, release with the left hand, and spin the head of the spear to hit into the left side of the opponent's face. Lower the body, take a step back with the left leg, and execute a left thrust into the chest. Release with the left hand and spin, thrust into the chest with a right thrust; from there extend the right leg one step, sweep the opponent's left leg, and knock down using the back end of the spear. Pull the right leg back, and execute a thrust.

Icchu-Santo 一擣三當

Lower the body, pull the right leg back one step and simultaneously thrust in. At the same time extend the right leg and smash into the opponent's left temple area with the back end of the spear knocking the opponent down. Release with the left hand, spin the spear, and thrust in to the left of the opponent. Pull back one step with the right leg and release with the right hand, get hold of the back part of the spear, spin it, and thrust left. Pull back quickly and thrust right repeatedly.

Hassai 撥摧

With the spear in Gedan, thrust into the opponent's chest. Release with the left hand, sweep the opponent's left leg, once again release with the left hand, return to the original position, and thrust in. Release with the left hand and smash into side of the face. Release with the left hand and thrust in.

Hiso 秘槍

Have the spear in Chudan no Kamae and thrust into the opponent's chest. From there extend the right leg and twist the body, using the back end of the spear to strike up into the opponent's groin. Pull the right leg back and thrust in repeatedly. Extend the right leg and once again use the back end of the spear to strike up into the groin. Pull the right leg back to kneel down, scoop the opponent's sword from underneath, and thrust in.

Tenchi-kaku 天地摧

Begin by thrusting in with the spear tip, pull the left leg back, and deflect the opponent's sword up using the back end of the spear. Release with the left hand, take hold below the right hand, and use the head of the spear to smash into the opponent's left temple area.

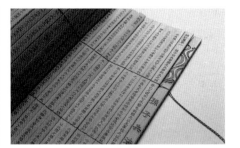

From there leap to the rear, use the right hand to slide down one shaku below the head of the spear, turn to face the opponent straight on and move in as if prepared to throw. When the opponent is close to you, aim the spear at the chest and thrust in.

Warning—if the opponent moves in towards you, it is vital to take a step back. If the opponent doesn't come forward, you should move forward one more step.

Happo-yaku 撥捕扼

This technique is for when you are thrusting in with the spear and the opponent is slipping by to either the left or right using a sword to deflect.

Start by thrusting in. The opponent uses the sword to deflect and slip by to the right. Then, use your wrists to roll the head of the spear so it redirects the top of the opponent's sword upwards, then thrust in. When the opponent uses the sword on the left or the right side to slip by, the power of the opponent will be lower, so it is important for you to scoop the sword up or down, and thrust into the opponent.

When the opponent uses the sword on either the left or right side to slip by, it is important to take advantage of that energy. This is the point when you should wrap up the sword by making contact with it, and when rolling the sword down it is vital to thrust in.

It is said that the spear as a weapon has very few variations, but that is not so. The idea behind yoko nagitaoshi is to use the side of the blade to knock the opponent down in order to thrust in; this is done by breaking the opponent's balance—make it painful and they will lose balance; that is the essence of this technique.

However, this technique should not be forced. Keep in mind it is better to gain a single victory using proper technique than to win ten times using wasted force. Just move lightly, and make it look nimble and agile. It is vital to be able to do everything without hesitating, without exception, and to use the hands quickly and gracefully. Of course it is important to be able to thrust with the spear, but by forcing it you are putting too much power into it; you are wasting energy and your thrust and your movement will become heavy and slow. Such methods against a sword leave you vulnerable and open to defeat. Make no mistake—such ways are not the way of Bufu. In fact, in the case of any technique you are practicing, it is necessary to absolutely eradicate any excess strength or power from your technique—in essence you must purify yourself of these ways.

When facing your opponents, especially in the case of the spear, realize the moment of truth, thrust in, and only after you feel a connection with something does the force naturally flow into it. That being the case, this is certainly true for the Yoroi yari.

Foster enlightenment
with the mind's eye
Grasp the hidden sword
effortless rewards await

For the most part, the art of the spear mainly flourished during the period known as the Sengoku Jidai (the Warring States Period; see Chapter 1) and as a natural result there were many ryuha, or schools, that developed in that era to actively teach the art. Nevertheless, among the multitude of schools that I have inherited, Kukishin-ryu was passed on to successive generations as secret transmissions, or Hiden 秘伝, for a longer period of time than the others, and its transmissions were not spread on a broad scale. As a result it re-appeared in the Tensho Era (1573–92) having emerged from Honryu as Kishin Sanpo-ryu.

Some of the various schools that appeared during this time include Hozoin-ryu, Otaki-ryu, Toda-ryu, Uchimi-ryu, Honshin Kyochi-ryu, Nakamura-ryu, Hanshin-ryu, Mokuge-ryu, Tanso-ryu, Nakane-ryu, Saburi-ryu, Oshima-ryu, Ippyaku-ryu, Riso-ryu, and Isshi-ryu, as well as the Hozoin Takada-ryu and others.

In the Keicho era (1596–1615) the Muhen-ryu, Honma-ryu, Magara-ryu, Kenko-ryu and Oroshi-ryu emerged. The Tenbun era (1532–55) saw the emergence of the Shijo-ryu, Sanmi Ichijo-ryu, and Hachijo-ryu. The Torao-ryu and the Kurama Shin-ryu schools appeared during the Eiroku era (1558–70).

In the Shoho era (1644–54) the Jitoku-ryu and the Daikoku-ryu emerged. In the Kan'ei era (1624–44) the Taneda-ryu, Oshima-ryu, Kashara-ryu, Kyoso-ryu, Muhen-ryu and the Hozoin Sanso-ryu emerged, and in the Genna era (1615–24) the Hikita-ryu, and the Shokei Shintai Muso-ryu emerged. In the Bunroku era (1592–96) the Muhen Yamamoto-ryu and the Icchuha Honshin Kyochi-ryu, among others, emerged. That being said, outside of Kukishin-ryu there are presently only two or three other- ryuha that remain.

As part of the inherited transmissions that have been passed on through Honryu Kukishin-ryu there is a particular group of secrets called the San-kokyu Kishinden that are really the initiation into the secrets of the art. The legendary lineage of these secrets has been transmitted from generation to generation, passing from the great-great-grandson of Minamoto no Yoshiie to the son of Tameyoshi; then this legendary secret was inherited from Minamoto no Yoshiteru, the son of Tanba Rokuro Tamemune who is the son of Tameyoshi, the 3rd generation of Minamoto no Yoshiie; to Minamoto no

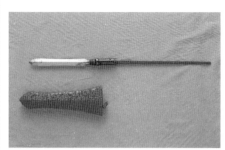

Yoshitaka, the fifth generation and Izumo no Kanja. The method of using nine vessels was completed by that time.

The family crest of Hatsumi is "one feather of a hawk." It is derived from the crest of Minamoto no Yoshiie.

When the San-kokyu, or three breaths, of the previous section are expressed as Kiai they are called Sansei-fugen. These three Kiai are more than simply a union of vocalization; they are actually joined in the heart, mind, and spirit as a single thought. With this in mind, the expression "Sansei" has three tones, of which the first is the Kiai of the sound of victory. This encompasses the Kiai of making the enemy lose the need to attack again, of making him believe he has won—it is called KanGiYaku.

The second Kiai is done just when you begin to attack the opponent. Make the opponent think that he may have just found an opening on you, and as he struggles to decide whether it is real or an illusion, his heart, mind, and spirit will scatter to the eight directions and he will collapse, unable to act upon his attack. This is the Kiai of expressing openings or opportunities everywhere—it is called HakuYakuSo.

The third is called the Kiai of Kyo, and its purpose is to realize the opponent's intention in the moment before the opponent applies a technique. Make the opponent know that you have foreseen exactly what he is going to do; this will cause him to doubt himself and create an opening to your advantage. Once you are able to capitalize on this you will be able to control certain victory.

The final Kiai I wish to mention is known as the Kiai of Fugon which is a fusion of the above three. Crush the opponent's technique and prevent him from using his abilities. This is the secret of secrets. The essence of the Kiai of KanGiYaku that emerges during the attack becomes the "YA!" sound of victory. There is a second sound that is the essence of the Kiai of HakuYakuSo—it is the Kiai of the sound of "AH!" that is projected when attacking. The third is the Kiai of Kyo, which means knowing the technique of your opponent, and has the sound of "TOA!" This interconnects with the Kiai of Yaku, Kaku, and Hei.

The Kiai of these three immobilizing attacks of unspoken deception together is "Umu!" and these three are said to be the three "crushes" of Kiai. The first is uttered to crush the Ki of the opponent. The second is uttered to crush the technique of the opponent. The third crushes the body of the opponent. When these three crushes are woven together they become the immobilization of paralyzing fear known as Fudo-Kanashibari. In any case, all schools have three Kiai of substance, three of deception, and three of adaptation, combining to make a total of nine. It is said that only a demon kami

 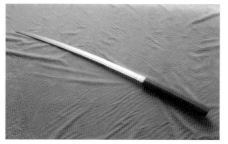

would be able to use these nine Kiai and that naturally leads to the Kuki Shin-ryu (Nine-Demon Kami School). Depending on the capacity of the warrior, Kiai may manifest as Kiai (miracle 奇合), Kiai (iron rails 軌合), and Kiai (life 生合). In other words, these roots are really the lineage of the iron spear stretching all the way back to Carmunger.

Men have nine secret openings, and women have ten secret openings. There is a saying that even though the nine openings are permitted, ten must be forbidden. It is here that the Nine-Demon Kami School of Kuki Shin-ryu (九鬼神流) can be heard to be the Kuki Shin-ryu of the Eternal Strange Divine Sect (久奇神流).

Gokui Gata 極意型

Ichimonji 一文字

The body is postured on the right diagonal, the spear tip is pointed down on the left, and the right hand is positioned above the head. Lower the right hand until everything is lined up. Thrust vigorously, then pull the spear back and spin the back end of the spear to the right. Pull the left leg back and sweep the opponent's left ankle, pull back one step, and with the spear head on the right sweep the opponent's right ankle, then thrust.

Kikusui 菊水

The body is postured on the same right diagonal as in the previous technique. Roll the right hand to the right. Roll three times, then using the head of the spear as if it were a whirlwind, thrust in for the opponent's leg with the whole body. Pull the spear back and thrust repeatedly. When pulling the spear back from the chest pull the body back at the same time by taking one step back. Use the back end of the spear when the opponent thrusts in, and pull the left side of the face to the left and thrust from the right.

Maki Tsuta 巻蔦

The body is postured on the left diagonal. The spear is in Chudan.

1. The thrust extends to the opponent's chest.
2. From there, sweep the opponent's right ankle using the back end of the spear.
3. From there, pull back. The opponent thrusts in.
4. Use the spear on the right to roll the upper part and thrust into the opponent's abdomen.

Onizashi 鬼刺

The body is postured on the right diagonal. The Kamae is in Chudan.

1. Thrust into the opponent's chest.

2. From there pull back one step. Pull the spear back a little using the palm.

3. Thrust into the opponent's chest.

4. Pull back one step. As before, the spear is repeatedly extended and then pulled back a little.

5. Move to thrust into the chest.

6. As in the previous technique, pull the left side out one step on the left diagonal. The spear is repeatedly extended and pulled back a little. Continue and thrust into the opponent's right leg.

Hiryu 飛龍

The body is postured on the left diagonal. The Kamae is in Gedan.

1. Thrust into the opponent's right leg. Leap back out to the right.

2. Swing the spear from the right around above and to the front, and thrust into the chest. Leap out back to the left.

3. Swing the spear around above, sweep the ankle using the head of the spear. Thrust in. From there use the back end of the spear to hit the right side of the opponent's face.

4. Move back on the right diagonal and thrust into the opponent's chest with the back end of the spear.

Tsuki-buse 突伏

The body is postured on the right diagonal.

1. Thrust into the opponent's chest. At the same time the tip of the spear is pulled back, pull the whole body back one step.

2. Thrust into the groin. Pull the spear back and at the same time pull the body back one step.

3. Thrust into the opponent's chest. Pull the spear back and at the same time pull the body back one step.

4. Thrust in again. This technique is such that the spear is pulled back so that the opponent cannot enter in with a thrust, and this is why the body is pulled back at the same time too thrust. This technique finishes in the form of Tsuki-buse.

Incho 蔭蝶

The body is postured on the right diagonal.

1. Thrust into the opponent's chest. Leap out to the right side. At that moment use the back end of the spear to sweep the opponent's left torso.
2. Swing the spear from Gedan no Kata and thrust in. Leap out to the right side. At the same time use the back end of the spear to sweep the opponent's left torso. This technique is done circling the body to the right; when thrusting it is done using the back end of the spear, sweeping into the left torso. This thrusting technique sweeps the torso using the back end of the spear so that the opponent cannot enter in with a thrust. Rotate to the right; this prevents the opponent from entering in to cut.

Mitsu-dama 三ツ玉
The body is postured on the right diagonal. The Kamae is Jodan.
1. Hit into the opponent's chest with the spear tip, with the right hand raised over the head. Repeatedly bring the right hand down, and thrust.
2. The opponent deflects the spear tip up. Use that motion and release with the left hand, rotate to the right, and on the opponent's left side sweep the leg. From there thrust into the abdomen.

Menkyo Kaiden Hencho Gata 免許皆傳変蝶型

Yoko Taoshi 横倒
The spear is in Jodan no Kamae. Begin to execute a thrust, but then rotate to the right to make sure not to let the opponent get too close. The last thing is to strike to the left side of the face with the back end of the spear. Rotate to the left above the head and strike to the right side of the face. That movement gets repeated. Striking to the side of the opponent's face and knocking them down is unorthodox.

Ryuto 龍頭
The spear is in Gedan no Kamae, the position is taken on the right diagonal. The right leg kneels and the thrust goes into the chest. Pivot the body onto the left diagonal, rotate the spear to the right, and sweep the left ankle. At the same time the left leg kneels and the thrust goes into the opponent's chest. This Kata has one leg up to defend against the opponent cutting in, and, just like the dragon rearing its head up, this thrust makes the opponent unable to knock the spear away with the Daito. It is also known as Tawara-gaeshi.

Tomoe 巴

The spear is in Jodan no Kamae. Spinning left and right above the head carving out a circle in the air, give the impression of striking to the opponent's face. The opponent ducks to avoid it. Here is when the thrust goes in once, twice, three times; this becomes a form of knocking him down.

Kugi-nuki 釘抜

This Kata has the spear in Jodan no Kamae. From a posture on the right diagonal the spear thrusts in and is deflected up. Using a motion that resembles prying out a nail called Kugi-nuki gata, on the thrust and deflection up, after the opponent moves to slip by the thrust using the sword, be aware of your wrists—in that opening you must thrust the spear in. This technique is called the spear of Sutemi.

Arashi 嵐

The spear is in Chudan no Kamae. Rotate the spear tip to the right as if it is a whirlwind, pivot the body onto the left diagonal, and from the right, strike with the spear tip into the left side of the body. From there use the back end of the spear and extend the left foot out one step and spring up into the groin. Pull the left leg back and thrust in, knocking him down; this thrust also uses the spear tip rotated to the left to resemble a whirlwind. It becomes a thrusting Kata. It is also called the triumphant art of defeating and capturing an opponent like a dragonfly—Kachimushi Tombo-dori.

Shinmyo 心明

This has the spear in Chudan; the body is postured in Kamae on the right diagonal. The opponent has a sword in Dai-jodan. Continue forward towards the opponent a little. If the opponent can move in to strike then that becomes defeat. Continue to move forward bit by bit, and at the last moment when the opponent moves in to cut, thrust in and knock him down. This is also known as Sutemi Shinmyo.

Taki Otoshi 瀧落

This Kamae is postured on the right diagonal. Shift mostly onto the right leg, using Kiai, and at the same time direct the spear into the empty space against distant opponents and throw to impale them with it. The spear is thrown from above the head; this is called Taki otoshi. Hold the spear about one-third of the way down from the spear tip, extend the right leg, and at the same time throw.

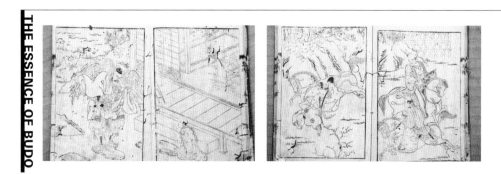

Yoko Nage 横投

This Kata is more than simply thrusting with the spear; it knocks the opponent down completely. The spear is held over the head with the right hand ready for a right thrust. The left hand holds the center and points it up overhead. When swinging the spear, move the legs forward and back rhythmically. The left hand releases and at the same time spin to the right three, four times, and throw the spear spinning into the opponent. After some practice this will stick right in, but when starting out the impact is into the side to knock them down.

Tachi Nage 立投

This Kata is for use against close-up opponents. Squat and hold the spear with the right hand five sun below the top of the Sendan-maki (the top part of the spear woven with rattan to facilitate gripping)—this is for throwing against the opponent. Extend the right leg and at the same time throw.

Nichi Getsu 日月

This technique is used when holding a spear and leaping into the midst of your opponents. It uses the back end of the spear. Spin the spear above the head two times to the right with the rhythm of Yoko Nage while holding five sun above the bottom of the Sendan-maki, and also swing once more to the abdomen. In order to be able to mow the opponents down, it is necessary to train hard and have good preparation.

Gokui Gata 極意型

Gokui gata are concepts that should not be conferred upon the general public. Nor are they to be pursued as merely techniques.

Within all of the fighting arts of the spear, the forms should come alive with the Kukan, or space, in a way that doesn't create barriers. As for the basic forms known as Kata, there is one called the "Secret Door Kata" which in Japanese can be read as "Hito Kata." While Hito Kata can also be heard to mean "One Kata," realize that instead of merely a singular, strictly defined Kata it should instead be seen as the Kata ho (方方) of "this way and that," which naturally becomes the Kata ho (型宝) of "Treasured Form." If you can see ho as coming to life through the character for treasure (宝), then the Hozoin-ryu (宝蔵院流) school of Sojutsu or the Tsutsumi Hozan-ryu (堤宝山流) school of Sojutsu become part of the spear, and as a matter of course you will naturally come to understand the feeling of Gokui. You should not think that it is always a simple relation-

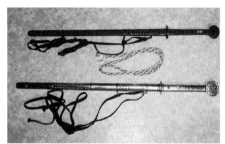

ship of one and one. Make a transition from one strictly defined way and enable yourself to go in multiple directions, morph into a giant butterfly, and flutter elegantly about. Make sure you unify the Hencho Gata (changing omen forms 変兆型), Kukan (empty space 空間), Chukan (universal space 宙間), and Chukan (loyalty that flows through all 忠貫) and whirl about, like you are dancing with these concepts showing your honor.

The Art of the Naginata 薙刃術

Let's look at the world of the Naginata, Nagamaki, and Bisento through the dramatic performances of Noh theater. In the presentation of the classic story of *Funa BenKei* there is a spectacular fight scene at sea between the hero, Minamoto no Yoshitsune, and the fierce apparition of Taira no Tomomori, who had recently drowned himself after losing a decisive naval battle to Yoshitsune. The ghost of Tomomori attacks Yoshitsune's ship and crew wielding a Naginata (written here with the characters for placate and blade; 凪刀), and kicks up a storm with his legs as he dances over the rolling waves of the sea.

The valiant performance with the very heavy Naginata evokes images of the brave fighter Chohan (長範) on the battlefield. The movements are performed with a wonderfully subtle grace and mysterious profundity for the hero. It is a very composed, dignified, and "heavy" dramatic performance.

The term Naginata (薙刀), can also be written with the Japanese characters for Naginata (長刀) or long blade, and that meaning also includes the Bisento. Additionally, if you write Naginata with the characters (薙鉈), meaning "to mow down" and "wide-bladed knife," it will hone your way of thinking until you see it as a fighter's tool. When expressing this through the Nine-demon Kami School of Kukishin-ryu, the nine demons of the Naginata are able to change into enormous monsters, mutating into a large hatchet, a huge axe, and the massive Nyoito, able to strike down upon and crush even the most impregnable iron shields and helmets, becoming the secret enlightened blade of the Bisento (秘閃刀).

At this point I would like to draw on the warrior legends of Scandinavia and relate a few of Odin's eighteen secret charms that were invoked to protect mankind. These include the ability to sap the power from the enemies' swords so that they inflict no wounds; arrest the flight of incoming spears and arrows; protect old comrades-in-arms when leading them into battle and inspire them so that wherever they are they remain

unscathed. Become a warrior hero who is able to praise and unify others.

Within Kukishin-ryu Happo Biken, the art of the Naginata is said to have evolved from the ancient Tang Chinese art of the Bisento. With that in mind, I would like to express the "to" of the Bisento as having the to (闘) of battle rather than the to (唐) of China. Even though it appears to be nearly the same weapon, the Bisento's blade is longer than that of the Naginata and there are some minor characteristic differences that give it a unique elegance, setting it apart from the Naginata techniques of other schools. Drawing the opponents in close enough benefits your weapons. If I am able to draw them in far enough, my body becomes Sutemi.

Here is where all your training and preparation for the assault, as well as the way that you carry your body, becomes vital. In other words, strategy is an integral part of winning. Through a cleverly implemented strategy of misinformation, the fundamental nature of opponents can be undermined. Through such strategy even the weak can attain victory. These are the illusion-inducing falsehoods of Kyo in the never-ending interchange between reality and deception.

> Small-mindedness
> > and impatience for victory
> Lead only to
> > self-demise and certain defeat

Realize that there is such a thing as winning through losing, which is called the prescience (Sente 先手) of retrospection (Gote 後手). This becomes the flash (Sente 閃手) of enlightenment (Gote 悟手) and is expressed through the following legend.

In the first year of the Hogen era (1156), Izumo no Kanja Yoshiteru, who was of the original line of the Genji clan, battled against a powerful rival and regent to the emperor, Taira no Tadamichi. After the Genji clan was defeated, Yoshiteru was forced to escape and chose to flee to the Inome cavern at Izumo. It just so happened that a monk named Tetsujo had escaped from Tang China and was also inhabiting that particular cavern. This monk was a warrior, a true master of the military arts of Tang China. And so Yoshiteru learned all the methods of combat that the monk had to teach. It is said that this is where Yoshiteru learned the art of the Bisento.

A similar legend says that while Yoshiteru was training in a cavern, he escaped to Tang China after it was clear that all was lost for the Genji clan during the Heiji Rebellion. This is where he met the monk Tetsujo and studied with him, learning from the master of the Tang Chinese military arts before returning to Japan a few years later. But this particular

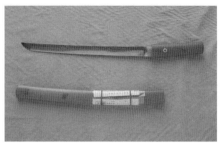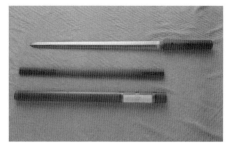

version of the legend is unsubstantiated and due to the long passage of time between that era and the present day, the real specifics of the matter may never be completely known. What is known for certain is that written in the ancient records of Japan is the fact that Yoshiteru did indeed learn from the monk Tetsujo.

In yet another legend it is said that Yoshiteru fought for the Minamoto clan during the Heiji Rebellion and after his clan was defeated he escaped to a cavern in the mountains of Iga where he learned this art of the Bisento from a man from Tang China. The blade of the Bisento is longer than that of a normal Naginata, making the way the body is used to manipulate it that much more essential. There are some definite points of difference between the two weapons.

The vital thing here is to realize how Yoshiteru survived through the turbulent exchanges of reality and deception that resulted from the turmoil of war; how this warrior survived by becoming a monk, living a life in which sometimes he was a warrior and sometimes a monk, living the life of Soryo Soryo (two lives and two journeys), the simultaneous life of a comrade-in-arms and a travel companion. Coincidentally, travelers to Kyoto may be fortunate enough to encounter the long-handled Chinese Naginata exhibition that is incorporated into a float in the Gion district and uses the power of the Naginata to ward off evil spirits. The crystal clear, cleansing light of the azure blue waxing crescent moon shines down on Gozan, the most important group of temples in Kyoto.

Sukui Age 掬上

This posture is out on the right diagonal with the legs spread and the hips lowered; this is Yoko Ichimonji no Kamae. The rest depends on what the opponent does. In the case where the opponent moves to cut in, pull the left leg back and cut up from underneath into the opponent's left side with the Naginata. In the case where the opponent doesn't come toward you, step forward with the right leg and cut up from underneath into the opponent's left side with the Naginata. In either case strike the opponent's lead hand and continue forward with the left leg, and cut up from underneath into the opponent's right side. This ends up being repeated a number of times.

Batto 抜倒 / Hataki Taoshi

This begins with Hasso no Kamae. In the case where the opponent is in Seigan, pull the left leg back, and from the opponent's left side cut down into the left wrist. In the case where the opponent is in Daijodan, come forward with the right leg and cut in below the left side. Roll the wrists and cut back into the right ankle. Then roll the wrists and cut

into the opponent's left shoulder. Draw back one step and return to the starting position. This is Hasso no Kamae.

Ashi Barai 足拂

Hira Ichimonji no Kamae. The opponent moves to cut in with a sword from Daijo-dan. Extend the left hand up high overhead as the right arm bends and receives the blow. Depending on the form when receiving, the opponent's sword will flow by. At this moment roll the wrists, pull the left hand back, kneel, and sweep the opponent's right leg. Roll the wrists and at the same time sweep the left leg, step back, and assume Zanshin. This is a variation of Yoko Ichimonji no Kamae.

Hatto 撥倒

Posture in Seigan no Kamae. The opponent's sword is also in Seigan. Shift the body to the left. The opponent moves to thrust in. Roll the wrists to face up, and cut up from underneath. This deflects the opponent's wrists or blade upward. Immediately roll the wrists, cut into the neck from the right shoulder, and roll the wrists again. This becomes a cut down from the left shoulder.

Kuridashi 繰出

This posture is Chu Seigan. Against the opponent in Daijodan, use Seigan and move back one step with the left leg. Make it look like you are moving back and shift the body out to the left side, roll the wrists, and cut into the opponent's left side. Then shift out to the right side, roll the wrists, and cut back into the opponent's right side.

Zengo Nagi 前後薙

Posture in Hasso. There are numerous opponents to the front and rear. Swing repeatedly across from left to right; that is to say using the motion of rolling the right arm for the strike to the right. Doing this quickly is called Naginata Furi Mawashi Kiri Kaeshi. In this technique you swing into the midst of the opponents.

Sashichigai 差違

From Hira Ichimonji no Kamae against opponents in Daijodan, thrust with the blade of the Naginata turned on its side. Roll the wrists, sweep the ankle, immediately thrust with the blade turned on its side, roll the wrists, and sweep the ankle. By doing this numerous times, all of the opponents will be knocked down.

Tobikiri 飛切

This begins by posturing in Hasso. If you can cut into the opponent's left side, use that reaction to leap to the left; if you can cut into the right side, leap out to the right. This becomes Tobichigai Kiru.

Bisento 眉尖刀

When I see the art of the Bisento, there are times when I feel it is more like the "bi" of a person's eyebrows. The eyebrows express the movement of human emotions together with mind, body, and technique. During the age of the Tang Dynasty in China, it is said that Emperor Genso (658–762) was so moved by the beauty of his favorite concubine that he commissioned ten pictures to be painted of her (known as the *Ten Eyebrow Pictures*), which came to represent the feminine ideal of the era.

In Japan there are also wonderful works of art that portray a passion for beauty, such as *The Picture Scroll of the Tale of Genji* as well as *The Tale of Heike*. Within those scrolls, there is exquisite attention to detail paid especially to beautification rituals. People often lose themselves in the application of cosmetics to beautify the face, first plucking out the unsightly hairs, then making the face white with powder and then painting on the eyebrows with a thick foundation—leaving the heart and mind abstracted. The Bushi of Kamakura held bravery above all and it is said that they never performed beautification rituals such as drawing in their eyebrows. Women's eyebrows are usually drawn in the shape of a crescent moon. It is as if women are following the phases of the moon. The art of the Naginata has recently been taken up by more and more women. Even after the hair on the forehead recedes and falls out, the eyebrows remain, and I am told that of all the species only humans have eyebrows. So how is it that these eyebrows still exist in mankind? When you've got sweat on your forehead the eyebrows redirect it to flow around to the sides and stop that sweat from going into your eyes—that is what has been left for us. That is to say, the tears or mercy of a warrior are clearly visible as the fighting spirit, as is the sense of righteousness, and reactions unrelentingly flow out.

There is an appropriate Kuji (nine-character sacred verse) that goes: Rin Teki To To Sa Gyaku Han Aku Zetsu.

Forms of the Art of the Bisento 眉尖刀術型

Oshin 汪振

This Kata means to become larger. The back end of the Bisento is heavy, making it difficult to move suddenly, so when cutting in just roll the wrists. It is essential to practice this Kata. Begin in Seigan no Kamae. Rotate in a large motion, cut in to the left side, rotate in a large motion, cut in to the right side—this becomes a way of training to cleave bamboo in half by cutting down from the left shoulder.

Kakugyaku 鬲逆

Rotate in a large motion intending to cut back across the chest with Gyaku Kiri; from the right cut back down across the opponent's left chest. It is disadvantageous for the opponent to block. The opponent's body just slips by and takes a step back. Do the same and this becomes a cut down into the right chest.

Chikusha 竹斜

Slice through bamboo at an angle, cut down from the left. Pull the right leg back, cut down with the right shoulder in the same way you would to sever the bamboo. Cut down again into the left side. This becomes a cut down into the right side.

Namiba 波刃

Chop down quickly numerous times to the left and right on an angle like the stormy waves of a raging tempest.

Batto 抜刀

It is said that this Kata is like Nukite. With the back end of the Bisento and the left leg forward make the opponent believe you are going to thrust, then move forward with the right leg, and cut down into the left side of the neck. With the back end of the Bisento and the right leg moving forward, make the opponent believe you are going to thrust and then bring the left leg forward. Cutting down into the right side of the neck requires thorough practice.

Gisen 曦先

This is a technique of the shadow of the blade. It begins in Chu Seigan. With the feeling of scooping up from under the opponent's wrists to above the head, the thrust extends

out. The opponent deflects to the right with the sword. Use that deflection to roll the blade face up, and scoop up into the wrists. Then pivot and sweep the right ankle.

Shinto 伸刀

This is a technique for extending the blade. Lower the body; the left foot should be forward, the right foot back. Merely by lowering the body, the body shifts a little to the rear. The opponent moves to thrust in. Shift the body forward, cut up towards the left shoulder on a diagonal from the right side, just lower the body, and then cut down from the left shoulder.

Seito 惺刀

This is a technique that comes from enlightenment. It begins with the opponent's sword in Daijodan. Assume Yoko Ichimonji no Kamae, and wait for the opponent to cut down. The opponent moves in to cut down with the sword. Pull the left leg back just the right amount, and hit the Tsubamoto, where the guard meets the blade, to knock down the opponent's sword that is cutting down and in from the left. If possible, cut into the opponent's wrists, but there are some cases in which you hit the Tsubamoto or the opponent's blade breaks, or you knock it down with Tataki Otosu.

Miken 魅剣

This is a technique of confusing. In Hasso no Kamae with the left leg forward the opponent attempts to move closer. The opponent is postured with a sword in Chudan. If possible, expose the left side a little; this creates an opening. While it is easy for the opponent to cut in, the opponent loses his composure and becomes uncertain of himself. Whether the opponent cuts in or not, cut up from the left ankle, and again lower the body. At the same time, cut up from the right ankle. This movement is repeated.

The Art of the Naginata, Techniques of the Bisento, Legend of a Triumphant Insect 勝虫相伝, 薙刃術, 眉尖刀技

Within the transmissions of the Happo Biken of Kukishin-ryu, the art of the Naginata was developed from techniques of the Bisento, and that level of refinement is markedly different from that of other Naginata styles. If I am able to draw the opponents in far enough, my body becomes Sutemi. It is here that you should know that good body

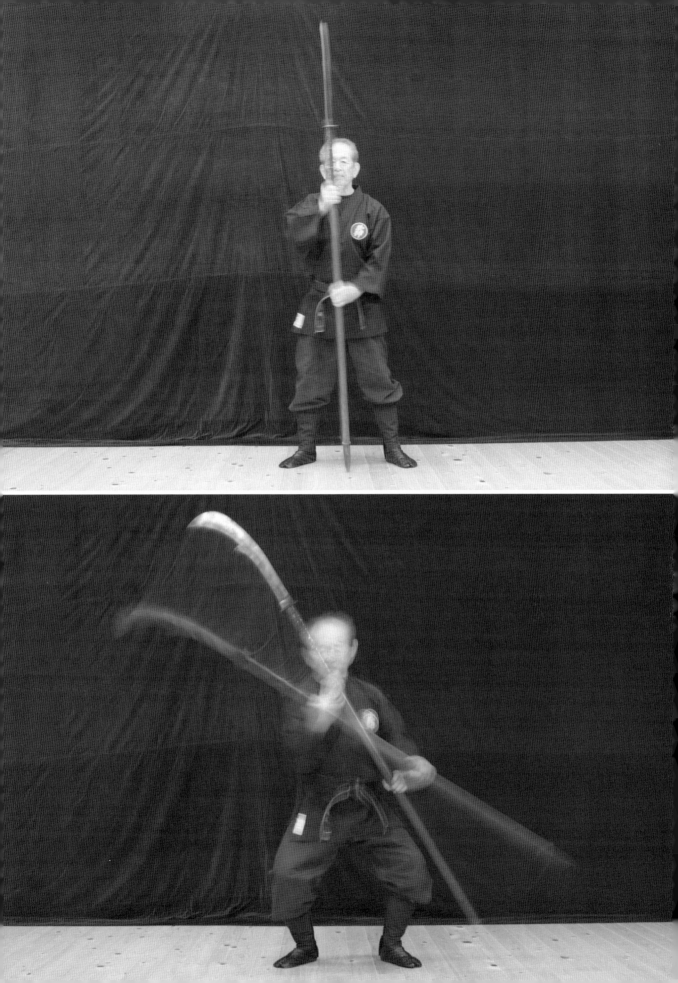

movement and a violent attack are vital. Victory can be achieved through conspiracy. With a conspiracy, even the opponent's sturdiest convictions can be undermined and become riddled with uncertainty. Through conspiracy the physically weak can emerge victorious. These are known as the illusion-inducing falsehoods of Kyojitsu.

> Small-mindedness
>> and impatience for victory
> Lead only to
>> self-demise and certain defeat

If you can attain the heart and mind of Bushin, your spirit will be in complete harmony and become the unified enlightened hand (Sente 閃手) of certain victory.

Legend:

As is the case with most legends, there often exist varying versions of which the actual facts are nearly impossible to verify. While that is certainly true of the following, these are the versions that have been transmitted over the years. Izumo no Kanja Minamoto no Yoshiteru, in the first year of the Hogen era (1156), was part of the rebellion against Taira no Tadamichi, the powerful regent to the emperor. After Yoshiteru's Genji clan was defeated in battle, he fled to Izumo Inoe cavern. Coincidentally, a monk named Tetsujo had escaped from Tang China and was also hiding out in that particular cavern. As Yoshiteru studied with this Tang Chinese monk, he came to learn the techniques of the Bisento. Another version that has been transmitted is that Yoshiteru trained in the cavern and after the Genji were defeated in the Heiji Rebellion he fled to Tang China, where he learned the art of the Bisento and then after a number of years returned to Japan. The blade of the Bisento is longer, giving it some definite points of difference compared with a normal Naginata, and making the way the body is used to manipulate it that much more essential.

Now I would like to pass on the power of Jinten Mineuchi, so that you understand the mysterious nature of striking with the weighty back end of the Bisento.

Oshin 汪振—Become larger

The same as before, into Migi Ichimonji no Kamae. Use the back end of the Bisento to bounce off the opponent's right leg. From there just keep the back end of the Bisento in under the right arm and strike with the blade into the right of the opponent's neck.

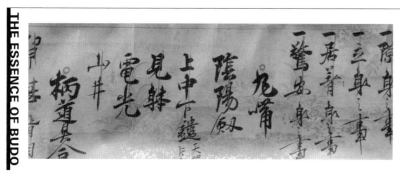 

Kakugyaku 膈逆—Striking back across the chest
The same as before, swing the blade around in a very large motion, strike in towards the area above the opponent's right chest with Gyaku Dageki.

Chikusha 竹斜—Strike as if to cleave bamboo in half
Seigan no Kamae. Strike down into the area above the left hand with Ochikaesu, sweep the opponent's right leg with the back end of the Bisento, then pass to the left hand and cut down on a diagonal from the outer edge of the opponent's left shoulder, just like you are cleaving bamboo.

Namiba 波刃—like the stormy waves of a raging tempest, Ichimonji, repeatedly chopping down with the blade using the left hand.

Batto 抜刀—Like Nukite Seigan.

Gisen 曦先—This is a technique of the shadow of the blade. Jito Seigan. The technique is to roll the blade using the wrists.

Shinto 伸刀—This is a technique for extending the blade. Jito Seigan. Change to the opponent's left side, change to the right side, left side.

Seito 惺刀—This is a technique coming from enlightenment
This has the opponent in Jodan and if it appears that the cut is coming down, scoop up from below with Sukui Muneuchi. If it appears that the opponent is coming in to thrust for the side, from above the right Hitosuji, cut with Hassuwari. Or from above the left Suji, cut with Hassuwari.

Miken 魅剣—This is a technique of confusing
From Ichimonji it appears that the cut is coming down from above using Hassuwari; in reality the crushing strike comes up from underneath. Crushing up from underneath and leaving the Bisento up where it is, drop it back down across the opponent from the right and crush. Make Taijutsu (body technique 体技) become Taijutsu (massive technique 大技).

This is the same as Chi Mi Mo Ryo Shyo In Gen Jitsu.

Ura Juhappon, separated into left and right.

The Art of the Jutte 十手術

The shogun Tokugawa Ieyasu said that people are encumbered with heavy burdens that they carry on their backs or shoulders for their entire lives. If that is true then I would like for us to look at the hardships in life through the duality of a Haiku verse that reads: "While it is the natural habit of water to flow down into a depression, as I fondly recall, before long it will begin its ascension." If you were to ask Jesus Christ, who himself carried the burden of a heavy cross on his back, "Isn't that what life really is?" what would he say? The answer has of course already been graciously given by Christ as "Yes," and lies in a pun with the Japanese pronunciation of "Jesus," which is "Ieyasu" and has the same sound as the affirmative answer "yes" in English. This is called the mount of Mumei (martial life).

The art of the Jutte (lit. the art of ten hands), as with all arts, is not confined simply to a matter of technique. In the realm of Buddhism, Muso Soseki (1275–1351) realized the enlightened vision of the *Ten Ox-Herding Pictures,* and if you read about the ten types of virtue in self-enlightened Zen master Suzuki Shosan's (1579–1655) treatise entitled *Moanjo* you will come to better understand the martial virtues of Butoku. From these ten virtues we can conjure dynamic images of the ten brave oxen ready for battle with fiery torches tied to their horns.

The Bushin (martial kami) pray: "Receive the benevolent gifts of the kami by cultivating the ten spiritual treasures of the ten spirits, be receptive to divine guidance and turn towards the heavenly path; once there, cleanse yourself of impurities."

The Art of the Jutte

I have been told that the art of the Jutte is also said to be the art of Juppo Sessho or the art of negotiating all directions, but those are only one aspect of these transmissions and we can easily open such a "light sketch" of the Densho to reveal 100 of them. This is also true with the Zen style of painting where anything unnecessary is omitted, and the place where it has been omitted is where the genuine illustration of Zen can be seen.

1. Kiri no Ha 桐葉

Within the art of the Jutte there is a technique called "Kiri no Hitto Ha (One Leaf of the Paulownia Tree)" and you should also know the expression "One leaf of the pau-

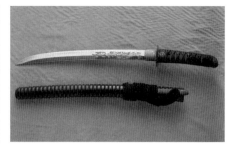

lownia tree falls to earth / The inevitable winds of change have come," as well as the Kabuki theater performances of classic Japanese dramas such as "Kiri Hitto Ha"(1894) and "Hototogisu Kojo no Rakugetsu" and the like, which were written by highly accomplished modern Kabuki playwright Tsubouchi Shoyo (1839–1935).

The "Tai,"or tower, of the paulownia tree is the crest of enshrined Kami.

2. Rakka 落花

Rakka, or the fallen flower, is a true transmission from the art of the Jutte. The flowers of the Bushi are the sakura (cherry blossoms), the tsubaki (camellia blossoms) and the botan (peony blossoms). See the way their petals fall to lie scattered over the ground, see the beauty in their determination as they fall to their death. Then, next year when they blossom proudly—it is those flowers we look forward to seeing again.

Rakka 落花—Cherry Blossom, Paulownia Blossom, Peony Blossom, Rakka Yojo Zangetsu

The opponent has a sword in Daijodan. Stand with a Jutte in Seigan. The hips are lowered in Kamae. The opponent moves in to cut down. Receive the opponent's sword. The opponent's sword will flow down the side of the Jutte, then pivot the body to position facing left, and with the right hand, wrap up the opponent's hands. Kick with the right leg into the opponent's groin; the sword ends up being captured down the opposite way.

Ura: the same thing done to the left.

People who are contentious fall to ruin. Strive for harmony, for peace. With the heart of justice, the martial ways of Bu cultivate a commonsense character and are able to overcome all obstacles, thereby becoming the art of self-defense. With the auspicious coming of the New Year, hang up a fresh Shimenawa (sacred straw rope) on all four sides of the Dojo, worship both the literary and martial kami, recite the poem below three times, perform Kuji, and endeavor through the training of the first class of the year—this is the way of teaching traditions.

> O Mighty Kami
> By the grace of your teachings
> Am I able to
> Rightly foster and protect
> My mind, body, and spirit

Kiri no Ha 桐之葉

One leaf of the paulownia tree falls to earth; the inevitable winds of change have come. (Note: this evokes memories of O. Henry's short story entitled *The Last Leaf* in which a young girl has lost the will to live.) I would like this to be a reminder of the fatal weakness that lay hiding in the leaves for the overconfident dragon that was vanquished by the hero Siegfried, in the classic opera of the same name.

The postures of the art of the Jutte are really the postures of the body. That is to say, the Jutte is held to the rear in the right hand with the left leg forward. When the Jutte is thrust forward, the left leg moves forward. With Jodan no Kamae, the right leg moves forward. The body is always kept lowered.

The opponent has a sword in Daijodan. Take up position with the Jutte forward and the body lowered. The opponent comes in to cut down from Daijodan. Leap by on the right diagonal, slip by the sword; the palms are the form for leaping in. Then strike to the opponent's neck with the Jutte using Yoko Uchi. The opponent becomes dazed and falls down.

Ura: techniques done to the left.

Mizutori 水鳥

Waterfowl playfully diving in a lake, enjoying themselves by the legless apparitions (rumored to be found next to the weeping willow trees). The numerous legends of the swan . . .

The opponent has a sword in Daijodan. Move forward with the left leg. The right hand has the Jutte to the rear. Lower the hips, take up position. This posture is like a bird diving into the water. Next the opponent comes in to cut down with the sword. Leap one step forward, strike into the solar plexus with the Jutte, from the legless apparitions. At that point the right leg kneels, this becomes a posture with the left leg up, and this is the playful form of Chinyufudo, the unwavering courage in diving.

Ura: the same thing done to the left. Grasp the wisdom of Ten Chi Jin.

Gorin Kudaki 五輪砕

The five Confucian virtues of benevolence, justice, courtesy, wisdom, and sincerity; the crushing military demon Buddhist spirit.

The opponent is in Daijodan. Have the Jutte forward, in Seigan no Kamae. Against the opponent's downward cut, open up the body to the right, then strike down with the Jutte into the wrist of the opponent's arm as it flows by. This is leaping in and striking in with the Jutte.

Ura: the same thing done to the left.

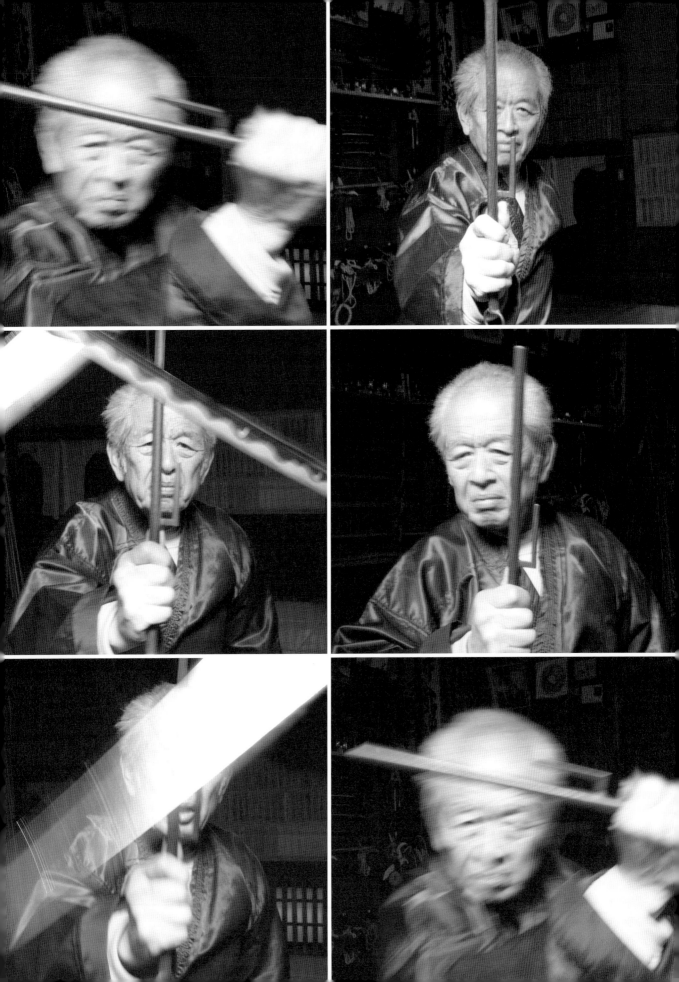

Mawashidori 廻捕

A flash of nothingness, the art of disarming with Juppo Kikatsu. Against the opponent's cut down from Daijodan use the right hand to receive, then make contact with the Hadome of the blade, or drop the body in underneath that and turn to evade. Kick into the opponent's groin with the right leg and knock the blade down (out of his hands), this is ToriOsaeru. On a broader scale this is ShikiEtari Jupposessho.

Ura: the same thing done to the left.

It is only once you are able to master the Taijutsu that you will become someone capable of beginning to master the art of the Jutte. At my level, I no longer have the feeling of holding weapons in my hands; through Taijutsu these become techniques for disarming.

Prince Shotoku (573–621), who was regent of Japan, which was also known at that time as the land of Wa (和), greatly revered the Three Treasures of Buddha and learned from his studies that "it is vital to achieve the Wa (和) of harmony and peace." I take that Wa (和) to be the Wa (倭) of ancient Japan, and then that expression can be read as, "It is vital to achieve a unified Japan." This is where true nation-building can be seen.

If you were to say that the Jutte and the rope were indispensable weapons or appendages, you can easily imagine the posture of Hitosujinawa Tajo Busshin (multiple bound heart) Jujyo (ten ropes). They would become entwined through the secret binding of Musubi.

Mysteries of the Art of Budo Taijutsu

With the art of the Jutte, unless you are able to master the mysterious wonders of the art of Budo Taijutsu, it will be impossible to see and appreciate the youthful beauty of the cherry blossom trees, the camellia blossoms, and the peonies that flower in the spring.

Within the art of the Jutte, it is important that the techniques of the Jutte should not be professed as in a lecture. Make no mistake, you the reader are probably thinking right now that the way to use the Jutte is to capture the sword that cuts down at you with the prong of the Jutte, but you should be aware that there are many different forms of Jutte. There are Jutte without a prong; Jutte that swivel about a pivot and open up into a cross; there is also one with something called Marohoshi, which is shaped as a shellfish talisman; there are some made with chains or firearms or even Metsubushi. In this way, the martial wind of Bufu was discovered on the infinitely long and continually flowing wind

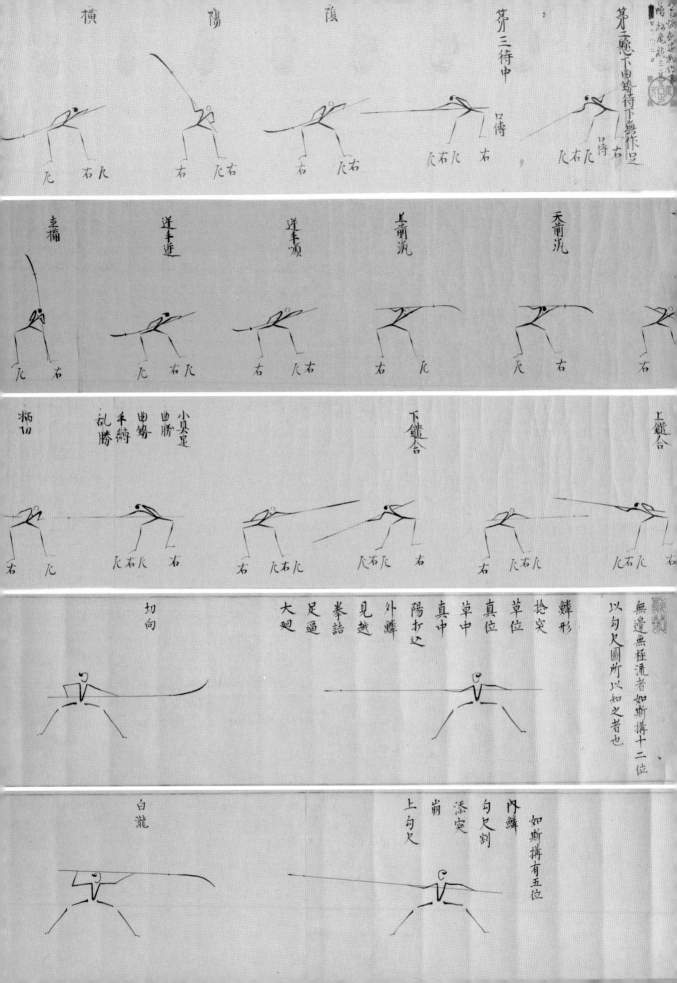

横　陽　陰　第三待中　第二懸下曲勢待下無作旦

立捅　逆手逆　逆手順　上前沉　天前沉

横切　乱勝　手縛　曲勢　曲勝　小貝足　下鑓合　上鑓合

切向　大廻　足逼　拳詰　見越　外鱗　陽打辻　真中　草中　真位　草位　捻突　鱗形　無邊無柩流者如斯搆十二位　以句尺圖所以知之者也

白瀧　上句尺　崩　添突　句尺割　內鱗　如斯搆有五位

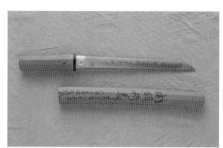

of antiquity that has hidden knowledge for mankind. It is found in the sexagenary cycle of the twelve earthly branches and the ten heavenly stems of the traditional Chinese calendar system.

Make the Kata of the Jutte come alive through the unconscious (written here as a pun for military awareness; 武意識), and couple that with things you must not miss. In addition, you can find Tetsubane, Tetsuto, Metezashi and Kakushibuki hidden everywhere in normal everyday life; much like the illustrations of the *Ten Ox-Herding Pictures* (written here as a pun for ten illustrations of heroism; 十義勇図) that hint at finding Buddhism in everyday life, and just like famed Zen master Ikkyu's (1394–1481) tea cup, there are hints at hidden things that can very quickly become weapons.

I am often told that in fighting, enlightenment is at your feet, and that brings to mind the classic book of Japanese prose known as *The Narrow Road to the Interior*. Be like a traveler who wanders for a time of one hundred generations; rather, know that enlightenment is here as well as also over there. When engaged in combat with the Katana, spear, Naginata, and sword, know that there are times when they can be cut and broken, but if you are able to be enlightened with the feeling of the Jutte, your life will pulsate and undergo a complete change. It is the same with Bojutsu, Hanbojutsu, and Zajutsu. The character of ju (十) resembles a clear plus sign, a positive, a power of language that makes it possible to change into anything—martial arts create multiple possibilities.

CHAPTER 3

Budo Vital Points

"Letter from a Budo Researcher"

This letter takes me back to an article written forty years ago in an educational magazine entitled "A Scratch of the Pen on the Present-Day Budo." I wrote about the historical event of Nitta Yoshisada (1301–38) who cast his Tachi into the sea of the Inamuragasaki coast at Kamakura and led his army to the opposite bank at low tide. The tides of Budo itself have also been changing, and my contribution to the magazine was about how Budo had been descending into showmanship. Just as Yoshisada cast his sword, I cast my manuscript, and my Budo friends around the world agreed with me. My penmanship was neither exposition nor fiction; it was a song to the brave individuals who transcend the common boundaries of life and death.

This is a chance to introduce the letter of the Budo researcher Kiyoshi Watatani. He also goes by the pen name of Tahei Tobushi:

I'm in complete agreement with your point on Budo. I admit that I'm an outsider to martial technique, but I'm completely disgusted with certain statements of so-called modern Budoka. For a long time I have been reading the densho of kobudo. Even if certain Budokas make salient comments, in general what they say is little different from the words of priests of Buddhism or Shinto. And even if there are Budoka who claim "the Sword and Zen are one," I know only one person who actually practiced Zen and the Sword together. That person is Sogen Omori. I believe if they do not practice sincerely or make insightful comments on Budo, what they say is simply banal and not worthy of attention. I believe that theory without practice is nothing more than mannerism.

Budo Changing to Sports

I have been asked, "Mr. Hatsumi, how do you view the concept of Budo becoming sports?" I answered immediately by saying, "Budo becoming a sport is a wonderful thing because you do not have to kill a person. This is the Yagyu-ryu concept of Katsujin Budo, or giving life to a person."

Warrior Naoe Kanetsugu was famous for being a nakimushi—one who cries easily. Olympic athletes shed tears of joy on winning gold—and with the five Olympic rings I am reminded of *The Book of Five Rings* by Musashi. When the athletes stand stoically to receive their medals, we can hear the sound of the Kuji (nine-character sacred verse): Rin

Teki To Do Sa Gyaku Han Aku Zetsu. The tears of the samurai—those are not tears of tragedy, but can be said to be the tears of overwhelming happiness.

Funsho Kojyu (burning books on the Chinese classics and burying Confucian scholars alive)

In the words of the thirty-second Soke of Togakure-ryu, Toda Shinryuken Sensei:

"Shobu ni Seiko, Fuseiko" (Victory or defeat does not determine success or failure).

"Kyojyaku Jugo Arubekarazu" (One must not depend on strength or weakness, or softness or hardness).

"Onore wo Ku ni shite Mata Haisu" (One must empty oneself and then arrange the body again).

Genuine Budoka pass through the road of conflict, and eventually become secluded from the present world. Some avoid mundane things and become monks, or walk the way of the saints, like the Koya Saints who travelled around Japan spreading Buddhism. Therefore, those who have experienced real conflict call on them for advice. Toda Shinryuken Sensei was one such martial artist. He sought the way of reincarnation which is said to have guided several other Budoka before him. At the close of the Edo Period he left his role of instructing in military tactics during a time of great disorder. The novelist Fumiko Hayashi wrote the masterpiece entitled *Horoki* (My wandering life). The actress Mitsuko Mori has brought this drama to the stage 2,000 times. My teacher Takamatsu Sensei entered the gate of the gods, and became a head priest for Kumano Shugendo. If you leave the life of conflict, you will survive into the next generation.

There is a way of living your life that is truthful. In the same way that Nitta Yoshisada cast his Tachi into the sea at Inamuragaseki on the Kamakura coast, and his prayers were granted by the current that swept his sword away, we must cast our bodies to the rough waves.

Humans have principles; we allow our lives to be guided by "isms," but when these principles begin to control us they become a dogma. I am reminded of the ancient rulers who burned books; I see visions of wars throughout world history and my eyes despair. In those flames are the dreadful stories and records of wars. In those flames I see that wars are a natural process of life. In the red fire I am writing a story in black ink. It is the world of fire and ink; of the red and the black.

Correct repetition of things must be handed down, and done so cautiously. To accom-

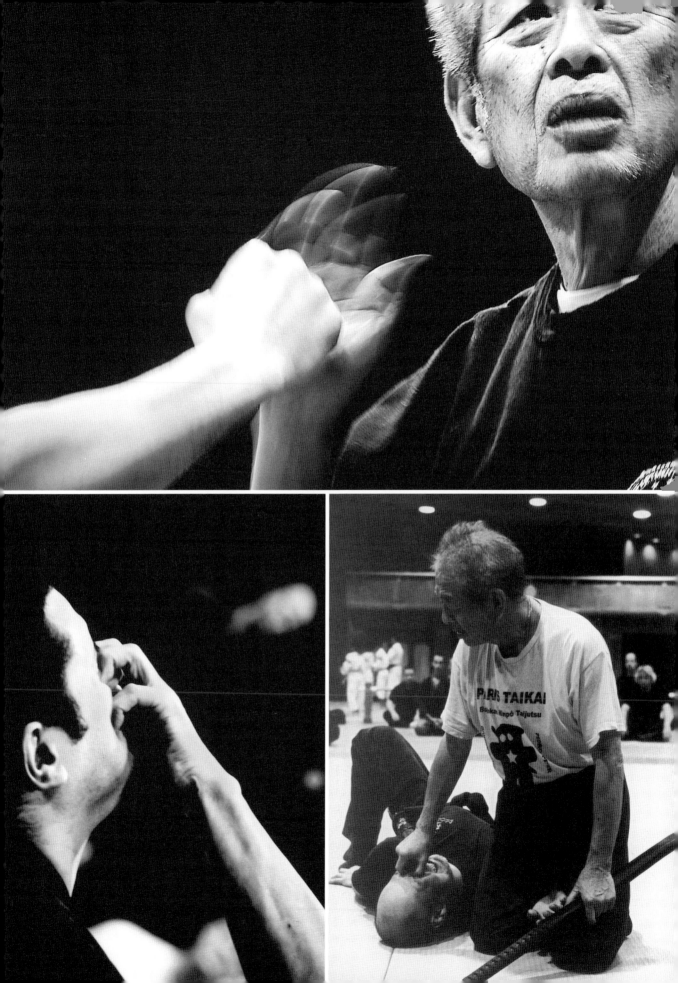

plish this a role of direct transmission is required. In that, you will begin to see the creation of nothingness in conflict and you will survive the conflict. However, it may be possible to explain the just and proper way of living as winning without drawing the sword. To explain this, I would like us all to have a look at a letter received from Takamatsu Sensei.

Takamatsu Sensei and the Kenbu (sword) Dance

It must have been at least forty years ago when I took seven of my students to meet Takamatsu Sensei while he was still in good health at his home in Kashihara.

Takamatsu Sensei, smiling away, handed each one of the students a scroll painting. Then he pierced his own arm with a needle, lit candles, and prayed to the kami of beautification whose physical manifestation is the needle and the stick. Then, in the Kashihara Dojo, he gave a mesmerizing demonstration of the sword dance. Incidentally, Takamatsu Sensei had once taken first place in the Japan Kenbu Taikai (exhibition) and his photo as a handsome young man was published in a Kobe newspaper, prompting the famous Kabuki player Jukai Ichikawa to ask him to become his adopted son. This episode is probably the reason why Takamatsu Sensei chose the name "Jukai" as his martial name.

I still cherish the lessons of my teacher, and one in particular stands out: Never sever a close tie. Of all the students I inherited from my teacher only two remain—15th dans Hideo Seno and Koichi Oguri. Sadly, not all students are so great—some have claimed to have trained with me for many years, when in reality they only had their picture taken with me.

Living in Emptiness (Ku)

Within Budo a very important concept is that of "Jyo"(eternity). In this one sound you can discover several other characters, such as the following ten: 常-eternity; 条-article; 状-shape; 情-emotion; 冗-uselessness; 縄-rope; 鎖-chain; 丈-stature; 城-castle; 錠-key. When you separate from "Jyo," and tear off its shell, you see Bufu-Shu Ha Ri. Within people, extrasensory perception (ESP) lies dormant. You must be aware of inner ESP, uncover what is hidden, and separate yourself from common conventional wisdom.

Zanshin no Kamae provides a good example of this. It is said that once you have completed your technique on your opponents you must remain with your body intact and in a state of awareness. Zanshin can also be seen as an advancing heart or a cruel heart. Namely, Zanshin no Kamae means never to forget that one must fight the enemy without

cruelty, and this is evidence of the mental preparation needed of Budo. This is one aspect of the essence of Budo.

Consider also Yugen Bu. The "gen" in "Yugen" simply means the black color which becomes mysterious; this is the color of Ten 天, or heaven. It is also the color of subtle and unfathomable differences. Gen also means the Huns who tormented the Chinese. If we derive the basis of "gen" we can understand there are many possible meanings, and many unexpected possibilities.

What must be handed down are those things that are dying out in society. However, these things still exist in nature. And what has been transmitted are the four seasons (shiki 四季), knowledge (shiki 識), and recognition (shiki 識); these things that must endure variation and maintain survival. And keep in mind the misery that results from those who must fight.

Sense of Survival

My training theme of 2008 was "Ku;" that is to say, Ninpo Taijutsu. I frequently taught Takamatsu Sensei's proverb: "You yourself must become Ku"—vanishing taijutsu, taijutsu that cannot been seen, taijutsu that becomes transparent. I was first taught this in the following way: "Taijutsu is that which sinks into the erogenous zone and disappears . . ." and many of the students at the time stood with grinning faces. I believe that this is the memory that I have, and then I disappeared while showing that taijutsu.

It is often said that my penmanship is quite erotic. This, however, is necessary for cultivating the sense of survival that exists in Ninpo Taijutsu. When you hear the word "seikantai," erogenous zone, and smile thinking of its direct meaning, you are already trapped in the snare of the ninja.

In the year of Hesei 21 (2009), I dedicated a figure of Daikoku-ten that weighed six tons, and it symbolizes six senses, and six worlds of humankind as the lighthouse showing the prestige of the virtue of martial arts at the Honjin (principal space) located in the southeast of Bujinkan Honbu Dojo. The figure connects the way (meaning the roped way and also the distinct way) with the Bujinkan Honbu Dojo.

Hiken Secret Sword

There are people who are attempting to discover the essence of things through kendo (the way) or kenpo (the method). But if you ask me, there is a limit to the "way" or the

"method." If we borrow the words, "Kiwamarinaki ga yueni gokui to suru" (as it has no limits, we call it the gokui), we can see that the gokui exists in biken, which is not a way (kendo) or method (kenpo). As in the words of Zeami: "Hisureba hana" (that which is hidden is beautiful); within biken there exists boundless hidden essence. Therefore, those that live within kyojitsu and uncommon sense possess a hidden sense.

My training theme of 2009 was the rope, which is one of the hidden arts, and I wanted those that grasped the essence to become people who could whisper the words of the bushi: "Kiyatsu wa hitosujinawa dewa ikanu" (to bind with a single rope will not control him; namely, things cannot be dealt with by ordinary means).

Written Transmission of Budo

Within the written records of Budo exists an element of the roots of kami and Buddhism. I will introduce one verse of these roots here. Within these records, an aspect of gokui is referenced to the self which is the light that illuminates the self from shadow and provides a connection with the divine. This illuminates from the origin of the proverb "never step on the shadow of your teacher; you will not receive a true heart to heart transmission if you do not respect such tradition."

If you see the letters in the secret writings as living entities, not just symbols to be memorized, then you will be able to see the miracle of the unconventional and mysterious balance of history and writings.

Book of the Four Strands of the Divine

When walking I am reminded of the song "Ue wo muite aruko" (Keep your chin up) by the singer Kyu Sakamoto. In America this song is known as "Sukiyaki." As in that song, stars in the small night sky are modestly playing that happy melody. Galileo or Copernicus might even be listening in heaven as Sakamoto hums that song.

Research on the universe continues and yet 96 percent of the universe is darkness. Even with the power of sight, insight, and intuition of humans it seems that we only understand 4 percent of the universe. Within Ninpo there is "Ankoku-toshi no jutsu" (the art of seeing through darkness), and there are those that will say "Hey, Mr. Hatsumi the Ninja, you can see through darkness, right?" and I answer by saying "Well, I can see you have a heart of darkness."

In the archives of the instruction from my master, there exist the writings of Shinmei

Shii. Those that possess the heart of the Budoka and read with the mind's eye will find them simple to read, but if you do not possess that heart then the long writing becomes confusing and the heart loses its ability to be mobile.

These are the writings of zanshin, and they must be read with a pure heart—and the hidden secrets of the universe are concealed in a place where even an astronomical telescope or an electron microscope cannot see. These writings cannot be transmitted in the typical form of an educational textbook. They must be transmitted through the harmony of heart-to-heart transmission; in a writing of beauty and cooperation; in the scattering of the petals of the beautiful flower of that which is hidden, blossoming into the next fertilization of truthful penmanship.

The Doctrine (the sect) and the Warrior Class

The religious sect and the warrior sect—within these two sects (mon 門) is the sect of life and death; of kyojitsu, inyo, the four inevitable stages of human life (living, aging, disease, and death), omote kimon, ura kimon, genbumon, seiryumon, suzakumon (vermillion bird), byakkomon (white tiger god), tatsumimon, koyumon, tenmon chimon, and so on.

If we understand shumon (religious gate 宗門) and bumon (martial gate 武門), these two gates will open. This is a belief from people outside the gates. They will say, "Isn't the character 'shu' 宗 wrong?" I will answer "No." Instead of the reading "shu" I will use the reading "so," and the character for spear (鎗). During the Warring States Period, the spear was unrivaled on the battlefield. The famous poet Basho wrote the haiku:

Summer grass
All that remains
of the dreams of ancient warriors.

In the Japanese folk song "Kuroda bushi," there is the following lyric: "Is this the sound of the koto (Japanese harp) of those that enquire? Or is this only a faint dream?" Akechi Mitsuhide, who was responsible for Oda Nobunaga's death at Honnoji Temple, experienced a short-lived rule and was quickly reduced to nothing, conquered by the seven spears of Toyotomi Hideyoshi, after which Hideyoshi seized control of Japan.

In order to take control of a nation, one had to take the head of the rival leader. Nowadays, the word for "firing" an employee means "to cut the neck." In order for a company to survive, one must be severe with subordinates.

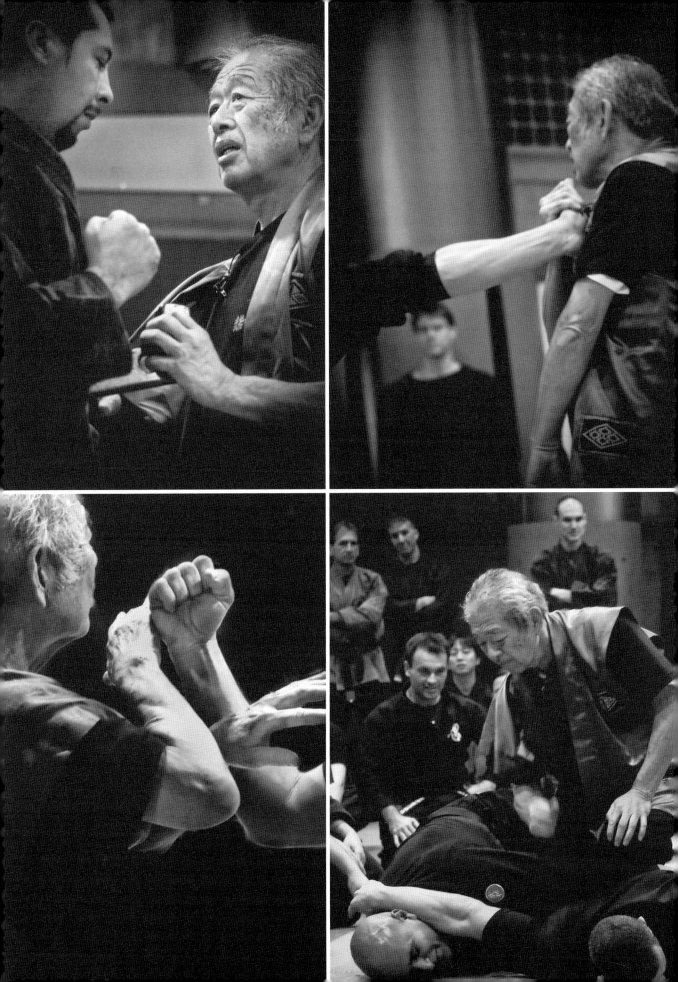

Begin at the last scene of the movie *Morocco*, and journey through the scenes of the movies *Manon Lescaut, Masada*, and *Helen of Troy*, and hear the chanting of the Shugenja, the ascetic mountain monks, during your pilgrimage. The chanting is like a drumbeat "Rokkon Shojyo" (六根清浄). Finish your journey at the beginning of the last scene of Kurosawa's *Rashomon*, taking shelter from the rain.

Those that seek the essence (gokui) of war don't find supremacy of the essence, but gain the simple grace of art for art's sake, in conventional wisdom. Technique or form should not be the goals in Budo, they should be a kind of taste. Rather than perfection, know that creating consistency of the martial wind is paramount.

The Thirty-seventh Anniversary of the Passing of Takamatsu Sensei

The year of Heisei 20 (2008) marked the thirty-seventh anniversary of the passing of Takamatsu Sensei. Let us therefore talk about the thirty-seven years of enlightenment that were experienced by Yamaoka Tesshu (1836–88). Yamaoka Tesshu's brother-in-law, Yamaoka Seizan, who was known to be a master of the yari [spear], was known also for his extreme training, and would wake at 2 a.m. to swing his fifteen-pound spear one thousand to five thousand times in Tenchi juppo, and perform countless leaping thrusts. At one time, it is said that he saw the sun setting, and thrust at the dark emptiness thirty thousand times until the sun rose again.

Seizan said that in order to obtain victory over people, the heart is more important than technique, and you must broaden your virtue if you win with the heart; in this way the opponent will naturally lose. Real victory is achieved not by technique but by virtue of the heart and warrior virtue.

Yamaoka Tesshu also in his later years developed a signature technique (tokui-waza) that he learned from the practice of the single thrust of the yari, and which became one of his strongest points. Yamaoka Tesshu was even called "Onitetsu," or "Demon Iron," as a master swordsman. One day, he was facing off with the practitioner Asari Matashichiro Yoshiaki. Yoshiaki's practice sword was not a wooden sword, and the long arms and the shining tip were the likeness of the eye of god. Although both Tesshu and Matashichiro were experts at the thrust, Tesshu could not escape the thrust of his opponent. But, incredibly, Matashichiro's thrust never came into contact with Tesshu's throat; rather he was struck by the energy emanating from the tip of Matashichiro's sword. He felt his spirit waning, and, breaking out in a sweat, could no longer maintain his footing.

Without thinking, he uttered the words, "I have lost!"

Tesshu reflected on the fabled words of Seizan: "To obtain victory over people, it is not technique but virtue," and walked the distance of 120 thousand meters to Ryutakuji Temple at Mishima in Izu district, to embark on Zen mediation under the priest Seijyo for three years.

At one time at the famous temple in Kamakura called Kenchoji there was a prayer that went like this: "I have been surprised and have fear of the enemy, how do I get rid of this mind?" If it seems that Matashichiro's blade is not yet positioned at your heart, then both life or death are stopping your heart. If life and death are on your mind, this is something that should not trouble the warrior. You must immediately cast out this mind. Essentially, have nothing—these are wise words indeed.

However, Tesshu was simply unable to find this nothingness. He visited the head priest of Shokokuji in Kyoto Dokuon and the head priest of Engakuji in Kamakura, Kosen. Finally, in Kyoto's Tenryuji he inquired to the head priest Tekisui, who let out a thundering roar—"You are actually fighting the opponent with a sword. You can avoid the fighting and not use a sword!"

Yamaoka Tesshu, on the thirty-seventh year of his following the way of the sword, in the year of Meiji 20, March 13th, at the age of forty-five, twenty-three years since first entering the school of Asari Matashichiro, was permitted the essence (gokui) of Musoken (dream-initiated sword technique).

Tesshu traveled on foot from Yanaka in Tokyo to Noda in Chiba. I still have a piece of calligraphy he handed to my great-grandfather which reads: "I was asked about the Way. I feel the gracefulness in the remote countryside." That was a long time ago, but what is mysterious is that I presently have the book of essence (gokui) written by Asari Matashi-chiro, which is quite possibly the only one that remains in existence written by the master. It appears in my book *Japanese Sword Fighting: Secrets of the Samurai.*

Yamaoka Tesshu was keenly aware of the oneness of the Sword and Zen (kenzen ichi-nyo 剣禅一如), but the sword master Asari Matashichiro did not study Zen. However, Matashichiro's talent with the sword reigned. As in the image of these two Budoka, it can been seen that Budo must not be confined to just the head. Those who only use their brains are like a candle—they shine brightly, but eventually melt. Tokui-waza (one's expert technique, signature move 得意技) can also be written as tokui-waza 特異技; the technique that threatens your benevolence.

At the time of the thirty-seventh anniversary of the passing of Takamatsu Sensei, I was able to have a statue of Daikoku-ten (in India called Mahakala; said to be the

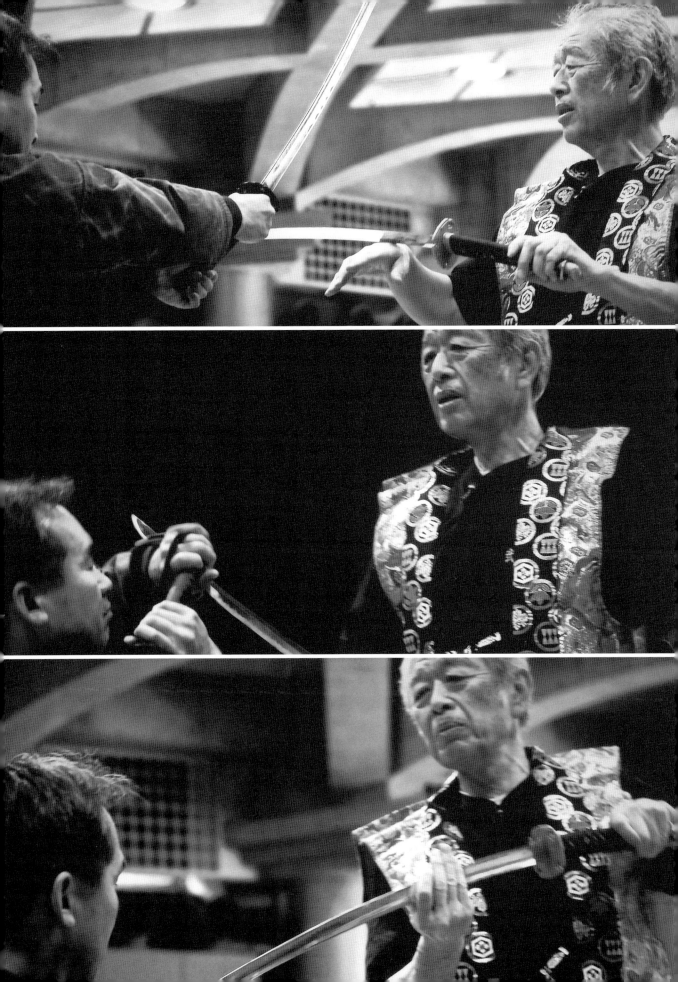

greatest deity of war) created in his honor. The name of Iko Butoku Daikoku-ten was given, meaning the Power of Warrior Benevolence.

Tesshu's enlightenment was also attained in the thirty-seventh year.

Become Mu!

When we express "Become mu (nothingness 無)!" it is best to understand that the meaning of the "mu" are numerous, such as Mugen (infinite 無限), Mushin (no mind 無心), Mujin (inexhaustibility 無尽), and Musho (without form 無象).

The concept of becoming mu is to hide oneself in an aspect of shingitai (mind, technique, and body 心技体) jutsu so that the duality of life or death must be released into space. When you show this spectrum it will become the seven colors of the rainbow. It is said that seven is an unlucky number; however, if you change that to seven prismatic colors, then it incidentally becomes a critical color. (The characters for "crisis/danger" 危 and "unique color" 色 when put together are pronounced "kiiro" 奇色, which is the same pronunciation as the word for the color yellow 黄色. In the same way, the characters for life and color when combined are also pronounced "kiiro" 生色.) Namely, you show it as yellow. If you look at the eight colors of the diode, among them you will see a vivid transparent blue.

My beloved readers, do you understand the zen of the radiance of the light-emitting diode? If you wish to understand the kukan (space 空間), then you must ask one of the ten great disciples of the Buddha, Subhuti, who understands the importance of Ku (emptiness).

Shu-ha-ri

Within the world of Noh, when you feel the martial wind at your back, Mugen-no, that mysterious perception becomes the source of courage, and becomes the very Noh performance that is not shielded by a curtain. For the players of Noh, the absence of a curtain symbolizes no beginning and no end—a limitless performance, standing naked, just like the Bushi poised without a shield, although able to cover all directions.

The word "Yugen" (hidden beauty 幽玄) is comprised of characters used in the talks by Lao-tzu and Chuang-tzu. In discussions of arts, including martial arts, one encounters the phrase "Shu-ha-ri 守破離." In order to understand this phrase you need to know that many people have differing ideas and it is easy to become confused. For example,

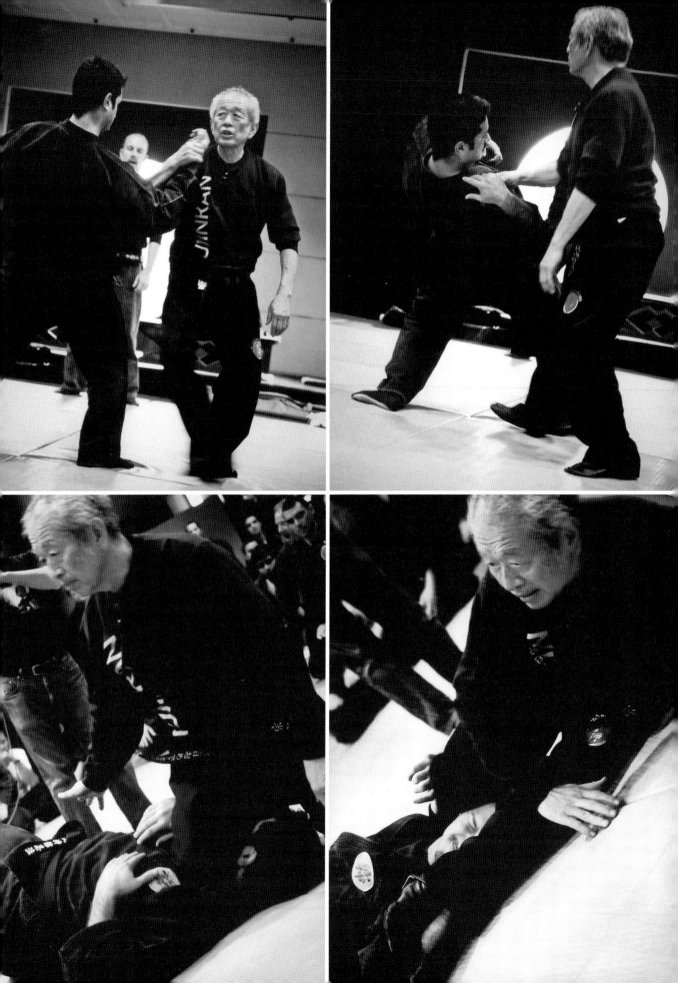

"shu" 守 is thought of as meaning to obey the teachings of your master; "ha" 破 to cast out the teachings of the master, to separate from the teachings; then "ri" 離 to distance from the master. And the concept of "shu-ha-ri" is regarded as the essence.

"Ri" is one's outlook on the universe as well as a perspective of nature. Tokugawa Ieyasu was called "Ri" (using the character for tanuki, 狸, Japanese raccoon dog) and he became the ruler of Japan. Just in the way that the character "Ha" 破 is comprised of the radical on the left meaning "stone" 石 and that of "skin" 皮 on the right, the Ninja will transform (to stone) and escape.

Well, even now I obey the teachings of my master, but this "shu" is the concept of obeying what is truth, the master's essential truth "Kaname," and to take those teachings to heart. The stone and skin elements of the character "ha" represent an aspect of transformation (changing into stone) and this aspect is used within the art of Tongyo-no-jutsu (ninja art of transformation/disguise). This transformation is used from a position of distance and therefore "ri" 離. This is done so that it cannot be revealed ("ha"). Mankind should know that "ri" is also the state of seeing the earth from the distance of a space satellite. It is important to try applying distance in thoughts and consciousness. Also, apply the practice of transformation between "Shuchuryoku" (concentration 集中力), and "Shuchuryoku" (orbiting ability 周宙力). Shu 周 means surrounding, chu 宙 means space/universe, and ryoku 力 means power/ability.

The founder of Hokushin Itto-ryu, Chiba Shusaku (1793–1856) wrote the following about Shu-ha-ri:

"There are three important elements called shu-ha-ri. 'Shu' is the aspect of protecting the style. In the case of Itto-ryu, the style will be Geddan Seigan (meaning "star eyes" 星眼). [Author's note: We must understand why Chiba Shusaku uses these characters for Seigan, instead of the usual 正眼. This is because Shusaku used to worship the star constellation of the Plough in the night sky.] If you are free from worldly thoughts and schools the style will be hira-seigan, and you are able to be free and maintain the style of self. 'Ha' means that you are not attached to this Kamae, and you are practicing to take it further by destroying the form. 'Ri' is to transcend both 'shu' and 'ha' and attain a level free of worldly thoughts."

Shusaku also wrote about the manner of how to treat those that do not regret defeat. A fighting scene of carnage imitates the faintness of the Sanshin no Kamae (mental preparedness 三心) consisting of Moro-tai (misty style 朦朧体), Yugen no Kamae, (elegance 幽玄), and Muso no Kamae (dream, vision 夢想).

These Sanshin no Kamae, while expressing the five words for enlightenment of Chi

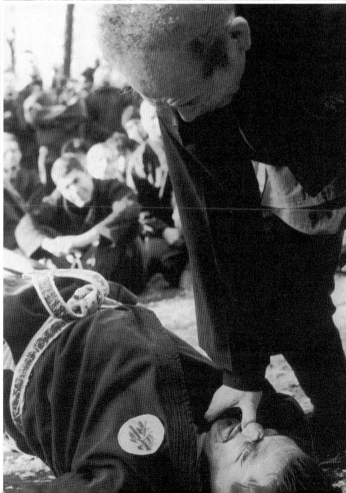

(earth 地), Sui (water 水), Ka (fire 火), Fu (wind 風), Ku (emptiness 空), are transcending the four seasons of consciousness.

A famous Japanese-style painter, Taikan Yokoyama (1868–1958), painted this aspect of ambiguity in his work *Metempsychosis* with his three brushes made of horsehair. These brushes resemble the three arrows of the warrior Mori Motonari (1497–1571), whose famous lessons to his three sons on how solidarity can overcome adversity echo to this day.

From the words of Chiba Shusaku, you can understand well the meaning of to transcend, "ri." Also, the sound of "reki" for the character for history 歴, that sound quality is ri; the sound of ri changes to reki. That footprint is transmitted in the dream-like phenomenon of the much-loved children's fable *The Tortoise and the Hare* by Aesop.

The Essence of Muto Dori

Budo and bugei are not about killing people. An aspect of the gokui is to cut away what is faulty. Fencing is about cutting away what is faulty in the mind, in the words of Shinkage-ryu's Kamiya Denshinsai Yoriharu. There are those heihosha (martial artists) who are respected as masters and who understood the foolishness of engaging in battle to further one's military rank or swell one's army size. Rather they avoided carnage and chose the path of the monk, hermit, or sage. We can call these people seijin, and they embody the three aspects of saintliness (sei 聖), life (sei 生), and justice (sei 正). Some of these famous sword masters include Ito Ittosai, Tsukahara Bokuden, Ko'izumi Nobutsuna, Toda Shinryuken Masamitsu, and Toshisugu Takamatsu Sensei. They lived with appreciation for the power of nature and the truth of genuineness of things as did the artist Paul Gauguin. They all are in agreement of the essence (gokui) of the extremeness of nature and the aspect of Muto dori, as well as the truth of "the underlying meaning" of "no fighting" with a simple perception of nature.

It was the thirty-eighth year of Showa, October 8th, that I was introduced to the following explanation in a lesson of Muto dori. Let's learn this as an aspect of the essence of Muto dori. My teacher stated the following:

"I believe that Muto dori is the crucial element of Budo." Whether the opponent's weapon is yari, ken, naginata, kodachi, bo, or even a bow and arrow or shuriken, you must study this aspect of Muto dori extremely well and practice this many times.

Consider an arrow being shot. It travels fifty meters in a second. When a baseball is thrown it travels forty-five meters in a second. If the opponent is swinging his sword

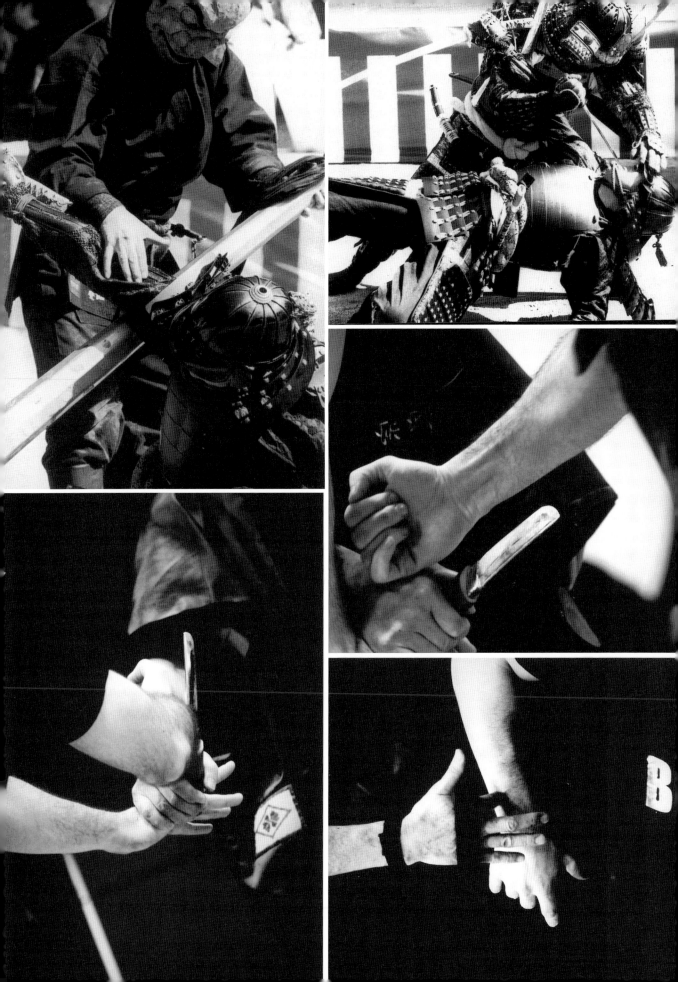

above his head in Daijodan, and we intend to knock the opponent's sword into his head, then we must attain a speed much faster than that of the arrow or the baseball, and we have only a small window in which to achieve this victory. Therefore, in the instant that the opponent creates a Kiai, you need to avoid the attack. Consider a baseball flying forty-five meters a second; the first twenty meters is covered in approximately one third of a second. Also, because the speed is not uniform, the closer it is the faster it appears, and the farther away the slower it seems. With this in mind it is good to practice evading.

Next, if a cut is executed by extending the sword out from outstretched hands, this is a weak method and will not cut effectively. If the opponent attacks in such a way, within Muto dori you can evade and at the same time jump and control the opponent's attack. As well as in the case where you have a jutte or a kodachi, steadfastly in this mind of Muto dori, you can change the body and jump in. This type of practice is very important.

Also, within judo, jujutsu, taijutsu, or even in the case of sumo, we understand that when thrusting the arms upward, they lose power, in contrast to the case where the hands are thrust straight forward. In weightlifting, it is simple to lift a bar with iron plates on each side to the chest with both hands, but not so simple to lift it above the chest. Within this truth, one can see the importance of a clear explanation of style.

My grandmaster mentioned the following: Since our ancestors landed in this country, we have yearned for the virtue of the nation. We respect Shinto, we made armaments, and with ethics, based on clans, we have been making the prestige of the nation glorious. For more than 2,600 years, we have inherited good traditions, and we have been blessed with them.

What I would I like you to consider here is that Bufu is not only thinking about winning against the opponent or bringing down the opponent. No matter how much the opponent wants to fight, you must not overreact, allowing the opponent to considerably take the initiative. But at that instant when the opponent attempts to escape, you must inevitably bring down the opponent. Within this is the truth of "katsumi" and the crucial study thereof. This is Budo.

Truth goes hand in hand with nature. You cannot gain the mysterious without nature. The average temperature of the human body is 37 degrees Celsius; this is normal, and in order to maintain this temperature, we dress accordingly. In weight lifting you start with thirty pounds and you gradually increase the weight until you can eventually lift twice the original amount. These types of truths exist in nature, and within practice these truths can only be acquired on one's own."

The Essence of War Exists in Jutaijutsu

The essence of the aspect of war exists in jutaijutsu. In regard to this, taijutsu forms the mysterious principles of the roots of the art of Ninjutsu. Why is that?

The sword is an instrument of killing and the yari is a weapon of thrusting people to death. Cutting before the opponent has a chance to cut, the thrust being a sign of an expert—With this thinking, the path of those who strive to be victorious, as taught in the art of war and the way of war, regrettably becomes the way of the evil sword and the evil spear, and ultimate victory is never obtained. The crucial point of war is the preparedness of heart and preparedness of body. This essence of war is expressed in the embodiment of the art of Ninjutsu.

Here, let's think about the two characters of "shori" (victory 勝利). These can also be written as "shori" (principle of living 生理), and can be considered also a principle of the divine. This concept of union of body and mind can transform into the posture of futen goshin of the Gyokko-ryu, and this posture is endowed with the eye of Bufu (martial wind). If you can exploit timing well, you can reach the state of Ryujin, the Dragon God who rides the martial wind of Hanno-bo'itsu-fusui.

Let's add the words of the French physiologist, Charles Richet. "Mankind are called homo sapiens (clever human beings) but shouldn't we change the name to homo stultus (foolish human beings)?" That would be what the zen priest Ryokan would call the ultimate fool (taigu meaning ultimate fool, 大愚 but this was also Ryokan's given name). If it is foolish it is ruined, but if it is Taigu then the path is opened.

"Kuraidori is equal": The teachings of Bushinwa are Within This

Within the levels of Budo practice, there are the Shoden or the Kihon Happo, San Shin no Kata. There is Chuden, Okuden, Menkyo, and Kaiden. The two characters that form the word Byodo, or equality, 平等 can be changed to Byodo, or Fighting Man 兵闘. The gokui or essence lies within these levels. It is fine to see them as the same.

The following story might be hard to believe, but I would like to tell you about the narrations of the "Mansen Shukai" of the *Ninjutsu Hitsudensho,* or secret writings of Ninjutsu. At one time, an instructor announced to his pupils, "OK, let's conduct the fifth-dan test." A woman who did not understand Japanese very well stepped out and took the test. "Splendid! You have passed!" congratulated the sensei, and without thinking a smile came to her face. However, not long afterward, it became apparent that she had been intending to take the fifth-kyu test, and had mistakenly taken the fifth-dan test!

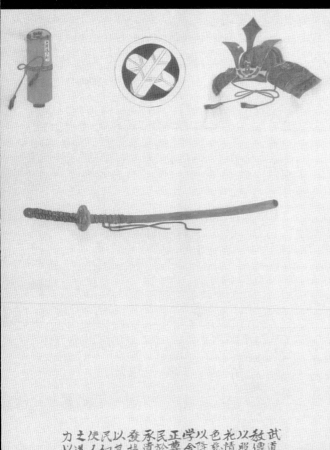

龍の昇天は精心力

武道者何人能弘正道也正道者何天地之自然而生民不可順失離者也武道之武何為
以教傳也茶惟上古神聖立極重統天地位蒼慈愛以萬物育蒼人花情竹性之養精神其所
以照臨六合統御宇内者未会不由斯道也寶柞以之衆窩国體以之安寧
以存自由平等皇化花惷竹性愛善乃若西風者未會服而聖子神孫尚不肯自足榮取於人以為花之香不更
學令此從彼夷化以之牽服於之衆窩国體以之安寧
正尊天位樣夷風陵夷褐乱相蹺武風文心以開大平之基之不明於世也蓋亦蓋亦笑我武祖撥乱反
民遵精沐浴恩鳳凡武風更祖師日宝受封於東土凡大和世
承民於蒙美風尊神道禧澤武備国威海外為雄臣子者豈可弗思所以推弘武風
發揚光德孕於日則偁留国家之所以為説也柳夫祀天尚尚來二千六百餘年世
以其風天功於日來也甚警孔子不子霸然他也我国中土之民風凡夜匪反昭大神摩利支天八
民以和武風之所縣以益大且明武不岐學問事業在天之靈亦將降鑒至古武
之道使人知武風之所以益大且明武昭大神摩利支天始其德資其本者
力以教国家窩之恩皇徒祖師之志弇堕神皇在天之靈亦將降鑒至古武道致以統冶

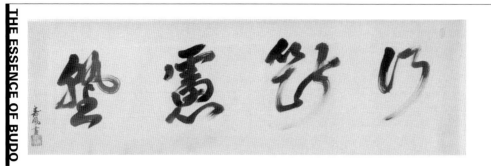

How could it be possible for a beginner to pass the fifth-dan test? It is apparently clear that she did pass the test. Within the Bujinkan, those who have not trained up to the level of fourth-dan are not qualified to take the fifth-dan test, and everyone knows this, but amazingly, on her first visit to the Bujinkan she passed the fifth-dan test.

My teacher Takamatsu Sensei would often say, "Whether they practice Budo or not, splendid people are still splendid people." Surely, these words are a good example of shi-kinseki hara mitsu dai-komyo (試金石腹満大光明). These eight characters mean the touchstone of a bright, full belly—that is to say, in Budo it is essential to have guts.

Those who possess guts have the combination of four powers—ishin denshin (communion of mind with mind 以心伝心), shinnen iryoku (will power 心念意力), shin-nen iryoku (authority 心念威力), butoku Iko (power of martial virtue 武徳威光), and through this combination we can recognize the state of kurai dori 位取り, where we sense the profound power of these four elements.

Kyojitsu Tenkan-ho

The gokui is a natural force as is the earth's orbit. We must first believe that we live on this earth. War is a matter of life or death, and therefore the teachings of the Fudoshin of Banpen fugyo exist in oral tradition. Within this lies the answer of the natural escape of death in the concept of Kyojitsu tenkan-ho.

In the consistent practice of Budo, at the time when the Fudoshin of Banpen fugyo is gained, the natural phenomenon of the union of nature will occur. Or rather, you have the ability to make this happen. Ultimately in the case of Fudoshin, generally, one might jump to the conclusion that "if we have fudoshin, shin-gi-tai (body, technique, and mind) are unmovable, and the stance is perfect, then we will not be disturbed by any opponents." This becomes not an orbit of the earth but rather the path of a demon, blending into the earth.

Let's recite the heliocentric theory of Copernicus. In this we pray in the morning and give gratitude in the evening, in appreciation of the daily compliance of the etiquette and code of the samurai. As in the beating of the human heart, the earth lives. And in result there is death, it therefore becomes important to have the readiness of heart to live together with the essence (gokui).

At times, nature may be severe or guide us with kindness, raising us, giving us direction. However, by destroying this cycle we are threatening an age of mindless warrior clones and inhuman soldiers. Even more so now, a correct and just human heart and soul is essential.

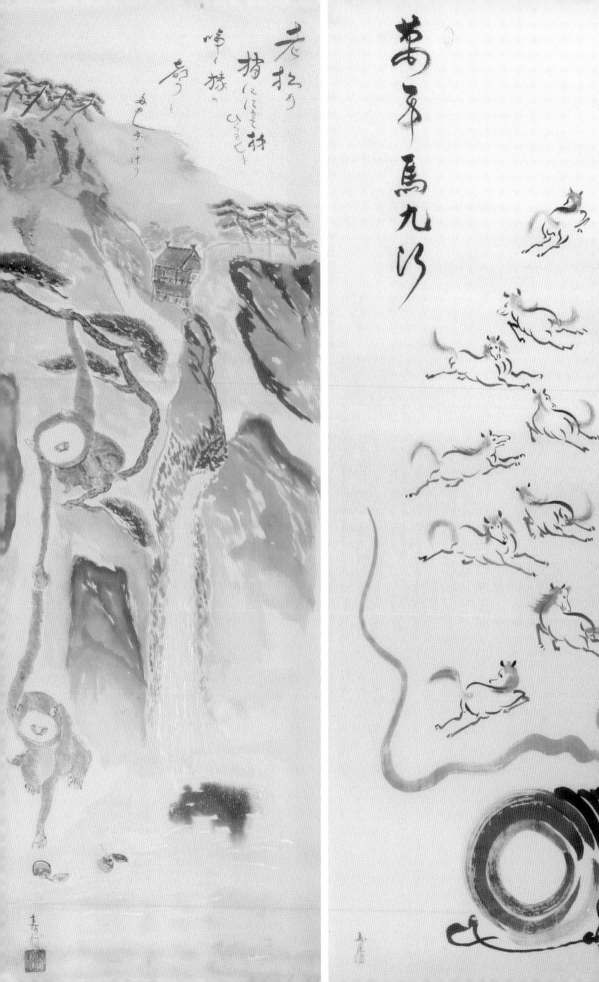

In this, the Sanshin no Kata becomes the knowledge and determination to strike out the opponent's offensive mind.

Gokui in the Movies

Director Kurosawa Akira (1910–98) at the age of eighty received a special academy award. Let's talk about that gathering. He famously commented, "I do not understand the concept of a movie." A comment like this is like the knockout punch in a boxing match or the home run in baseball—it appears without warning. Within the films of Kurosawa, *The Seven Samurai, Throne of Blood, Sanjuro, Kage Musha,* and *Ran,* appear many samurai protagonists who entered the world of death in many interesting ways.

Director Ozu Yasujiro (1903–63) said, "The end of a movie is the beginning." In the movie by René Clair called *Under the Roofs of Paris,* the opening image is that of a townscape of chimneys and roofs. Similarly the movie by director Ozu Yasujiro, *Tokyo Monogatari,* opens with a scene of roofs and chimneys. *Under the Roofs of Paris* was created in 1930, and it is said that *Tokyo Monogatari* was a 1953 creation and one can say they are both lost in time. Within these masterpieces there is a blossoming point of time forgotten. This deep impression of timelessness is felt in the masterpieces of Ozu no matter how many times you view them: *Late Spring, Higanbana, Bakushu, Ukigusa* (Floating weeds), *An Autumn Afternoon.* You can see the Zanshin of the warrior in the performance of Chishu Ryu.

The director Billy Wilder would say, "There is no perfect person." I believe that to be true. The Bufu always floats drama on the clouds.

What Goethe Gained

I learned in a book about director Kurosawa's comment, "I don't understand the concept of a movie." What would Goethe say? Doctor Faust studied philosophy, law, medicine, and chemistry, but grieved that he never did understand the truth. And then he turned to dark magic to gain this knowledge, and that turned out to be a disaster. He began thinking suicide was the only option to view another world.

Viewing this image, Mephistopheles would have seen this as the way of the devil, with the protagonist begging for forgiveness, but the Lord responded by saying, do as you will. In this Goethe continued to live with the devil's temptation. Love, catastrophe, and love. Surely, as director Ozu Yasujiro stated, "The end of a movie is the beginning." Like the samurai, Faust remained true to his principles. When we view his life we can see into our

山系一貫

為初元先生

own souls. Realization of this is like a rebirth. Even though we die seven times, we can be reborn and defeat our enemies.

Those humans that strive with great effort to seek the evolution of creation, the progress of development, and without becoming the *Goldfinger* of James Bond reach out with open hands to the saving hand of god. This can be seen as the five rings of the Olympics of Chi, Sui, Ka, Fu, Ku. Let's think of "0" in 007 as a hole. The two holes in 007 are the eyes, and if combined with 7 more holes the total number becomes nine. The discovery of one more hole is one plus nine, or in Japanese "ku no ichi"—the elements that comprise the kanji character for "woman": 女 (くノ一). I hope that more great men such as 007 will be born on this earth.

In the way of Buddhism, rebirth in paradise is within nine levels, nine levels of Amitabha's Pure Land, and nine qualities of the human. To derive this way of floating with the tide is the kuji of Amitabha.

The Essence of Koto-ryu

Within Koto-ryu there is a method of attaining enlightenment called Shin Shin Shin Gan 神心神眼. This is can be changed into Kanjin kaname 肝心要, and this change can also be seen at "tengan," or the eyes of heaven.

Regarding the field of vision of the ball of the eye, this is the center point of Shin Shin Shin Gan. This is something that the third-century alchemist Hermes would have surely agreed with. He would say that everywhere there is a center, a circle without centrifugal force, that is projected onto the eye. The famous Japanese philosopher Yuji Nakamura would say that the form of gokui overlaps into the aspects of philosophy; this is the logic of universal feeling.

Humans remain consistent with the martial wind, and human experience will be transformed when we practice fighting techniques. Masters are forever floating in suspension in the astronomical phenomena of the transmigration of souls.

Takamatsu Sensei, Enlightenment by a Dream

Often in the densho there is a mention of becoming enlightened via a dream. Let me introduce you to a Kuden that was told to me by Takamatsu Sensei regarding a butterfly.

On a page in my previous book, *Unarmed Fighting Techniques of the Samurai*, there is a painted picture of a cat intently watching a butterfly. There is also a calligraphy by

Takamatsu Sensei: "Single-Minded Perseverance." Incidentally, the butterfly is the family crest of the famous samurai family Heike.

Many years ago, Takamatsu Sensei lived in China under the Manchurian Dynasty. He later wrote his memoirs, which I still have in my possession today. This particular passage is memorable to me:

When I was twenty-six years old in China, Ren Somei, the uncle of the previous emperor, took a liking to me as a master of Japanese martial arts. I was then invited to teach around 600 people and was training every night. At this time, I was challenged to a duel by an experienced and well-known fighter from the Shadong Province who was known to attach about thirty pounds of weight to both ends of a roku shaku bo (long thick stick) and spin it every morning around 100 times. He was a master of kenpo known as the Cho Shiryu from the Shaolin Temple. I refused the challenge on two occasions, but he still kept challenging and there seemed to be no chance of refusal anymore.

One night, I had a dream of a red demon that was trying to hit a butterfly with a metal stick. The butterfly kept smiling and evading in every direction (happo). The demon eventually grew extremely tired and fell over. When I woke, I was enlightened. "This is it, this is the gokui!" I thought, and I responded that I would accept the challenge at any time. I was twenty-six years old, and I weighed 75 kilograms. He was thirty-two and weighed 140 kilograms, and was 187 centimeters tall.

It was June. In a dojo of twenty tatami-mat size, per the agreement, the bout began. He was skilled at jumping in every direction and I was able to do so as well. Before long, he thought of finishing me with a single blow. I was able to control my hands and close the distance and thought as in the gokui that I would be able to finish him with a single blow, and then we closed the distance and became bound. He jumped in and I shifted to both sides. If I could move in on his suki (weak point) then he would have to jump up high. This went on for about an hour. He began to break out in a sweat on his forehead. I never usually broke into a single drop of sweat even after teaching sixty people in the middle of the summer, and I did not show any sweat this time either.

Finally, Ren san declared a draw and the bout was over. After this bout, we both became sworn brothers. Over the following years we developed a close friendship, and he would come to my aid in many adverse conditions.

The most important thing human beings can do is smile. In fighting we must

never get angry, never stare with our eyes, and when we must face death, know it comes in various guises and is never a surprise. On the contrary, animals cannot smile. When they sense death, they show their fangs with fury in their eyes, and let out an unashamed cry. Animals are both fierce and cautious, like the ninja.

The Mongolian Tiger, Takamatsu Sensei, and the Cat

At present, I have several great warrior friends around the world, and as the martial wind blows, it brings happiness day after day. In the passing days, I have come to rely upon the following letters that I received from Takamatsu Sensei:

Showa 37 Nov. 7th
Mr. Hatsumi, you possess the following strong point in the capacity of a Budoka: "It is said that humans who overcome the mind will become true masters." [Author's note—"Seishin," as in mind or spirit, can be written in many ways to include such meanings as "Just Heart" 正心, "Life Heart" 生心, or "Pure Heart" 精心.]

Showa 36 Dec. 12th
On the 11th, I saw you on television. It was a great performance. The most important quality in a human is courage. The other day I was discussing this with a pupil. In the past, I must have taught several thousand people, but I have never met someone with such courage as you, Mr. Hatsumi. If you have courage, then you can accomplish anything, any technique. I have had experience of scores of bouts and been in the place of real combat, without facing defeat, and I believe it is because I have had some courage.

Someone who knew Takamatsu Sensei when he was known as the Mongolian Tiger had the following to say to him after meeting him several decades later: "Hello, Mr. Takamatsu, it has been a very long time, and I'm surprised, you who were once called the Mongolian Tiger; it is great to see that you have become a cat." Takamatsu Sensei smiled and responded, "Yep, I became a cat, it is great to be a cat. As a cat you climb up and can sleep in the warm lap of a woman. I am like the panel of sleeping cats in the Toshogu Shrine at Nikko."

The American author John Steinbeck would say a genius is a young boy who follows a butterfly and realizes that he has climbed a mountain.

學海無涯

佛說
阿彌
陀經

Kubi-uri Onna (The woman who sells heads)

It is said that Oda Nobunaga kept an enemy general's skull as a sake cup and drank from it when intoxicated with victory. Within mankind, the defeated enemy's head is severed and displayed as a symbol of victory.

There is a story called *Ueda Shichihon-yari*. It tells that before the battle of Sekigahara (1600), in the fiefdom of Ueda in Shinshu, the warriors of Tokugawa Hidetada carried out the first attack (Ichiban yari) in the siege on the castle of Sanada Masayuki. When the battle was over, six of the seven bravest samurai of Tokugawa took a head of their slain enemy and boasted victory.

The seventh, Mikogami Tenzen, later known as Ono Jiroemon Tadaaki, was mocked by his fellow samurai for not taking a head. "Mikogami," they scorned, "though you are a well accomplished swordsman, you did not carry a head from this battle." Tenzen replied, "In the midst of battle and bloodshed, you will agree there is little time to take the head of an adversary. But rest assured, my friends; if you return to the battlefield you will find no fewer than six slain warriors with my mark etched clearly on their necks behind their ears with my sword."

In the aftermath of a battle, there existed a woman who would gather the heads of the fallen warriors to sell them. She would sever the head from an armored warrior's body, adjust the hair, clean it well, stitch the wounds, and disinfect it. When the fallen warrior's relative would come looking for it, she would exchange the head for money.

The ukiyo-e artist Tsukioka Yoshitoshi (1839–92) was famous for capturing the harshness of battle in his portraits.

Heart, Technique, and Body

Heart, Technique, and Body

Even during the Edo Period, when warfare had all but ceased in Japan, an outsider sneaking a look into a dojo might have faced a serious beating, or worse, death. These were considered preventive measures to keep corrupt people from using the techniques and forms practiced there for evil purposes. The martial way is not a killing technique. Such preventive measures were for those people who could not see that the martial way is the way of "giving life." Those who detach themselves from common sense are not insane. They are the "living," or the noble.

The heart, body, and mind necessary for the martial way were gleaned from years of true combat and were passed down by oral transmission from those experienced warriors to only those deemed worthy. Other necessary or important information was written down and passed on in the form of martial scrolls.

Recently I have been teaching the importance of a person's talent, spirit, and capacity (utsuwa 器) for unifying the heart, technique, and body of the martial way. In the past, it would be fair to say, there was no determined structure or method for passing on the true martial way. Therefore there was no way to objectively explain or understand the martial path. The majority of people believed that the martial arts were conjured from fantasy or were created by the artisans of dance and theater.

There is a recent trend to view violence as abominable, as something to avoid or disdain. There are many people in this modern day and age who mistakenly equate martial arts with violence and believe them to be bad. The martial arts were also mistakenly perceived as such to some extent in the past. This double misconception (gokai 誤解) is the foolishness of the world today being unable to enlighten (gokai 悟怪) itself.

In history, the strong, often referred to as thugs or ruffians, used martial force to gain lands, and some even became powerful enough to challenge the empire. Under their power, however, the common people faithfully pursued lives of peace. Animals too, create flocks or groups and live and survive together.

Even among actors, there are those who started their careers portraying villains, gained praise for their performances, shed the villainous roles, and became great leading men. Toshiro Mifune is one such actor. He portrayed a Japanese yakuza in director Akira Kurosawa's *The Drunken Angel*. Another such actor is Kou Shimura, who is known for his stellar performance in *To Live*, also directed by Kurosawa. Jack Palance, Anthony

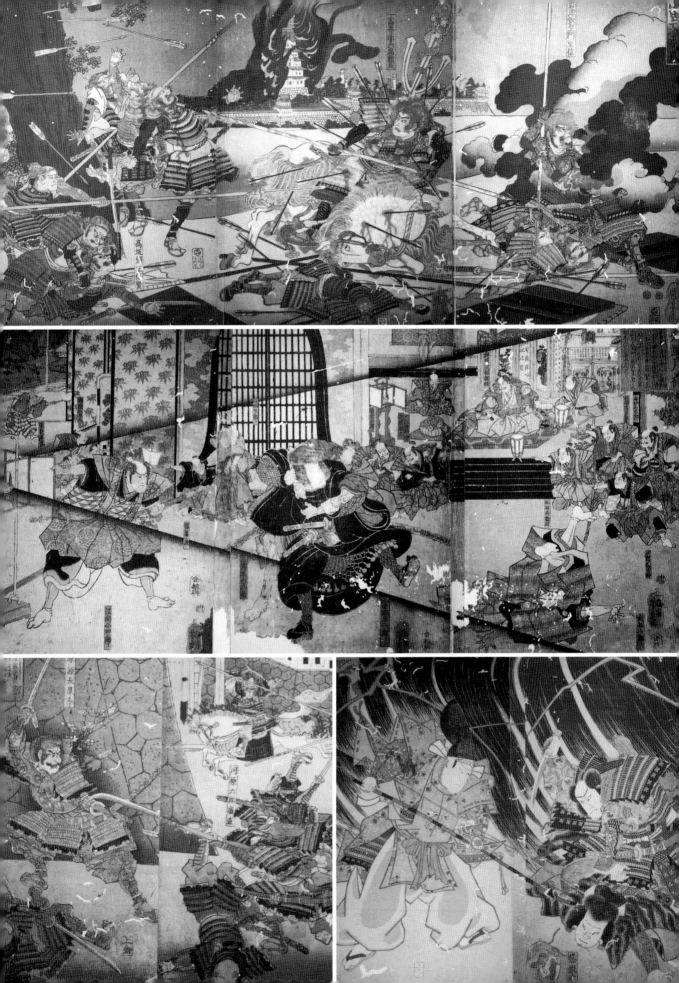

Quinn, and James Cagney also come to mind as performers who first debuted as villains. I wonder how the great pacifist Gandhi would respond if the philosopher George Sorel were to tell him, "All revolutions are achieved through violence."

Training Protects Warriors from Mental Illness

One warrior friend spoke to me:

> I wonder how many "martial arts warriors" really understand the sickness that comes from taking life? You have always said that the purpose of martial arts is to *protect* life. Professor Humphrey said the same. It is so true. I have learned that the special Bujinkan training methodology—combined with Professor Humphrey's philosophy—is like an antidote to the sickness of killing another human being.
>
> This is of great importance. I finally have a small understanding of why we train like we do—so differently from sports martial arts and "paper" Budo.
>
> Because a warrior must kill to protect life, the training can protect the spirit of the warrior from the sickness that comes from taking life. I learned this lesson a little late, but because of you, I can teach young warriors this important point. Thank you.

Play and Combat

When I first started going abroad (playing outside), I used the word play. It was the first step in enlightening people to the essence of the martial way. This behavior caused people to point their finger at me and call me "Cute boy!"

If you watch the actions of puppies, kittens, or any young animal, you will understand. The same behavior can even be seen in human children. Their playfulness is really combat training (playing) for when they mature and must fight, live, and fend for themselves. Once we mature and separate from our parents, we look back on those playful childhood days and realize how much play and true combat overlap. Hence, we discover for ourselves the terrifying nature of play.

When you read that the master of Yagyu Shinkage-ryu, Yagyu Munenori, performed Muto dori (unarmed sword receiving), you must be able to grasp that this is really the Muto dori of evading fighting. If you grasp this, you will come to understand the true righteousness of Muto dori: "To catch the weapon that threatens life, it is necessary to have the ability to foresee it." Therefore during training, to prevent injury, I have people

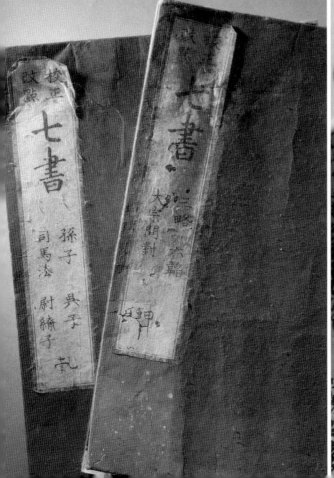

use soft shinai (practice swords). If the characters for Muto dori 無刀捕り are changed to "No Fight Catch" (無闘捕り), the meaning may become even clearer.

I hear the words of the great scholar Confucius: "Those that understand play have life's greatest treasure."

We must pour our hearts now more than ever into performance skills and performance abilities to fully express ourselves in our martial demonstrations. This is one form of transmission. We must become not only masters of the Eighteen Fields of Martial Study; we must strive to be as master Kabuki performers in master roles. We must not bring shame even to the Eighteen Fields of Kabuki!

The Words of a Woman Artist

A ninety-one-year-old woman artist stated: "I think painting is about throwing away those paintings that you have finished." Without doubt, the same thing can be said of training. Nearly every day I teach my students, but I have never taught them the same way twice. During training, I tell them to throw away and forget any and all that they may have previously studied of the common or uncommon. By forgetting and leaving all behind, we create the metabolism necessary to maintain the heart, technique, and healthy body in order to stay true to and see the martial wind through to the end.

Thus the inner-secrets song of the martial way and life, "Riding ahead of the flood, the chestnut shell floats because it has entrusted itself," will vibrate within and rejuvenate our bodies.

Returning the Teacher's Gratitude

The author Kamo no Chomei writes in the *Hojoki*, "The flow of the river never ceases, nor ever does it return to the source. The bubbles that collect in the pools at once disappear, bind together, but never do they remain long." I would add to this, " . . . and the coming clouds never cease." Because dragons summon the clouds.

The painting *The God of Wind and the God of Thunder* by Ogata Korin has become the symbol of the Rinpa style. The vibrations in this picture flow from the clouds and thunder of the masterpiece of the same name by the artist Tawaraya Sotatsu. These vibrations

The Densho of Kogen Itto-ryu ▶

今ぬるくお空思ふな

　　　　　　み江守れ

あ江川ことを

志川りる月

髙野源茴正

髙野源英正

髙野源蕃正

髙野佐三郎

源豐正

rode the thunder and lightning to be revealed in Ogata's painting. This vision became the picture that gave birth to the Rinpa style. Beyond even heart-to-heart transmission, this is vision-to-heart transmission, similar to transmission of the martial path. In this way, the landscape of martial clouds and fortune can be drawn.

One day in spring I heard from Toshitsugu Takamatsu Sensei that as a young boy he was made to write and rewrite the scrolls many times by order of his teacher Toda Shinryuken. At the end of the conversation, Takamatsu Sensei said to me, "Hatsumi, I have transmitted all to you. Thus I have finally returned the gratitude of my teacher." Gratitude can be read as sound. And from that day forth, I have hummed that sound. I hear these words of compassion from far away now at the age of seventy-eight. I am alive and active today because of my teacher's gratitude (shion 師恩). And yet again, because of the gratitude of my students (shion 子恩). Then we can see the cross of the "four gratitudes" (shion 四恩)—teacher, self, and student along the vertical pillar; and father, self, and mother along the horizontal pillar.

The Cow Artist

The Japanese artist Togyu Okamura was born, like Takamatsu Sensei, in the year of the cow. Past the age of eighty, he leaves us these words: "Even now, one must not forget the beginner's heart. Even if the paintings are clumsy, I would like to draw living paintings. This is very difficult, but it is my sole wish and reason for living. Art is never completed. It is really a question of how much you leave undone at the end. In the short life I have remaining, I will cherish this and strive every day" (essays from *The Walk of the Cow*).

Furthermore, we can feel this harmony reverberate in the words of Zeami of Japanese Noh theater when he says, "At eighty years old, return to the beginner's heart."

I feel greatly the words of the artist Togyu. I have expressed my martial arts in many forms. But I feel Takamatsu Sensei transmitted to me the martial path like that of a strolling cow with four stomachs (intentions). The gait of the cow, gyuho 牛歩, can be written as the walk of the honorable and brave, gyuho 義勇歩.

Takamatsu Sensei liked to draw. He once said, "Even if I were alone at the bottom of a well, drawing brings me so much pleasure." The smoke from the cigarette becomes a spirit cloud. I see in it the smiling face of Takamatsu Sensei. He walks the ancient path in the land of the gods and never has he vanished from before my eyes. "The point is how much we leave undone in living this life. This is the real flavor or charm of a person," my teacher speaks unto me. This open-hearted acceptance is part of the beauty of the warrior.

Known for his "spiritual peaks" images of Mount Fuji, the artist Daikan Yokoyama is said to expound the secrets of the divine heavens and earthly energy and as such, in his words, "Even if you can draw mountains and water, or flowers and birds, if you cannot draw the entirety of space and time, it cannot be called art."

It is said that Togyu Sensei detested crooked ways and always strove to conduct himself honestly and truly. Like a compassionate father, he was kind to all he encountered. He was like the saying that Takamatsu Sensei would often recite: "The compassion of the flower, and the character of the bamboo."

Many strive to understand the inner secrets of the martial way. But if you search only within the field of the martial arts, the picture will never come into focus. If you were to ask, "How then do I get a clear focus?" I would respond thus:

As martial artists following the path of the warrior, we need to equip ourselves with the "heart and eyes of the divine" as our navigation system. The two paths of the martial arts and the warrior way are kyojitsu as we foster our firm yet flexible intuition. This is one path to the inner secrets and their embodiment. Each era has, and needs, its own inner secrets.

Cherry Trees Are Cherry Trees and Plum Trees Are Plum Trees — is it really so?

Every person has their own individual traits. As such, people often expound the necessity of an education that develops individuality—a quite correct opinion. Every child has unique traits that mark his individuality. Cherry trees are cherry trees. Plum trees are plum trees. Taro (a common boy's name) is Taro. Hanako (a common girl's name) is Hanako. It is said that we should bring each person's individuality to fruition.

This is the natural principle of making good of what one has.

But when we look at flowers or the green of a pine tree, is it really proper to think that they are all individuals? Within the same species of pine tree, some trees have beautiful branches and other pine trees have less aesthetic branches. To be certain, we could call this individuality. But perhaps it would be better to encourage the good traits and, since poorly shaped trees can be fixed with proper trimming and guidance, reforming them would be the true form. If you view Japanese bonsai, you will understand this well.

In the past, to pass through the spiritual gate and the martial gate would be like charging from the front Devil's gate (kimon 鬼門) to the back Devil's gate. I have a memory of this route on my navigation system.

Many people, regrettably, have a tendency to view the martial way as a sport. The martial way is not a sport. Education that stresses competition of academics and individuality has become the education of competition. In this environment, children do not have the opportunity to develop as true humans. An example of the martial way (武風) would be such that from birth to six years old, the child is developing a strong and healthy body. From six years to twelve years old, children would be taught proper behavior and manners. From the ages of thirteen to eighteen, the child is prepared for and engaging in battle. When these periods, collectively called the "martial competition," are met successfully, a path equal to the Eighteen Fields of Martial Study opens unto thee.

"The venerable old man speaks, 'Righteousness is a martial virtue and the basis of the martial arts. Martial law and strategy are the branches and leaves of martial virtue.'" (From Nakae Toju's *Questions and Answers of the Old Man*.)

Spirituality precedes and leads the people. If we look on the navigation system for the road, we see a dojo and ask for directions. Is it here? The teacher responds, "The traditional dojo is measured in the size of fifty tatamis (gojyujyo 五十畳)." The dojo of "enlightened ten life" (gojyujyo 悟十生)! Even a demon at eighteen years of age is handsome, homely girls are pretty when they are young, the sweetness of cherries, the sourness of plums, the bittersweet taste of first love, the venerable old man whispers, "You are yet young." Can you envision the *Budo Shoshinshu* (The code of the samurai) by Daidoji Yuzan?

The *Ten Ox-herding Pictures*

A friend of mine gave me a tea cup that I really enjoy using. It has a Zen circle in the bottom and the Zen parable of the ten oxen drawn around the side. It is the work of an abbott of the Myoshinji lineage, Yamada Mumon Roshi (1900–88). The *Ten Ox-herding Pictures* is a work intended to illustrate the Zen practitioner's progression towards enlightenment. In the martial way, there are stages for the practitioner as well. Generally, the stages are from first-dan black belt through tenth-dan black belt. These stages are connected with the stages of the ox. "The old days"—it is nice to reminisce about them while sipping my green tea. The way of tea, the martial way, and Zen are all connected through the circle. It is pleasurable to muse about the ten stages that connect one through zero.

Relaxing and sipping tea from my ten-oxen teacup, it is just this deep serenity that fosters the fighting spirit on the battlefields of the Warring States Period. It is the moment when tea and Zen are one.

The martial way is culture and at the same time it is an art. This is not to say that cultural art is superior. If practitioners of the martial arts are fixated on ideas of strong and weak, life will be fleeting and in vain.

Please analyze the number ten. Ten is made of 1 and 0. Zero represents all. One is a connection to zero and is but a form of zero. Therefore, every living being is simply a connection. The monk says, "You are you and I am I." The ring of kyojitsu in the Buddha's phrase "In heaven and earth, I alone am exalted," can, if the characters are changed, be heard as "Revolving, Purified, Revolving, Self Courage, Elegant, Exalted" (転浄転我勇雅独尊).

Strength and weakness, hard and soft, kyojitsu, and light and dark are things of the world of in and yo. "There should be no strong or weak, nor soft neither hard. Therefore separate from this heart and enlighten to the single character of nothingness." This tells us that only by becoming nothing will the bright inspiration be born. Therefore, when I speak of being in space, I say, "I am a UFO."

People often use the words "righteousness" or "justice." Let's take a closer look at this concept.

1. There is the justice that, at first glance, appears as common sense but is, in fact, not sensible at all.
2. There is the justice where the uncommon sense (absurd) and the common sense.
3. There is the justice where the uncommon sense (absurd) and the uncommon sense (absurd) collide.

It is important to recognize these three aspects. There is not just one form of justice to be understood only through common sense. It is important to view all three forms.

The Hidden Sounds of the Octave

The octave is made of the world of the eight notes CDEFGABC. Strike the two C notes in unison, what a beautiful sound indeed! These eight sounds correspond to the Eightfold Path of Buddhism or the Eight Basics of the Martial Way. Between the two C notes, the other notes, DEFGAB, lie waiting in silence. These are the six sounds of the illusional world; hell, hungry spirits, beasts, asyuras, humans, and heaven. They become purified through the six sounds of charity, morality, forbearance, diligence, meditation, and wisdom, that are the basis of training for humans.

The octave, the two C notes, represent the form of the teacher and student; and of martial friends as well. In death, the two make a pilgrimage to Shikoku and pay their

respects. As the martial artist would say, "The hidden sounds of the octave teach us the sounds of the inner secrets."

Enlightenment is rung in with the striking of the two C notes. First, the door to the Kihon Happo opens. Then, the curtain rises on the Happo Biken. The octave starts the music and the San Shin no Kata is transformed suddenly in the famous movie song of Sir Carol Reed's *The Third Man*.

In Japan, the royal family traditionally has three divine instruments (known as jingi, 神器) of the mirror, jewel, and sword. I regard these as the three techniques of man (jingi 人技): meat eating, vegetable eating, and the eating of mist. In the Warring States Period, this could correspond to man eating (danjiki 男食), fasting (danjiki 断食), and the Way of the Mist. Thinking about the Sanshin no Kata in this manner is quite interesting indeed.

The Seeds of the Martial Way

The legendary thief, Ishikawa Goemon, shouted out before he was allegedly boiled alive, "Ishikawa and the sands of all the beaches may disappear, but thieves never will!" When I first started accepting students, it was not truly for the purpose of teaching but rather for my own self-study and training. And now after fifty years of scattering tens of thousands of seeds around the world, two hundred and ten trees have emerged. It reminds me of the saying, "The farmer sows the seed and the crows eat them." But in this case it was the humans that ate them.

Here we sum up the evolution of the martial way. Some of the scattered seeds slumber where they lie. If some continue to sleep, some get eaten in their dreams. Some fail to sprout and thus decompose. Bears hibernate in the winter. Snakes, frogs, and the seven turtles that I have kept for forty years, all go to sleep in the winter.

Even now, birds eat the seeds I scatter. But I never scare them off. I just watch them. For this is a natural principle. These birds then excrete the seeds. From the excrement, new sprouts arise and give us a view of the maturing true power of the tree.

When the martial wind blows, all the trees' leaves shake. In the growth rings of the giant trees is left the stamp of the achievement of the inner secrets.

In his youth, when he was known as Takezo, Miyamoto Musashi was hung up in a pine tree by the monk Takuan and scolded. With the setting of the sun, the crows gathered in the tree top and cawed "Aho aho!" (stupid, stupid!) Grandma Sugi looks up at Takezo with fury in her eyes. Perhaps she had hay fever? This story is well known and loved in Japan.

THE ESSENCE OF BUDO

My fifteenth-dan martial friends, these 150 brave trees grow thicker with each ring as they mature. They create shade to protect us from the strong rays of the sun bursting through the ozone layer. Birds flock to the big trees. Why is this tree a pine tree (matsu 松)? Humans have to wait (matsu 待つ) spending a life in forbearance and diligence. Many inner secrets are discovered only when we bear that which is most difficult to bear. This I wish to say unto you.

It has been twenty years since they aired the television program *Ninja Jiraiya* in Japan and now it is being released on DVD. The Master Yamaji Tetsuzan shouts, "Dokusai, throw away your evil desires!" The bird henchmen of Dokusai all lose their nerve and respond, "That's right!"

Toscanini and the Audience

The Italian conductor Toscanini (1867–1957) stated that "music is for listening." In that case, I say write the martial scrolls in a musical score! When Toscanini conducts the orchestra, his back is to the audience. It seems to me, the orchestra is his ally and the audience is an attacking enemy.

The fifth-dan test in the Bujinkan is performed by a practitioner who has attained the level of fifteenth dan. The recipient kneels with his back to the fifteenth dan. The fifteenth dan raises a sword and with the release of martial intention, or perhaps a shadow kiai, he brings the sword down. Those who avoid the sword are promoted. This is the conductor of the martial symphony in the world of consciousness.

Even now in my old age, the shadow of Takamatsu Sensei is intimately connected with my existence. His shadow becomes the leaves that create the shade (hagakure 葉隠れ) in which I rest. These days are an expression of this fortunate path. I have a great sense of ease that Takamatsu Sensei is looking over and protecting me. Under his giant tree, I proceed with my pen. Toscanini sought inspiration from the shadow (audience). I too live by the power of the shadow. The expression "Fall back three meters so as not to tread on your teacher's shadow" comes to mind.

The Art of Changing Thought and the Art of Changing Struggle

They say there are only three philosophers who have written theories of women: Arthur Schopenhauer's *Views on Women*; Simone de Beauvoir's *The Second Sex* (it begs the

178   Chapter 4   Heart, Technique, and Body

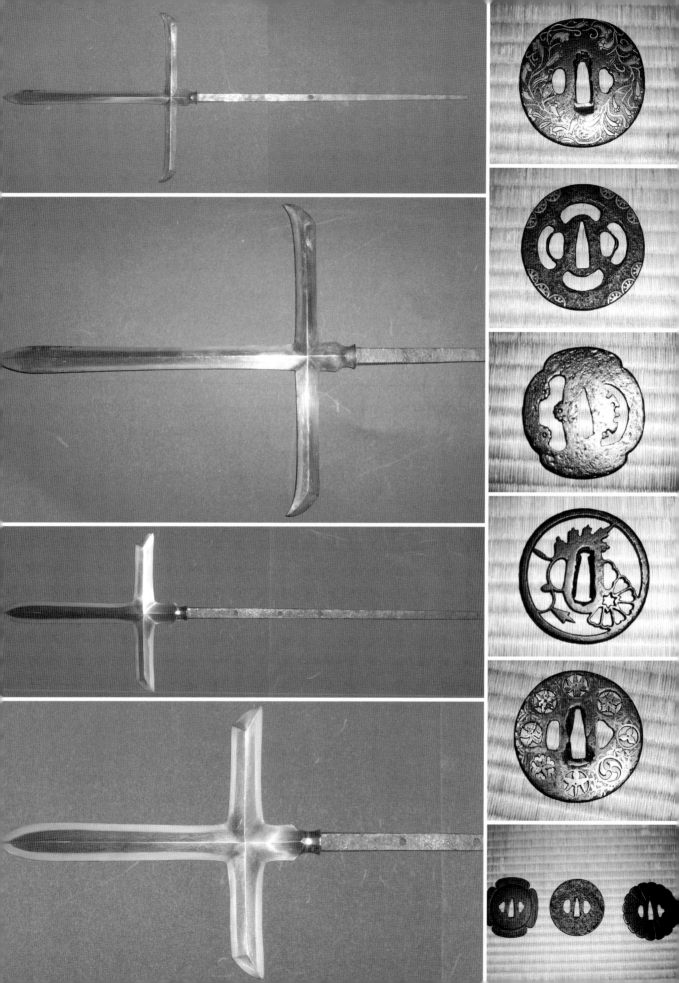

questions, What is the first sex? What is the third sex?); and Georg Simmel's *Cultural History of Women.*

It is sometimes said that physically, the ratio between men and women is seven to three. On the other hand, spiritually and mentally it is the reverse: three to seven. When we speak of seven and three, it brings to mind the method of disguise used by the ninja Shichiho Sanpo (Seven Directions, Three Laws). When we change the characters for disguise, they can be read as the "art of changing thought" 変想術 or perhaps we can interpret it with different characters as the "art of changing struggle" 変争術. You may be nodding in agreement.

The deity of war is sometimes shown with three faces. For example: Asyura Malishiten, Daikokuten. To the left and right of Daikokuten's face are the faces of Benzaiten and Bishamonten. These three come together to form a guardian deity.

Now I am expressing the inner secrets in three ways—through painting, pictures, and a combination of pictures and calligraphy. It is my sincere wish that people can grasp a feeling of the inner secrets. I would like to continue with these three methods. Here we use the word manga 漫画 for picture. Change the characters and it becomes "infinite pictures" 万画. Flip the order and change the characters and it becomes "perseverance" 我慢. Indeed, it is because we persevere that we receive the power to draw the infinite pictures.

Writings of the Inner Secrets of the Martial Way

Miyamoto Musashi left his writings of the inner secrets in his work *The Book of Five Rings*. But no matter how many times one may read the five scrolls (earth, water, fire, wind, and void) of this work, one will never grasp the inner secrets. In Buddhist teachings, consciousness is the sixth element added to the elements of earth, water, fire, wind, and void.

Musashi's works on consciousness can be seen in his drawings and sculptures of Fudo Myo-o. The characters and words he used to express the inner secrets are drawn in the world of space and consciousness. Not written words or letters but "images" (written with the characters: intent, eye, different, express 意目異示). If you rely only on written words (expressed as well as "winning words"), these words can only have their one express meaning. For example, in the word kyojitsu 虚実, kyo is only kyo, and jitsu can only be jitsu. You will arrive at the final station standing all alone. Consciousness is the conductor that leads us to the transcendental world.

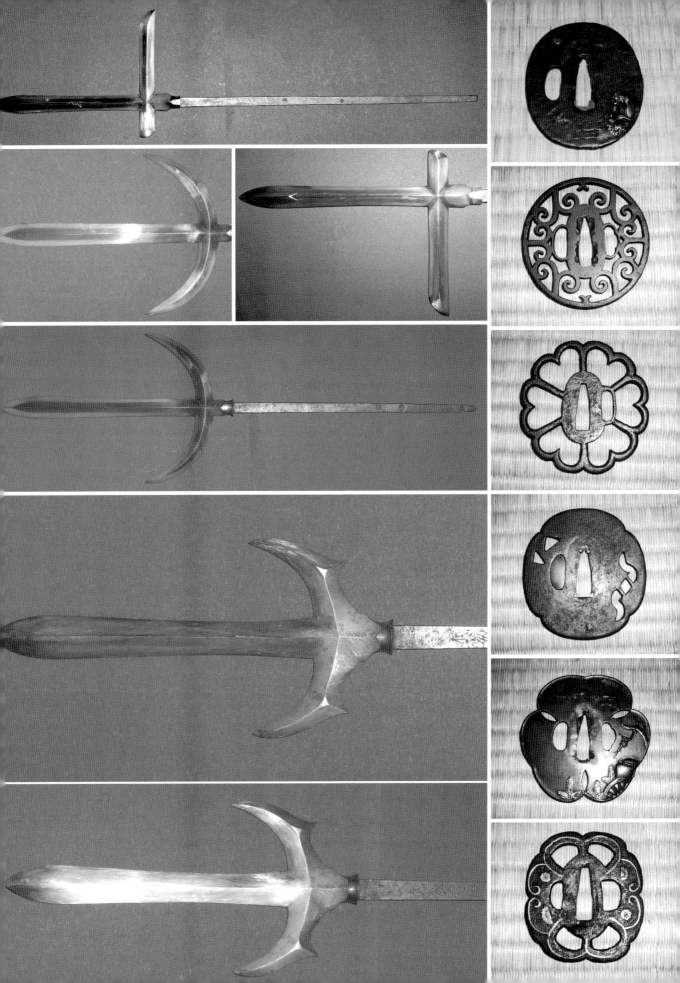

I have previously mentioned Yamamoto Tsunetomo's words, "The way of the warrior is in finding his place of death." It is important for every person to be aware of the time of death, persevering through consciousness. The giant elephant, sensing his imminent death, leaves the herd and proceeds to his place of death. The character for elephant (象) can be written as "giant form" (巨象). We can thus understand the form as the great master at the moment of death.

Viewing Musashi's *The Book of Five Rings* and Ihara Saikaku's *Japan's Perpetual Treasures* and *World's Secret Calculations* as martial writings is interesting indeed. Saikaku was a commoner poet and writer of the ukiyo-zoshi (popular novel). His works have the sense (saikaku 才覚) of the warrior. During war or peace, the world is always in turmoil. It is important to view with both eyes open the fact that we are only living in the space between life and death.

One Life in Nine Deaths; One in Ten Thousand

There is the saying "One life in nine deaths." For the warrior's attitude, to face defeat, to have an honorable death; from these sounds of ten deaths (toshi 十死) we recall the wàrrior (toshi 闘士): the Fighting Bushi. In other words, hidden within the rules of the poetry of the fight (toshi 闘詩), "kuji (nine characters) are forgiven but juji (ten characters) are not." Therein lies the profound meaning that fighting is unforgiven. The eight jewels of the "Legend of the Eight Dogs" shine forth.

Ten years ago, in the past, inherent in the expression "worth ten thousand deaths" the inner secrets left by the warrior who escapes one life in nine deaths, and passes through the one in ten thousand gates, disappear.

The one-eyed warrior asks, "Are you the one who has vision that can see through all?" "The world's four (shi 四) gates of religion, philosophy, thought, and education are closed. The gates of the genbu (Fantastic Warrior 玄武), shujaku (red sparrow 朱雀), seiryu (green dragon 青龍), and byakko (white tiger 白虎) lead you from the gates of death (shimon 死門) and become the gates of good fortune," whispers the enigmatic feng shui master. The bright path, the labyrinth, the dark procession at night, all lead to the gate of life. Flash. Strobe. Shutter. Lightning. The famous Japanese photographer Ken Domon releases the shutter.

The one who travels freely and is inspired, like lightning, through the eight hundred thousand gates; we must ask this leader, this inspired rider who opens and closes the gates at will. He will respond to the one-eyed warrior, "The inspired leader who passed

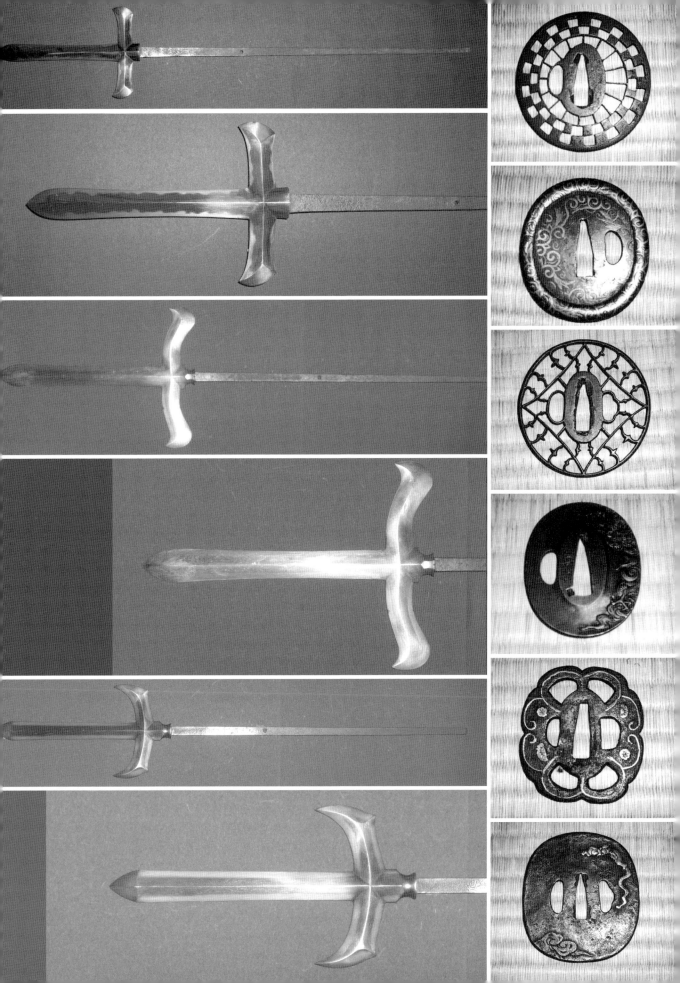

through the mysterious gate, we shall call him a martial artist." And then, "My spear strikes first!"

Waves

I would draw your attention to the drawing of the Genji warrior Nasuno Yoichi entitled *The Winning Tide* (Nagi no Kachidoki). The artist Kyoun Kawanabe is the successor to Kyosai Kawanabe, who is well known as the teacher of the famous English architect Josiah Conder. It is a drawing wherein the warrior Nasu no Yoichi, while on horseback in the ocean enduring the waves, shoots an arrow through a target on an enemy's boat. The splendor with which the waves are rendered is overwhelmingly beautiful. The meaning of "to knock over or defeat" can be said to be inherent in the word for waves, nagisa 渚. This is a point of utmost importance.

Nasu no Yoichi's superb archery did not only hit its intended target (a Japanese fan) but it pierced the heart (kaname 要) of the army of the Heike and led the Genji army to victory.

Martial Artists and Zen Teachers

There are many stories of martial artists gaining enlightenment with the guidance of a Zen master. There is a saying, the sword and Zen are one. It is also said that martial and Zen are one, tea and Zen are one, art and Zen are one, and bad and good are one. I write the characters for "as one" as "one aid" 一助. In reality, Zen is but one aid to the sword. Martial artists must not believe everything that the Zen master tells them but should use the teachings only as an aid.

Analyzing the character for Zen 禅, we see that it is made of two parts, shimesu 示 and tan 単. Shimesu means to express and tan is a counter. We should interpret tan as guts; an expression of your guts. The famous monk Takuan leaves us the following words in his work, *Reiroshu* (The collection of exquisite sounds) :

"Desire, life, and duty are the most important things in this world. Desires exist to support life, so life necessarily ranks higher than desire. But duty is another thing altogether. There are times when we should not begrudge our lives for duty. This cowardliness is unacceptable. We must be willing to lay down our lives for duty or honor. This is the reason we are born. We must not take life lightly. Therefore we should pay careful attention to the true desires that respect true duty and honor; the treasured desires."

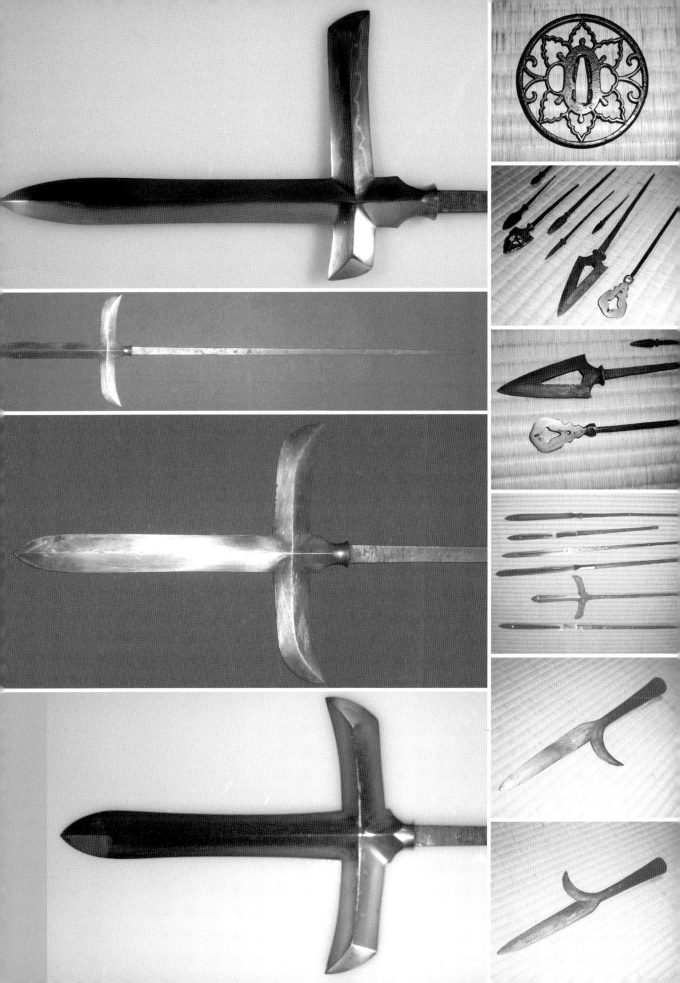

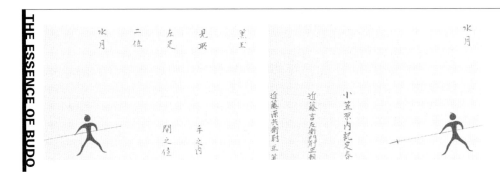

Although he never formally entered the power structure, Takuan expounded the teachings for the power structure. He was a monk of the Rinzai tradition and was exiled to Dewa district by the government because of the "purple robe incident." (In this incident, Takuan co-authored a scathing admonition of the shogun Tokugawa Hidetada.) He was later pardoned. He was a poet and well versed in the tea ceremony. The work that best represents him is his *The Unfettered Mind: The Mysterious Record of Immovable Wisdom.*

There are also the writings of Suzuki Shosan, a practitioner of the Nio-Zen, or grimacing Zen, entitled *Myoanjyo* (Guiding stick for spiritually blind people). Shosan served the Ieyasu house and was a decorated general in two battles, Sekigahara and the Summer War of Osaka Castle. He entered the priesthood in 1620 and built many temples of the Jodo Shin-shu sect for the Ieyasu house. He also built one temple in honor of his own sect, Soto-shu. But never taken by any of these, he preferred non-secular pursuits. His Zen wind blows with the feeling, "The heart that thinks of oneself, suffers. The heart that thinks of others, is free." Below are ten precepts for living found in the *Myoanjyo*:

Knowing life and death; therein resides enjoyment

Reflect on oneself and know oneself

Experience events from the other's heart

With sincerity, aid the sick

See the place of things and the character of each

Leaving the household behind, there is virtue

Forget yourself to protect yourself

Rise up, be discreet

Destroy the heart to foster the heart

Forget the small gains, receive the biggest

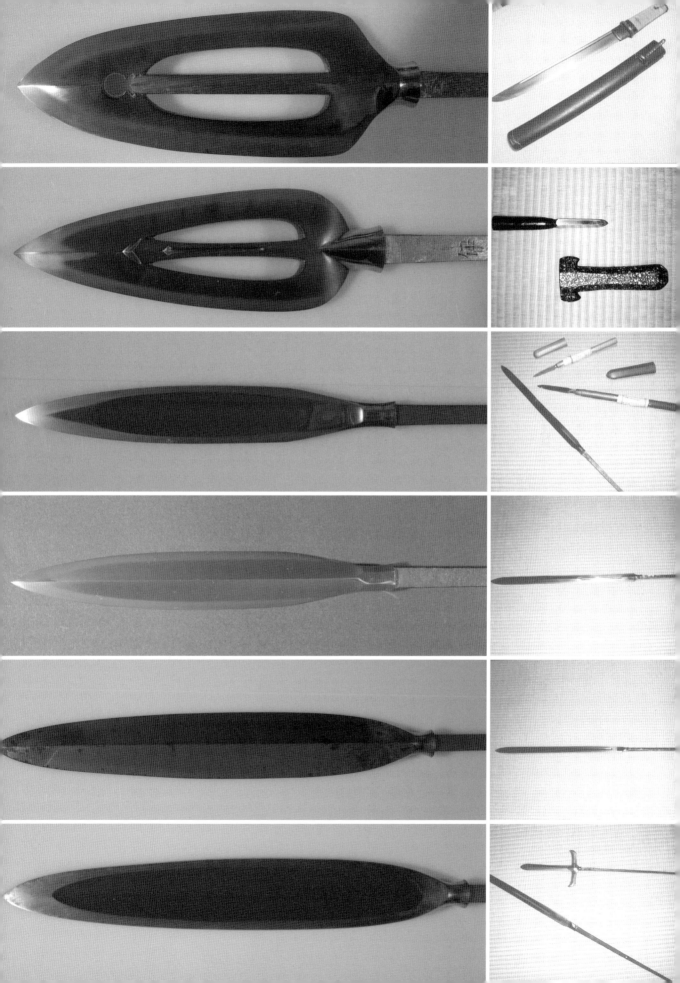

In his work *Muchu Mondo* (Questions and answers in a dream), Muso Kokushi expounds the sinfulness of war. To lay the souls of the dead to rest as well as to teach virtue to the people, he erected Risho pagodas of the Ankokuji Temple all over Japan, and opened the famous zen temple Tenryuji in Kyoto.

As for me, I erected a monument for my teacher, Takamatsu Sensei, in Toyooka village. Alongside of this, I have placed two monuments, one to honor the nine lineages that I inherited from Takamatsu Sensei and one to honor the Bujinkan. I opened it to the public in 2008 as the archbishop Hakuryu Jyuso.

Interpret Misfortunate Years and Devil's Gate as Soaring Years and the Gate of Life

One of my students, in a New Year's greeting, once said to me, "This is the year of my great misfortune (yaku doshi 厄年). I went to the temple New Year's day and received blessings for Sensei as well." "Thank you so much for your thoughtfulness!" I replied with a happy heart. The misfortunate years are those years in life where the likelihood of encountering great suffering, disaster, or life-threatening situations is presumed high. One must be cautious and prudent during these years. The misfortunate years are, for men, twenty-five, forty-two, and sixty; for women, ages nineteen and thirty-three. The years directly prior to and after these years are also considered unlucky as you enter into and come out of the great misfortunate year. One must exercise diligence in these years as well. We often go to the temple to pray to the gods and receive blessings to cleanse ourselves of the misfortune.

When I was forty-two, in the year of my great misfortune, Takamatsu Sensei passed away. At this time, my only thought was, "There really are misfortunate years." But now at the age of seventy-eight, I look back at that misfortunate year and realize another possible interpretation—that in my misfortune I became one with Takamatsu Sensei. Rather than an unlucky year it was an auspicious, transitional year (yaku doshi 躍年).

One could say that the perseverance of the suffering, sadness, and disasters of the misfortune year becomes a medicine (yaku 薬). It is certainly good medicine. The misfortunate years are a time in life when our capacity gets broadened, and can be a time of enlightenment. In the game of mahjong as well, when you receive "yaku," it leads to winning.

Along with the misfortunate years, many people also worry about the Devil's Gate (kimon 鬼門). Located between the signs of the cow and tiger, it generally faces

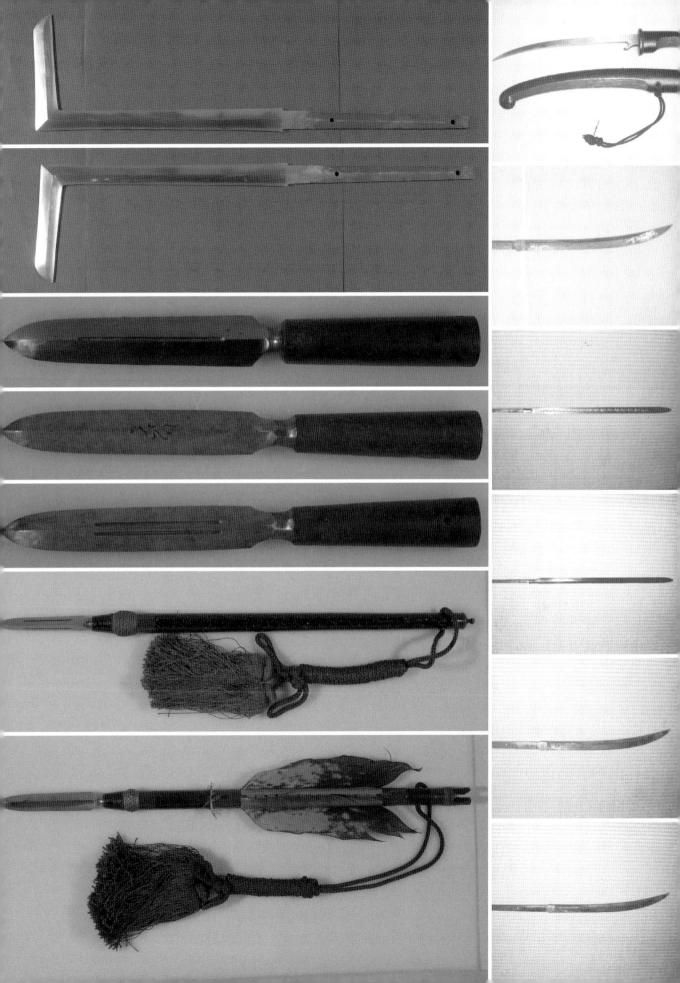

northeast and is considered unlucky or ominous. In Kyoto and Tokyo, it is said that when the cities were built, temples were erected in these directions to ward off evil. But let us view the Devil's Gate (kimon 鬼門) as the Gate of Life (kimon 生門). Having the guts to see it this way will turn this gate into tomorrow's gate of life energy.

Change in the Kyojitsu Phenomenon

It is said that if you cup a bee in your hand while chanting the mantra, "Amo issun no tama mushi" that the bee will not use his stinger against you. In the same way, if you place a scorpion in your mouth and close your mouth, the scorpion becomes still and will not harm you. This is the ura waza (reverse technique) of the inner secrets expressing great mysterious nature. A perfect reflection of Jean Henri Fabre's *Souvenirs Entomologiques* (in Japanese, "Mysterious Insects").

We could think of this as nature's way of teaching us the immoveable heart. In ancient writings, Amo represents the god Amaterasu Omikami (Great God of Heavenly Light). The tama mushi (also known as the scarab, the jewel beetle) is hailed as the insect of immortality in Africa. Even now I cherish the immortal beetle that Colonel John Bon, who served in wars in Africa, sent me. It is not just an insect, but a "soul" insect.

Sometimes we hear about the person who wouldn't hurt a fly committing some terrible act. Well, recently I heard that honeybees are experiencing a syndrome that causes the collapse of their swarms. As such, the production of fruit and vegetables is declining.

Great nature (daishizen 大自然) is changing from era to era (daishizen 代自然). To be able to survive and live in the midst of this constant change, it is important to comprehend that which is the essence. To this end, I believe it is important to vary this theme of change every year. Each year, for nine years, I taught the inner secrets of one of the nine lineages. Then I taught for one year about the space within the nine lineages. Next I instructed my students about the space, as it is connected with twisted intention; in other words, the natural martial wind (bufu) theory of the art of situational (jotai 状態) rope (jotai 縄体). If you ask me what is next, I will reply, "Rokkon Shojo."

The Natural Aspect of Sex and Violence

Violence is the living demon of which we can only catch glimpses. From soldiers to mercenaries the times change. When using weapons, the master makes magic, with weapons to be seen and weapons unseen. The movie director Billy Wilder filmed fantastic scenes

PAST AND PRESENT PHOTOS OF THE AUTHOR

with his brilliant use of small props. Likewise, the Japanese director Yasujiro Ozu also used small props that were just as important as the actors to create regal and refined scenes.

There is always the fear, with armies composed only of men, that some will turn rogue and commit rape and other acts of atrocity. There is an army composed of only women stationed in Liberia, Africa, that has a better reputation than that of the men's army. Yet, even so, there are other opinions about it, and some readers may be nodding their heads in agreement.

Ordinary people cannot live according to the flow of their natural instincts. They feel this way because they have no discretion. If you think of it like this, all of the terrible events, anxiety, and fears that arise from internal and external causes will be blown away and disappear.

It is said that General Yamanaka Shikanosuke from the Warring States Period prayed to the crescent moon shining from behind the clouds of war during the brief time of his rise, "Give me hardship, give me suffering." Here we catch a glimpse of his warrior period and it brings to mind the paintings of the artist Tsukioka Yoshitoshi, *Hundred Forms of the Moon,* which were created during the last days of the shogunate (an era in which peace began). The prince Shotoku Taishi states, "Hold peace righteously." This could well be heard as a call to the sakimori, the protectors of the borders of old Japan, as "Harmony is the greatest of virtues."

Machines (kikai) and Humans

In his work *Machine Man,* La Metrie, the French philosopher, claims that humans are very complex machines. They are machines that can wind their own springs, accumulate experience, and walk on two feet. The same theme can also be found in the philosopher Descartes's *Mechanistic Theory.*

Today, with the martial arts becoming robotic and the use of unmanned weapons proliferating, I think we should adopt a "Living Mysterious Being Theory" as our guiding principle. If we fail to do so, we could find ourselves plunging into a terrifying new era.

This becomes a time of opportunity (kikai 機会). The three hands of the clock tell us so. Hours, minutes, and seconds become the Sanshin no Kata, the Sanshin (three hearts) embedded within. The five elements—earth, water, fire, wind, and void—see us through to the end of the fifteenth-dan road. To express this in the scrolls, katakana, hiragana, and kanji are used. There is also the use of the Kamiyo (mythological age) characters, and the ancient Izumo characters, old Wa characters, and more. Word processors and computers,

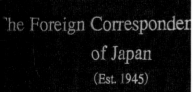

The Foreign Corresponden
of Japan
(Est. 1945)

社団
法人 日本外国特派員

unlike humans, have no self-recognition or vision.

The sound of one kanji can vary up to eight ways. In the Nara period, they called Bushi protectors or guardians. Do not let this escape your notice. The emperor Tenmu also created a naming system based on eight categories.

The Strong Who have Passed

The deity Amida lives in the paradise of the west and shows us the infinite glow of life. Yes, thinking of it, when I look from the place of my birth, Takamatsu Sensei lived to the west in Nara prefecture. I was twenty-seven when I rode the train to Takamatsu Sensei's house in search of the inner secrets. Until then, that young boy had been running the dark streets of ignorance. At that age, the deity Amida, in the guise of Takamatsu Sensei, welcomed me. Little did I know that it would be the journey of my death. I was walking recklessly on the road of suffering and hardship. Thanks to the compassionate face and soul of Takamatsu Sensei, I am here today.

In the sutras is the story of Amida. Amida was born a king and later became a monk. Taking the name Hozo, he became an ascetic and trained in the martial wind. Acquiring the infinite wisdom and a compassionate heart, he vowed the forty-eight vows (to save humanity) and created paradise in the West. Thinking of it, when I was twenty-seven, rather than experiencing the idea, "The way of the warrior is in finding his place of death," I believe I died and was reborn. If you view it this way, I am only fifty years of age now.

The characters "the heart of the Buddha, enlightened heart, and single intent" 物心、悟心、一念 are written in the inner secret writings of the Koto-ryu Koppojutsu. We get a feeling that they originate from these roots.

I had some friends and students who were diagnosed with cancer. Knowing their time of death, they persevered through body, heart, and consciousness, and left us for the sacred land. When I gaze at their forms, they appear in my eyes, curiously, like the statues of Buddha carved by the monk Enku, with gentle smiles on their faces. Hiroshi Tanaka, Iwao Sagawa, Higashiura-san, Bonnie Malmstrom, Bing Ford, Glenn Morris, Dick Severence, Alan Collin, Butch Johnson, and more . . .

I answer to them, the way of the warrior is in seeing the warrior through till the end (士貫). You, who have passed before us and gained the inner secrets, you are the truly strong, the warriors, the samurai. Like in the Japanese movie *Okuribito* ("Departures"), we pray for their martial merit (infinite life), and keep them forever in our hearts and praise them ever forth.

The Tree of Inner Secrets

The Guardian deity for the Genji clan is the Benzaiten in Kamakura.

The Guardian deity for the Heike clan is the Benzaiten in the Itsukushima Shrine.

These are said to be the guardian deities of the rise and fall of the rival Genpei (Genji 源氏 and Heike 平家) clans. Daikokuten is said to assure victory and be the highest of the guardian deities in India. In front of the Bujinkan community center stands a six-ton statue of Daikokuten. It shines with the golden characters, "martial virtue."

Siddhartha Gautama became a monk at the age of twenty-nine. Later, gaining enlightenment under the bodhi tree, he became the Buddha and went on to teach according to the level of his listener until eighty years of age.

Next to the memorial for Takamatsu Sensei, I planted a single bodhi tree. I intend to wait for the days of my eightieth year under the shadow of the leaves (hakage 葉陰) of this tree.

In the year 2009, the theme for the Bujinkan was "Talent, Spirit, and Capacity" (utsuwa). This is the teaching, according to each listener's, each student's ability. The aura I wish to impart becomes a spotlight revealing the heart, technique, and body of the martial way. The years of compassion draw near.

Voyage of Space Battleship Noah

It has been fifty-two years since I inherited the nine lineages. Although I have not yet reached the other shore (higan; enlightenment 彼岸), I feel that my earnest desire (higan; the forty-eight vows of Amida) has been realized. I still remember the spirit of the words Takamatsu Sensei spoke when initiating me to the scrolls. Today they are the most essential, the necessary eyes of the divine. "Hatsumi san, you are my beloved student, do your very best" (ganbatte—keep going). Even now it seems he speaks these words to me.

One day, it seemed that Takamatsu Sensei realized that I did not, or was unable to have any children and he said, "Hatsumi san, even if you don't have any children yourself, if you have a fateful meeting (connection) with any child, love is the most important thing." At the moment, Takamatsu Sensei's wife was bringing us tea and she added, "That's right, Hatsumi san. Just like he says, even if they are not your own children, love them just the same." This sound echoes in my ears today.

When I first embarked on my voyage around the world, I wished only for people to become aware of the true martial arts. I kept love in utmost importance as I traveled, teaching everyone single-handedly, man to man. Perhaps this is the love of just having

people know the art. Now after learning of this eighth ocean, I have decided not to board the famous animated Space Battleship Yamato, but I shall board the Space Battleship Noah. Sixty years ago I plucked the song *Harbor Lights* on my steel guitar, now I strum it on my ukulele.

The memorial of the nine lineages that I received from Takamatsu Sensei and those teachers who have gone before is a lighthouse. It shines forth brilliantly the fighting poetry of spirit and life. The Bujinkan memorial forever radiates the light of those martial artists that have, with whole-hearted devotion, pierced through their martial life with (selfless) spirit.

This is the light that, through the martial arts, expresses the unending love between buyu (martial friend) and buyu. The systems created by man crumble one after the other. In the midst of this, the Space Battleship Noah embarks to save the earth. To the sound of popping champagne corks, it launches into the eighth ocean.

I cannot say why, but the marching theme from the soundtrack of Japanese director Yasujiro Ozu's *An Autumn Afternoon* echoes in my ears and brings this old heart back to the life of my youth.

THE MEMORIAL FOR TAKAMATSU SENSEI

The statue of Daikokuten near the Bujinkan dojo

APPENDIX—Original Japanese Text

極意とはなんぞや

　万変不驚という言葉がある。宇宙の年齢は？　最近137億歳だという答えが出た。伝統のあるもの、歴史のあるもの、それらは今日まで長く続いているだけに、一瞬のＤＮＡの生命力の生死明暗ともいうべきものを間近に見る思いがする。

　だが、それらは人類史の長い年月の、一瞬に過ぎない。いうなれば火打ち石がライターに変わったようなものである。

　変火、その結ばれた火縁は第一の火、第二の火、第三、第四、第五の火となり、木火土金水を変化生滅させる。そこにも極意の変化する一端を見せる。そこで、火を扱う人類にとって肝心なことは、火は魔物であり、化物であるということを知って、その実像に迫ることである。極意という化け物は、井上円了の研究の世界や三遊亭円朝の語りの世界にも現れてくる。

　「その人が得意とするものを極意とししなはったんやな」と師の高松寿嗣（1889–1972）先生が言われたように、極意とは特定のものでなく、限りあるものでもなく、名人、達人とは限らず、と言おうか、突然変異もありの、名人達人ならぬ「冥人」と化した人の魂の骨姿が、粉骨砕身して極意の世界に花秘となって見せるものである。

　極意の法に虚実転換の秘があるが、無限なる虚、偉大なる実の、虚実展観がある。奇命に結ばれる、天なる観神観眼の瞬間瞬間に見る紺碧の空、根碧の空、その完璧の壁を見通す両眼・龍眼・霊眼が、生と死の二つの眼となる。

　武術を求める者のほとんどすべてもが、勝ちこそ極意であると思うものだが、さにあらず。負けの極意を会得せぬ限り、勝つことの真の極意には到達せぬものである。勝ちを＋とすれば負けは－、言うなればプラスとマイナスの接点で灯を見せるような現実を知ることである。そして勝ちと負けが接触し、光がシャープ・アンド・フラットのサウンドを聞かせ、奇くことである。

「大愚」良寛の極めたもの

　極意とはまた極位であり、極会であり、極異でもあり、異極に輝く武徳威光の星のようなものである。人は極めたと思い込んだら、たちまちそれに囚われてしまいやすい。まさに獄意。地獄、餓鬼、畜生、修羅、人間、天の奇道に迷う。大愚が妙愚座に一変する。そこに坐る者、名僧も愚僧も瞑想に入る境地を見る。

　そこで、違った視点というよりも盲点から、武道の極意を見つめてみよう。和歌、俳句に巧みであり、のびやかな書でも知られる禅僧、良寛（1758–1831）。この世の権威を排し、大愚良寛と自称し、日頃から子供たちと遊び戯れていたといわれる彼の心象映像の極意から、その心胆を見つめたとき、凡人には、彼が「大愚」と謙遜しているのだろうと思われるのだが、さにあらず。賢明な彼の心眼には、世の真実がまざまざと見えていたのである。子供と遊ぶというのは、「三つ子の魂百までも」、または「三歳の法」からも言われるように、子供とは限らないものだ。子供と言えば、日本では大切なものを、虎の子と言う。

　日本では古来、愚かなることは、「ビッグ・グー（愚）」「巨人」として称える言葉であった。大愚は大ばか者にあらず、たわけにあらず、栄賢を称える頓智遁行の言葉が秘められているのだ。例えば愚の骨頂という言葉があるが、これは愚の「骨調」（グーを英訳音としたグーなる妙愚の骨法術）として捉えていただきたい。さて古典の軍略兵法を参考にしても、実際、現代の戦いの確率は低迷し、皆無（怪武）に近い。しかし、マンガの古典

（個典）が現実になって、当たることがあるのは何としたことか。

　良寛が大愚と自称したのは、真の愚を具えんとしても、大愚になれずという、大愚の境地への憧れ、禅夢を獏（夢を食らう獣の、獏である）然と称えたものであろう。

　徳川家康（1543-1616）の生格、生き様を端的に表しているとされる「鳴かぬなら、鳴くまで待とう、ほととぎす」という心象の句、そして中国の太公望（軍師の呂尚）の「釣れるまで待とう」の深層心理を真想心理と見てみるとよい。

　大愚に対して、枯れた武人・耄六はどうか。

　素晴らしい芸、武芸をめでるときに、「枯れた技だね。枯れたいぶし銀のようなお姿じゃ」と感動したときに発する表現がある。高松先生が耄六という画号をお使いになったのも、そんな趣意から出たものであろうと思う。

　宮本武蔵（1584-1645）も、真鎗真理の中には、このような姿象を求めていたのかもしれない。それを表すかのように、「枯木鳴鵙図」を残している。

極意と伝承

　武道の極意について記された本は決して少なくはない。だが、それらの多くは、経験した自叙伝的なものであると見なすほうが望ましい。知識も過ぎれば痴識になってしまう、という武道・武芸・兵法界のミステリーゾーンがあるということを見失ってはいけない。

　しかも、極意について実際に記した人物であっても勝負で敗れているという事実がある。とはいえ、負けることは、良き伝承となる。誤りや間違いに気がつき、それを後世に正しく伝えてこそ、武道の真実は継承されるものである。

　さらに言えば、極意の中には間時に見る心眼もある。徳川家康のように、負けるという間化する極意によって天下をとった人物は少なくない。それに対して、勝つことばかりに邁進する者は、「毒才者」となって死道に走り、士道を取り違えた自殺行為に走った喩えもある。「負ける」を「ふ」と読む。「ふ」は「賦」、すなわち「もののふ」の「ふ（歩）」である。将棋の歩は金になる。変進も知らねば、一人前にはなれぬ。

　一人の武芸者があるとき、「馬の尻の方を歩くな」と言ったという。馬脚で蹴られるからだ。自然界には、たくさんの死角盲点反射が潜んでいる。それを避ける極意の一つを表すのが、馬の裏脚の道理虚実である。それは言うなれば、遭遇反射に対する口伝である。私は二頭の馬を飼っているが、要は馬の質を知り、愛を伝えることである。私は一度もクッキーとトビに蹴られたことはない。

　極意の平仮名に返り点を打つと、「いごく」となる。そう、「動く」である。動くとは、万変変転である。固定した、思いこみや常識にとらわれたために、極意を失うからである。地球に北極南極がある。武象の極は東西南北をはじめとし、十方にある。基本八法に動示意極、動時移極、道似威極もある。終支の亥極そして十二支の子に移ごきを見る。子は大黒天である。

　武道をはじめとする古文書を読むときは、固定した観念で読むと、その多極的に変化する勝字や活字の空間の秘伝を読み違えることになってしまう。極意の書というのは奇本的なものであり、正しく師伝を守り、修行するところに、基本が生本という、心技体一如の生きられる極意が自ずから授かるものである。

極意と四天王

　「極意というものは、その人その人の得手としたものを極意としたものやな」と師の口伝を遠くに聞く。古代では秘文を杉の甘皮に、神代文字で断片的に記録して残している。私の継承した流派の武風の極意は、その時代の風に吹かれ、宮沢賢治流に、雨にも風にも負けず、灯し続けられてきた。それは風前の灯の下で書き記され、語り続けられてきたものであろう。

　極意を護る姿を四天王に喩えるならば、この四天王の血の流れとでも言おうか。その血役の形、象はA型、B型、AB型、O型の四系。血液型にのって生き続けたその血で書き記されたものである。この四型は神明四羅の秘文の喩えとも言えるだろう。また、四天王の姿とも喩えられよう。また四大文明を守る姿とも言えよう。そして四大文明の推移を語る語り部にも思えてくる。

　私は本書で、古くは断片的に残された秘文の偉大さのように、極意とは断片的に残された一つの灯りの輝きとして表現したいと思っている。なぜならば、極意とは言葉をもって長々と説明するものではないと思うからである。故に本書は、文字よりも絵と写真を多く使用したのである。

極意はない

極意はない、と言ってもよいだろう。なぜか。極意は無信の無心の空間の世界から、突然飛び出してくるものであるからだ。有るかと思えばなく、無いと思えば有る、秘妙なる術なりというゼロのサウンドが答えてくれるからである。

よく紙一重の差で極意があると言う人がいるが、極意はその紙一重の隙間に存在しているのである。「極意は語るに尽きず語らず」の腹芸の教えもうなずけるであろうが、極意に対する答は、そこで紙一重の隙間の間の広さに表現されるものだと言おう。童視（同志）に見せる一種の絵本として力を注ぎ、読者の皆さんに「殿寿」するものである。

巻物には絵を描いて極意のイメージを発揚するものもある。極意の書を記すにあたって、私は大愚フィーリングをもって、枯れた表現にすべく工夫している。

極意の未地（道）は、人間が生まれた瞬間、否、戦国の世にあっては生まれる前から、遠くにある卵子に向かって、はるばる遠泳をする精子の時から始まっているのだと思ってよいだろう。そこに、二羽鳥が先か、卵が先かというこという質問が生まれる。なぜ鶏ではなく二羽鳥と書いたかというと、メスオスの鳥でないと、ヒナが孵らないからである。

捨身技

「托す」という言葉がある。これは捨身技とも言えるのだが、タックスとなれば税金で、「説金」は社会を守る一つの定義である。ここで、説とは道理を話して意を通すこと、金は金言の意味である。大切な寿要（環境を守るための）と表現して、次に大切な需要護身経済となっている。スエーデン語では、それが正しくサイクルされれば、タックタックということになってくる。

極意を伝授することも、人から人へと、人に対する敬意から伝授する行為となる。人は、托される、そして托すことのできる人との出会いが大切である。そうして生まれたギブアンドリターンの極意のネットワークが世界に広まれば、争いがなくなるはずである。ここで托すというのは、生体は自分一人で生きているのではなく、つながりにヘルプされることを知れということでもある。それは人とは限らず、生物、自然に托し托される姿勢であり、これを人としてのマナーと極意自覚しない限り、実行はできない。

托鉢をもって修行僧は家々を廻り、食をいただく。禅寺での食事は、慈悲と布施の鉢をもって僧堂に行く。ドミニコ会、フランチェスコ会、カルメル会の修道士も、喜捨を受ける生活を送りながら、人々に救いの道を説いている。

虚実とはいかなることか

武士、武人というが、武士とはいかなる者だろうか。

日本でさまざまな制度改革を行った、第三十八代、天智天皇の時代（668-672）、心の正しい者として、農民のうちより生活に不自由を感じない身体健全なる者を選んで武人とした。「武」という字の本体は「正」と書くが、まさに武の核には、心身の正しさがあるのである。けっして闘争せしむる強者を武人に選んだわけではないのだ。

「正しい心に、敵はない」という言葉がある。しかし、敵があり、その敵が向かい来たるときは、敵を傷つけないように避けるべきであって、避けがたきにおよんで初めて決死の勇気を出すのが本体だ。すなわち両刀をたばさんで何時でも来たれというふうを見せるのが虚であり、避けて通るというのが本体の実であり、この虚実がなければ、武士道の武風もないわけである。

ここで、師との談笑の一つ、耄碌の話。足を踏まれたとき、「あなたの足が、わての足にのってまんがー」と問えば、争いが失せる。そして争いなれば、腰も曲がっての極意歌を知る。

体術にても、引くと見せて押す、押すと思えば引く、左と見せて右に投げる、というふうにする。それは商人が、売りたいように見せながら、それでは引き合わないから売らないと見せかけ、儲けのよい値段で売りつけようとする駆け引きにも似ている。これを虚実というのであって、虚実は許されてはいるが、過ぎると心を読まれるから、過ぎぬようにし、不足もしないようにする。ここに極意の武風が生じ、幽玄な様、妖なる様、玄なる様、妖術幻術も見通すことができる。そして神技や、エイリアンの特異技も象じさせるのである。こうして、極意のさまざまな姿象、要術を現実に許伝されたい。

困難や危険に遭遇したり、不遇の時にいるならば、その一服の時間の鉢を逆回しにしてみると、茶事、そこに古事古伝の極意を指す時間が記されることがある。これ

ぞ運命を左右逆転させる時称（自称）虚実転換法とも言えるのである。

要に祈って開く武運の鉄扇

　私が高松先生に教えを受け始めてから、はや半世紀が経った。77歳、「奇寿」も過ぎ、さらに人生を生きていなければならないことを運命づけられているようである。そして、復活祭に見る「武士道とは死ぬことと見つけたり」の人生から抜け出すことができたと思う。というのも、その年齢にて、私は本書を含め、二冊の武道書の著作を講談社インターナショナルから依頼されたからである。

　ある日、私の戒名とともに、「神忍院殿白龍大日武晃大居士は80歳までの寿命あり」と告げられたことがある。なんとありがたいことか。お釈迦様が入滅なさった同年80歳まで生きていられるとは。言うなれば、釈迦の教えは今でも生きているではないか。世阿弥も80歳にして初心に返ると言っている。

　武士道は士貫ことと見つけたり、士風を貫くことこそ胆なる武人の姿であろう。

　アランやヒルティ、ラッセル等が幸福論を書いているが、武道家から見た、幸福の虚実についても触れていこう。ヘーゲルが言うごとく神は自己意識であるならば、幸福は自己意識なのだろう。

　「己が身を己が心で痛ます　心の乱れいまぞ鎮むる」という、武道の古歌をよくよく味わうことである。

武人の道の教え──高松先生の手記と共に

　高松先生は、高松家の長男として生まれ、七人のお母さんに育てられました。本当のお母さんでないお母さん（継母）にも子供が生まれました。高松先生は、老いた継母を最後まで面倒を見られたそうです。死期が近づいた継母は、まさか寿太郎にこんなふうに面倒を見ていただけるなんて、と両手をついてお礼を言ったといいます。

　ドラマはそこから変化してくるものです。そして、日本の戦前の空気に包まれながら、清国など激動する外国でも生活なさいました。

　私ですか。わが家は、男は私一人、姉が一人、そしておばあさんと、父と母という構成でした。幼年期の私はおばあさんに背負われたとき、足が地上につくほどに

なっても、おばあさんにおんぶをねだっていた「尼えん坊」だったと聞いています。

　酒を飲んでいないときは、文字通りもののあわれに感動する、仏のような父でしたが、酒が入ると一変して、刃物を振り回したり、物を壊してしまう酒乱に変貌してしまうので、それを押さえつけて寝かせるため、自然に武道の必要性を味わったのでした。私が少年の頃に武門に入った理由のひとつは、そこにもあります。

　このようにして、子供の頃から、酔って帰る父の足音を百メートル先に聞いて、危険なものを隠し、そして刃物を振り回す父の白刃を捕って、父が寝るまで見張ったり押えたりしていました。いまや人並み優れた私の勘覚も、この時期に父に直伝として教えられたものと思い、父のことを我が師匠の一人として感謝しています。

　同様に、神仏に手を合わせて願うということも、自然の行法となりました。

　演劇家のスタニフラスキーが「生活から出発しなさい」と言っていたが、それは武芸者についても当てはまることです。

　第二次世界大戦の前と後では、世相が一変しました。そんな世相も、私を武道への道を歩ませました。武道への道を歩みつつ、私は世界の名画から、たくさんのことを学びました。「道」といえば、ジェリソミーナを演じた、ジュリエッタ・マシーナーの、ペーソスとユーモアのあるしぐさが大好きでした。それに似た歌舞伎の名女形の芳沢あやめの一言「あどめもなく、ぼんじゃりとした」を表わすマリリン・モンローの姿を見つめたものです。フランク・シナトラ歌う「マイウェイ」のサウンドにも聞き入りました。

　私の友人で、作家であり医師でもある宗谷真爾さんは、『動悸と人形』という本を出版しています。道をつくったり、道を歩くのが人生です。そういえば「アスファルトジャングル」という映画もありました。映画館の映写機からスクリーンに向かって放たれる光に、煙草の煙が踊るとき、そのノスタルジックな雰囲気に浸ると、映画館は能舞台だと思われてきます。

　大谷嘉輝さんとロスアンジェルスではなく、ニューヨークの五番街を歩き、冷麺を五分で食べた思い出もあります。駐車場は十五分で料金が割り増しになるというので、二人ともあっというまに平らげたのでした。その時の冷麺の味は、いまだに思い出せません。早食いは武士の習いとして大事なことです。

＊

　高松先生と私のとりの話をしましょう。鳥には「青い鳥」「鳳凰」「不死鳥（フェニックス）」「三本足のカラス」の伝説がありますが、高座や舞台の最後につとめる「とり」ということもあります。これは私の修業中のとりの、私が41歳の時の、先生とのお話です。

　高松寿嗣先生の「幸福の栞（しおり）」の言葉は次のようなものから始まっています。——

　皆さん、互いに憂いを捨てて、幸福を得ましょう。

　皆さん、幸福は人生最高の満足です。

　悲しみとか不満を捨てて、思い直すのも幸福です。

　災害、病害を前知して、覚り改めることも幸福です。

　この一節は、高松先生が、私へ武道を転授伝承させる、残寒の春の日だったと思います。

　極意とはどんなところにも存在しているもので、武道の極意の栞も同じこと。これらはみんなつながっているのです。幸福を拾うことは武道を拾うことで、武道を拾って歩いた私の青少年期がそうでした。修業する心を正しい方向に転換する心が大切ですね。

　振り返ってみると、これを羅針裸心する自針の自覚がないようでは、武道の極意も幸福の極意もありませんな。

＊

　次の項から、高松寿嗣先生との、とりの問答の際に、高松先生が語られた言葉を一言一言掲げてみましょう。

正義の心

　第一に、神仏とはなんでありましょうか。没後、神仏となった歴史的偉人たちがいますが、人は彼らのことを信仰するのではなく、崇拝するのであって、そうした造物的人格化した物体を神だと言ったのは、数千年、数百年も昔の人たちに教えるための目標としたものにすぎません。

　神とか仏とは、不正を畏れ、人を恐れず、迷わさず、

　権力に怖じず、真に正義と真理の理念の極意をもって自然生命体を警せしめ、人々に迫るものであるべきです。そうでなければ、神仏とは言いがたいのであります。

　さて武心和をもって貴しとなすと言うならば、「正義と生義と聖義」の和魂が武士の家紋として描かれます。

　このことから、次のことが言えます。正義の心が即ち神であります。神霊であります。またその教ゆるところが感情的でなく、正義的であり、一国家的でなく世界的であり、一民族的でなく、人類的であり、否生物的でなければならんと思います。いわゆる自然界の生命体ということになるのでしょう。そこに極意生存説が鮮明に見えてくるのです。

　この点から判断しても、神仏は自然的正義を供えたる宇宙の偉大なる正霊と言えるでしょう。

【筆者注】私は、正義と正義、非正義と正義、非正義と非正義、この三つの正義の象を三心の型（かたち）とあてはめてみた。

　私は知らず知らず、1982年の渡米の際、「①アイアムノージャパン、②アイアムノーカントリー、③アイアムユーフォー」という言葉を発していたが、いま地球を、宇宙からの視点でとらえ、地球規模で地球を守らなくてはならない時期がやってきている。

運命を転化する道

　偉大ということは、その大きさ、偉さに限りがないという意味であって、これを我らは、今は量り知ることができないのであります。故に、天災地変は、この自然界の定めを無視していることに対する、正しい神の警告であると知ることであり、また争うものは滅びると知ることであります。地球資源の乱獲からのアンバランス、温暖化に対する自然界からの反撃が見られます。

　地球は寒冷期に入っているという説もありますが、この自然の変化に対し、自覚がないと、神に審（さば）かれる時が来るでしょう。それは物事が過ぎるからであって、過ぎることや不足なことは正しいとは言えません。改めることが十分でないと、地球その世界は行き詰まりの状態に置かれているのです。

　今や、自由主義、社会主義、共産主義の淵に流れる資本主義から、宇宙主義、自然主義、そんな主義の輪廻が地球を廻しているように見せています。

【筆者注】さらにいえば、それらの主義の手話が、主義ではなく、和義産義への変化を望み見る。その一例が欧州共同体である。「和をもって貴しとなす」のスタートラインについたが、世界は漂流して産義潮流にのって生きていく方向を見つめることであろう。そして、生義の島に辿り着いて、正義のユートピアが見つかるであろう。ここで、信仰という意味を、神交・神行・進行と転意してみると、神ながらの生き方にのることができるのである。

いまや正義の神は滅亡を宣告していると思われる。正しい心をもって生き、運命を転化して幸福の極意に到達できるようにしたいものだ。

格帥（覚醒）して幸福になる

人間には善悪の判断力があります。間違いのない判断をして、悪いことは直し、改めるべきことは改めることが大切です。個性という、人間各自がもっている特別な性質のために、すぐには直したり改めたりすることは難しくとも、習慣づけると必ず改められます。こうしたことによって、盛衰興亡が生まれるのです。

その表れは、仏の前身の鬼のようなものであって、鬼子母神のごとく、やさしく人を守る仏の姿に化身した、かつての鬼は数知れずあるものです。

人間は正義に改めることにおいて、また自然環境の再建が早くでき得るように互いに改めることにおいて、自然界の復興ができ、幸福となるのです。この危機の中で、家族が滅亡の淵にさらされ、悲境の極みに達していることをよく見つめ、覚醒しなければなりません。悪いと判断して悔い改めることは、生きんがための正義なのであります。

宇宙間のあらゆる生物で、この世に生まれてきて、生きようとする欲、すなわち「生欲」を抱かない者はありません。人間もすべてが生の欲望をもつことは当然であります。しかしながら、欲を欲するがゆえに過ちがあってはなりません。そのために私は、以下、営業的にも、法律的にも、病理的にも、宗教的にも、また、建築や住まいや結婚などの面からも、宇宙観において、人生の生活で必要な一切について、問いに答えさせていただきたいと思います。

【筆者注】両手を火鉢において、火箸を握られ、そう

言って喝。そして微笑まれた高松先生のお姿が目に浮かびます。この問答があった当時、橿原神宮駅前の木を切ろうという都市計画があったのを、高松先生が反対して、その木を切らせなかったことが思い出される。

——人間は生まれ落ちると同時に、みな「生欲」を有するものでしょうか？

日常的には、生欲を考えてはいないかもしれませんが、必ず生欲のために、空腹を感じ、食欲を満たさんとするのであります。人は必ず生欲を有していることを何よりも明らかにするのは、人間が死に直面したときに、はじめて一時的であっても、長く生きたいという欲意が生じるという事実です。

世界の戦いの歴史、そこに描かれた戦士たちの死に様、それは主君のため、一族家族のため、愛する人のためと、いろいろな形で語り継がれています。その霊に対し、敬意を表することは大切だと思います。

【筆者注】平成20年には、私はすべて供養することができました。私が修行して、いま生きているのも、先に生きて死んでいった人々のお陰であると、報恩感謝の思いから、九流派の供養塔として一塔、武神館道場の供養塔として一塔、それを過去と未来を繋ぐ灯台として建設した。

師の語りが続く。

歴史的に、人間は精神の支配に従って行動するものであって、そのために生欲とか苦楽とか喜びとか悲しみがあるのであって、もし何事をも考えない精神が普通の状態であるような人ならば、生欲が最も大切であると考えるでしょう。

精神が己であり、己が精神でありまして、精神から離れた己はなく、己から離れた精神もないわけです。従って、戦士たちは環境によって、精神は、生欲よりも犠牲的行動を重んじたとき、心体一如に散ることができたのでしょう。

これを聖欲とでも言うのでしょう。

——それでは、精神の狂った狂人は精神がふつうでないのだから、生欲もないということになりませんか。

精神の狂いの場合は、知能の働きと知識が別々に行動するのです。ふつうは知能の働きを知識に受け入れて、身体に命令を下すのですが、別々の行動では、知識が生

欲を感じても、知能がその方向に働きません。言い換えれば、宇宙の正霊と自己の霊とが別々に行動しているのです。その証拠に、狂人は必ず自己に尋ねて、自己が答え、またその答えを否定しています。故に、空腹だと思うと、食うか食うまいかと自分に尋ねるものです。

知能は食うように勧めるものの、知識は食うてはいかぬと言い、また食欲は精神合一的にしていない故、栄養分が充分とれずに害になって、食べている割には栄養になっていないということになるのです。知能の狂いがあると、実の伴った生欲ではありえません。

——それでは、吾々相互は、何を目的として生欲を満たそうとするのでしょうか。

生あるものは必ず自然に生欲がありますが、その生存中に、より以上の幸福を望んで、幸福な生涯を送ることを目的としているのでありましょう。

幸福とは、精神の満足であり、それには盲点や死角（死覚）、そして思い違いの満足もあるということを知ることです。そして、錯覚と不幸の線にも気づくことです。

【筆者注】肝心なのは、現実を見つめ、生活空間の共存を知ることである。そして、欲というものを、世久（良く）するための欲と正すことが大切なのである。

——それでは、精神の満足を求めるあまり、修業に熱心であれば、悪いことになるのでしょうか。

何事によらず、一心これを貫く心得における忍体とは、心を養い、技に励みて末永く、辛棒こそ真の忍者なり、の護道を歩くので、幸福に導かれこそすれ、悪くはならないものです。しかし、護道にはずれて、例えば自己の才分を失い、生活に苦しむほどまでに神仏に奉納することが、報恩感謝の行いであり、また救われる鍵であると思いこみ、財産がほとんどなくなるまで奉納することは、奉納される側の人を喜ばすだけであって、神仏とはほど遠い所に行ってしまうのではないでしょうか。熱心と熱狂との違いも知るべきです。

一般に、日常生活において幸福な生活をしたいがために、物質的欲望を満たし、同時に精神的欲望を満足せしめようとして、無理な活動をするのですが、体力、気力、財力は人それぞれ限りがあるため、それが具わらない者は、無理が生じ、こと志とは反対に、不幸に陥る恐

れがあるのです。

美しい刃波と輝く日本刀を作る際も、鉄を熱し叩き、不純なるものはすべて取り除き、澄水に浸したところにこそ、名刀が生まれるのである。

——正霊と知能、知識はどう違うのですか。

正霊と知能、知識はそれぞれ別物でありますが、密接に関連しています。まず知識は自然意識の作用です。知能は意識の指名によって知識を習得せしむるものであって、知能の働きの強弱によって、賢愚などが判断されます。知識はたいていは、その専門にのみ限られた、狭い範囲のものです。つまり、経験のない知識は価値の乏しいものであって、知能さえ普通に働けば、本人の心掛けと努力と教育とによって、いかなる方面の知識も得られることとなります。

宇宙の正霊とは、この知能に働かしめる力であって、ここにおいて知能に区別が生じるのです。聡明な知能、あるいは常識や礼儀をわきまえぬ劣等な知能というように。正霊の偉大な力の協力がなければ、判断力に間違いが生じやすいのです。

現世に学問をしても、就職をすることもできぬ状況や、知識が生んだ、人よりも大きい自然まで殺す武器の出現を見ても、考えさせられるものがあります。

——生活と経験と知能とはどういう関係にありますか。

知能の働きによって、試みたり試したりして、経験を取り入れることができるので、知能と生活は密接な関係があります。

また人間はみな等しく、生きんとするために生活しつつ、老衰して死するということは千古の法則であって、何人もこれを免れることはできません。人間はなぜ死するかというと、私は、人間の発達には限度があり、内臓の諸官中、心臓はもっとも遅く発達し、しかも老年まで発達を続けるものの、限度があるために人間も死するのだと思います。知能の発達には限度がなく、この知能に身体は支配されるのですが、知能にしても、老衰と共に弱められていくことは確実です。

私の唱える武道は、正しく生命を維持していくことが人間の価値であること、そして正しからぬ生活では生命を維持していくことができないことを明かすものです。

正しく生命を保持するためには、身体の保護、精神の保護を必要としますが、人間は誰しも安楽に暮らしたい

という欲心があります。その欲を満足させようとするために必ず心身に無理が生じ、その無理が重なって、不幸な世界に陥ったり、遺伝として子孫にまで及ぼすこととなります。従って、正道とは人道であることを基礎として、誠の幸福な道に手引きをすることです。

現在の戦争の後遺症を見ても、うなずけることと思います。残心を武風によって、その爆風爆雲の行く所までを計れるようでないと、自然の生命まで脅かされる時代です。

——高松先生から、日本の古神道に伝わる「天津踏鞴秘文」のなかの神心神眼の医学書および、それに基づく古代からの宗門と武門の祭事を伝授されておりますが、医学は、意学と同一のものであると思います。故に医学がさらに発達すれば、そのような注意は不要になるのではないでしょうか。

それは大きな間違いです。人間はもとより生物には、自然に直すことのできる治癒力、抵抗力があります。例えば犬は傷口を己の舌でなめて直します。人間は、そうした力が及ばないと知ったとき、はじめて病気であると気づいて、医師に診察を受け、投薬を求めるのです。ところが、医師の投薬では直すことのできない、心の病というものがあります。この病に犯されると、我が身一個人だけでなく、家族、親戚、知人にまで悪影響を及ぼし、思わぬ災難を招いたりします。ところが、正しい道には、天災地変を含めて、敵（天敵とでもいうべきか）がないということを、私は経験上、確信をもって言うことができるのであります。

【筆者注】私がアフリカを旅したとき、ランドルバーで野獣の住む危険地帯を走った。プロのインストラクターが、ここは安全ですから、と車を停めてコーヒーを飲みましょうといったが、私は危険を感じ、やめなさいといった。それでも彼が大丈夫というので、二台のランドルバーは不気味にそこに停まった。私たちが車を降りてコーヒーを飲もうとしていたとき、地元のインストラクターが藪の中に入ると、近くに大サイがいるのを見つけ、あわてて逃げ帰ってきた。みんな、「地元のプロがわからなかったのに、どうして先生は危険なサイがいるのか、わかるのですか」と不思議がっていたものである。

——天災とか地変ということは、今日の科学者でさえ予知できないのが現実です。武術的に、なぜそれを前知することができるのですか。

正しき者には超越ができるのです。そして、水は必ず下に流れる道理で、心が正しければ、必ず直覚とか直感にて知ることができるのです。心が正しければ、心自体が真理になりきっているからです。その直覚は、直接的であって、しかも確実であります。少なからぬ人が、大なり小なり、そうした直感的な正霊の働きを経験したことがあるのではないでしょうか。

【筆者注】同じくアフリカでセミナーを開いたとき、忍法はこの世界まで消すことができると語った。その夜、月蝕となり、セミナーに参加した者たちを驚かせたことがある。

——武風心、宗教心というのは自分の安心立命のためのものであって、他人にそれを信じるように勧める必要はないと思うのですが。

【筆者注】私が百歳の高僧と対談した際にうかがった、悟りとは「あなたはあなたです。私は私です。それでよいのです」という運築を思い出した。

人間は人格が具わると、温厚篤実な人になります。そして、おのずと、博愛の人になるものです。すると、自分にとって良いことは他人に教えよう、他人の苦しむところを見て、力の限り救助しよう、となるものです。大富豪を見ても諂わず、富んでいても傲らず、人性を超越するのです。

【筆者注】平常心の一片である。日本には八百万の神という表現から、嘘八百という喩え、江戸八百八町という言葉まであった。

武風的な宗教

師言は続く。

——武風心、宗教心は一種の礼儀ですか。

人間として礼儀はなくてはならないものです。礼儀なき人間には価値がありません。先輩とか恩人とか目上の人に対してはもとより、普通の人、目下の人に対して

も、人間としての礼儀を忘れてはならないのです。人は平等であるからこそ、なおさら礼儀の必要性があるのです。人間から礼儀を取り除けば、他の畜類と変わるところがなくなってしまいます。かようなことになれば、強い者勝ちの、混乱した世の中になってしまうことでしょう。

私は世界を廻っていた時、礼儀の礼を零として〇の心を第一としていた。Θの心構えである。ちなみに禅のお接待にもΘを用いる。

武風心、宗教心は、言い換えれば、正しい心の教えであります。自分は正しい心の持ち主であるから、べつに宗教の教えを経験者から受けずともよいはずだと言う人がいますが、自分が現在思っていることが正しいかどうか、それは研究の必要があります。たとえば、もし自分の子供が医術の効もなく、死に直面しているとき、そんなときには生死を超越した、武徳威力を見せる人としての行動力と徳姿が表れるのではないでしょうか。

人には、欲というものがなくてはなりません。その欲のあるうちに心の洗濯をすることが必要なのです。この心の洗濯は、衛生上の入浴をすることと同様に、当然必要ではありますが、生涯しなくとも、生きていけないものではありません。また、一日に数回入浴しても害になるのと同じく、信仰心のない者は幸福の生涯を誤ることがありますが、信仰も前述したように、度が過ぐれば狂信的となって害になります。本能と煩悩とは紙一重です。

私が説く信仰には、狂信の恐れがありません。正しい信仰ですから、度が過ぎることはなく、熱心になればなるほど人格を高めることになるのです。

【筆者注】この熱心とは、根通心（ねっしん）である。根に通じる心だ。熱と真と説き、日本刀の作刀に似たものがある。

この信仰とは、宗教的な、思想的な、哲学的なものから超越した、武道家としての神交（しんこう）（間を会得するためのものです。

【筆者注】ここで神の一字を新・進・辛・心・深・親・芯・真の八字に変えてみよう。

宗とは、「しゅう」とも「そう」とも「むね」とも読む勘をもちたい。また宗の字を主・秀・拾・習・衆・襲・終・修・舟・収・囚・臭の十二字に変えてみるとよい。

——「自分は信仰するつもりだが、眠りたいときに寝て、食べたいときに食べ、そして栄耀栄華に暮らしたい。そうでないと、自分は幸福とはいえない」と堕落論を吐いたものがいます（……喝）。

そうした暮らしを手に入れるのは容易なことです。しかし、その前に天地自然の実体を知っておく必要があります。天あって地あり、日あって月あり、陽あって陰あり、というふうに、幸福の裏には必ず不幸があり、不幸の裏には必ず幸福があるのですから、人一倍の苦労や努力をすることによって、栄耀栄華の本質に導かれた生活が送れるようになるのです。そして、自分の生涯というものに満足することができるのです。

【筆者注】ここで「栄養栄我」かつ「栄要映我」と書き加えよう。

——その本質の実体とはいかなるものですか。

実体というのはけっして単独のものではなく、繋がっていることにその特徴があります。上手と下手で繋がり、強い物とか弱い物も繋がり、楽には苦が繋がり、愛には憎しみが繋がり、浮かれる者があれば憂うる者があり、怒りには憂鬱が伴い、素直には僻みがあり、残酷性があれば慈悲心があり、満足には不満があり、勝てる者があれば負ける者があり、喜びには悲しみがあります。それは痛みが生につながり、生体の防禦と言われるようなものです。

このように表と裏、明と暗が、大なり小なり、人間の本性にあることは原則であり、それは日輪の晴れやかな日もあれば、うっとうしい日もあるごとくです。満足も過ぐれば害となり、怒りも過ぐれば精神的にも肉体的にも病変を起こします。

宗門と武門、これらの実体には繋がりがあり、切断のできないものです。これが真理であり、その程度を知っておかないといけません。この覚りを手引きするのが武風、俗に言う宗教であり、不動心という言葉が了解されてこそ、人間は超越できるのであります。それが武風一貫して、不動心が富動心虚実転換と同一であると自覚できる実体でもあります。

——それでは、この実体を二つに切断してはならない、ということですか。

絶対に切断は出来得ないのです。地球上の生物が、太

陽の力だけでも、あるいは月の力だけでも育たないように、人間と宇宙がつながっているということを自覚することが本来の姿であり、それに気がつかないということは、人間本来の姿ではなく、宇宙の原則に反することです。

　宗門、武門に見るごとき、その分かつことのできない繋がりのことを、仏は方便と言い、俗世間ではベニスの商人ではありませんが、法便と言い、武道的には虚実と言うのです。

【筆者注】物事の正体と言うとき、その正体を見て、そこに招体を読み取り、消体を察知できるようであってほしい。宗門、武門、そのゲート・門構えは名カメラマン土門拳のシャッターが正しく捉えている。

――信仰の生活を送るとなれば、残酷なことを一切してはいけない、けっして偽りを言ってはいけないという拘束が生まれ、人によっては、これまでの職業を辞めなければいけない人も出てくるのではありませんか。

　人間生活にも虚実があります。仏法では、それを方便と言っております。仏法では、人を偽ることに関して、己の利益を得んがために人を偽ることが悪いのであって、他人に利益を与えんがための偽りは、方便といって、罪にはならないのです。たとえば商人が、商売の駆け引きとして偽りを言うことは害にはなりませんが、度が過ぎるようでは信用を失うこととなり、悪い行為が己に帰ってしまいます。武風的には活便、喝便、勝便とも言っている。

　また食用に供するために、職業として、たとえば牛や豚といった生物を殺すことを残酷であると言うことはできません。そうした生物は大切に育てられて、死することによって、食肉となる責務をまっとうするのであって、そうした食肉の生物の命を必要に迫られて奪うことは、やむを得ない虚なのです。

*

　幸福の栞は、武道の極意の道につながるものである。私が、四国八十八ヵ所ならぬ世界武芸八十八ヵ所巡った結花（結果）を見たからである。

師と弟子

　一子相伝とは、万物が帰一する自然現象でもある。その

れは万に一つであることも意味する。すなわち、師の跡を歩ける者は万人に一人という天意がある。

　師と弟子、それは時には演出家と俳優のような関係で修業するとよいと思う。その演劇作品、いや縁激作品ともいうべきものは、その時、その時代により、異なる様式や形態で生きており、事実がいかなるものであったかは、時実の双実、奏曲に聴かねばなるまい。

　そのストーリーは、驚きや刺激や恐怖が伴う妖怪談に満ちていたりすることがあり、要快、もしくは用絵の手法で絵画的に伝達することもある。

　青い、幼い、青の心の情報化の時代も過ぎた今、平常心の心構えで、怪談や落語のごとき、真偽を織り交ぜた、さまざまな情報を吟味できる心身を養わなくてはいけない時代になってきたようである。

　わが師、高松先生は言われた。忍体とは心を養い、技を励みて末永く、辛棒こそ真の忍者なり、と。辛は神意を聞くことに通じている。

　高齢者になった今、私はその言葉を幸鈴者と思いなし、サンタクロースの橇に乗って鈴を鳴らしながら、世界の各地から尋ね来る弟子たちの、その心の中へと走り続けている。身の養生、心の養生、識の養生ということが、生あるもののための要生となるからである。

抜かず勝て、抜けば切るなよ

　宗教とは衆教でもある。世界的に宗教を見た場合、たくさんの宗教が、それぞれ異なる神を奉じてあり、日本の宗教（神道）においては八百万の神と言っていたことは、基本八法と同じで、まさに現代社会に大きな意味のある、普遍的な世界観を持っていたということになると私は思う。日本は古来から、地球の中の小地球という、象徴的な意味合いがあったのではないだろうか。地球の変化によって、いま世界の少なからぬ人たちが地球合衆国の意識を持ち始めている感がある。

　戦国時代以降、権力をもった武士の長、すなわち大名が各地に大きな城を築き、その周りに家臣や商人たちが集まり、町が形成された。それを城下町というが、本来は自然環境や人々の心身を浄め、平和を守るための、浄化町の役割があったはずだ。そしてまた、町の周りに壁をつくっていなかったのは、日本だけに見られる光景なのである。

　それだけに、権力を手にした者がいい人であったら、

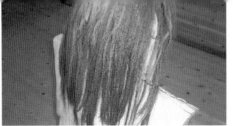

「封建制」というのも、人や自然を守るものであって、決して一方的にあくどい制度だとは思えない。多くの人がそれを過去の遺物であるとして、良しとしていないが、武士の社会の場合のランゲージは「包剣制」であって、だからこそ、武士は行列の時にはいつも柄頭に袋をかぶせ、紐で縛っている。それは武士が刀を抜かないという心意気であり、争いを好まぬ構えであった。「飛び道具は卑怯なり」の一言もうなずけると思う。

武士道の極意の一つとして、「抜かず勝て、抜けば切るなよ、ただ忍べ、命をとるは大事とぞ知れ」という歌が伝わってきたのは、そのためである。

山本常朝（1659–1719）の書き記した『葉隠』の中でも、「武士道とは死ぬことと見つけたり」という言葉はよく知られているが、「死ぬ」ではなく、「士貫」が本来の姿であり、武士道を貫くことなのである。そこで私は『葉隠』ならぬ『戸隠』の伝書を読めと弟子に語る。

それは不浄な心を斬り捨てて、正しく生きる術であり、不浄な世界を浄めると同時に、そのために世界を大眼して生きることが、これからは重要になっていくだろう。私はそれを六根清浄ならぬ「禄魂 笑浄」と言いたい。集団においては団結し和することも大切だが、一人大人の大黒柱としての生長が必要とされる時代が到来したのではないだろうか。

極意とは生きるための知恵である

武芸者というのは、お釈迦様が言われたという一子双伝「天上天下唯我独尊」であって、ひとり士道を貫くことを心がけねばならないのである。武士は、争乱生死の境にいつも存在していることを自覚し、そんな日々を生き抜くことができるための生命の養生反応を、自然の中でも養ったのではないだろうか。だから、山の中に入って籠るにしても、木の実や山菜などの食べ物のある、快適に生活できる場所を選んでいたであろう。自然は化け物である。山に入るのは化け物退治の修業の始めでもある。

俗世間から離れ、超感覚を身につけるため、山の中で武芸者は、例えば手を鍛えるとか、足場のないところであっても自由に動ける訓練などをした。自然の中における稽古は、足場がないだけではなく、風雨に襲われるなど、現代の冷暖房の設備の付いた、板敷きや畳敷きの道場における稽古とは雲泥の相違がある。両極に生きた自然の中では、そうした変化に即した勘生が、実戦する時に必要な無から有を生み出す勘生という知恵を授かったのであろう。

鳥や獣を相手に稽古することもある。それらは人間にない超感覚をもっていて、どのようにつかまえるのか見抜くのは容易ではなく、また鳥獣たちは察知力が強く、素早い。これを見極め、極めを捕る。それが俗世での化け物たちとの遭遇にも屈しない、生きた過程となるのである。

極意とはそのように、時に応じて生体反応ができる、生き抜くための叡智なのである。今や、テレビなど映像の前に座って、映し出される画像を眼にしているときでも、なにかそれ以外のことが見抜けるようでないと、生きていけない、そんな時代になっているのである。ブラウン管も薄く薄くなっていく。

江戸時代の禅僧、桃水和尚（1612–83）は立派な寺を捨て、名利を擲ち、乞食姿で草鞋などを売り、自然人になって生きる人生を選んだ。説教を超越して人里を離れたのである。自ずから人間の道、仏道に則り生きたというより、この行為を衆生に知らすべく導きの姿に化したのであろう。説教も捨て、勉強も捨てた現代人に、何かのサゼッションを与えている。

ともあれ、ここで私が宗門武門と記しているのは、宗教観、武道観について語ろうとしているのではない。それは教えでなく、門、ゲートなのである。土門拳のシャッター音なのである。

陰と陽

高松先生は、えんを切るなよ、つながりが大事だと、常々おっしゃっていたが、最近、そのことがよくわかってきた。陰と陽はつながっている。男と女はつながっている。朝も夜もつながっている。生と死もつながっている。天と地はつながっている。明と暗もつながっている。表と裏もつながっている。宗家も代々師弟もつながってきた。

そこから愛も喜びも命も生まれてくる。そうしたつながりを知らなかったら、極意というものを発見したり、生み出すことはできない。次の時代は生まれてこない。

ちなみに武神館の五段のテストでは、前にいる人間が、後ろにいる敵の殺気を察知できるかどうかを試験する。前と後ろのつながりは、腹、即ち、へその緒のつな

がりと思うことである。そこで武人としての生命が成長し始めるのである。「神」は「ひも」とも読めることからも、うなずけると思う。古代、命を玉の緒と言った。

私の場合も、高松先生とのつながり、そして両親とのつながり、それだけによって、ここまで至っているのである。今や思想、宗教の違い、人間の意識の違いによって、世界の混乱が生まれ、強まっている。それを解決する道の根底にあるものは、つながりではないか、と私は思う。極意とは、いつの時代ともつながり、またどんな社会ともつながっているものなのだ。悟久意である。ところが、人間というのは、ともすると、そのつながりを見失っているのではなかろうか。

こうなると、陰と陽というより、縄の分類ともなってくる。空間につながる縄識の世界を見つけることができる。平成21年のテーマとして、武道体術も縄のようにつながっている常体を発見するよう、私は指導している。それは武道の本体を、縄のような状態の動きで、常動（縄道）に復するということである。武芸の縄識体術とも言う。

世界中で、これまで、戦うものの意識というものは、みなその時代なりにドラマがあった。それが風化され変化された。まさしく風媒花だが、たまたま日本には武士道というものができた。しかし、修行をしていくと、武士道という片道切符ではあまりにも無残であり、生きる判断につまずきやすい。時代によっては、どうにもならない一種の波動によって、波に呑まれてしまうおそれがある。

そこで、武道と武芸の二つの虚実という真実（誠）に生きることを実勘した。武道家と武芸者という道の、二道の虚実（文武両道から武芸両道）を持たねば、本質的に極意の意味するところには到達しないのである。二道は荷道なり。徳川家康（1543–1616）の遺訓に、「人の一生は重荷を負うて遠き道を行くが如し。急ぐべからず」とある。速度制限の安全運転を示している。

戦いと兵糧

窮地を切り開くという言葉がある。師は言った。「人間、食べられれば病いに勝てるのや」「食べ物のある国はいつまでも戦うぜ」と。

また、過ぎし日、師が言った。「あの国はな、食い物が豊富やさかい、戦に負けまへんで」と。その通りだっ

た。私は私なりの配合の、玄米、黒豆、小豆、しいたけ入りの飯を主としている。また、あえて調味料は少なくし、自然のままの食事をベースとしている。食と性と排泄、そこに誕生のネクストワンという産心が生じる。

極意の唄

極意の唄を聴いていただこう。そのリズムとサウンドは、演歌なのだろうか、それともシャンソンなのだろうか。ジャズなのだろうか。カンツオネなのだろうか。ロシヤ民謡なのだろうか。世界各地の民族のサウンドなのだろうか。詞韻である。

まず、この唄は心に響くものとして聴いていただき、そして聖歌ならず生歌として身ていただきたい。世見（世間）を見生き（見聞き、見気き）、今や人の意識ではコントロールできない、無人兵器の時代に変貌している、その一瞬の光とともに消えていく、そんなことがないように、永遠の灯の唄を聞こう。

*

強弱柔剛あるべからず、故に此の心を離れ、空の一字を悟り、体又無しとして、之に配す（戸田真龍軒）

なす技を己が力と人は言う。
　神の導く身と知らずして（高松寿嗣）

敵来るとも相手すな。手向かえば意にまかせ、
　最後には捨身とぞ知れ

松も色より、貝石山よ、思いこめたる岩に契りは、
　唐戸淵（藤原千方）

抜かず勝て、抜けば切るなよ、ただ忍べ、
　命をとるは大事とぞ知れ

心こそ、心迷わす心なり、心に心、
　心許すな（沢庵禅師）

月影の照らさぬ里はなけれども、
　ながむる人の心にぞ住む

大水の先に流るる栃殻も、
　身を捨ててこそ浮ぶ瀬もあれ

身の備え、勇をあらわす武の中に、
　真の極意は心なりける

武の秘とは、敵の力を利用して、柳の風の心ともかな

棒先で虚空をついて、我が手先、手ごたえあれば、
　　極意なりける

心眼で悟りて捕れば秘剣とて、
　　いと極楽に糾し得るなり

戦いに勝たんとばかりあせりなば、破れを生じ、
　　負をとるべし

千早ふる神の教えはとこしえに、正しき心、
　　身を守るらん（高松寿嗣）

底知れぬ波間にうつる水鏡、心知られて辱しと思う

底ひなき、渕やはさわじ、山川の、浅き瀬にこそ、
　　あだ波はたて

ゆく末は、我をもしのぶ、人もあらん。
　　むかしを思う心ならいに

澄む水の心となりて備えなば、鏡の如くうつる相手ぞ

柔術は、敵の力を利用して、柳の風の心、ともがな

体術の極意は、平和の基礎と知れ。学べば、
　　不動心の道にありける（高松寿嗣）

仁王尊、陰と陽とを形捕る、拳の動きぞ、
　　呼吸なりける

忍体とは、心を養い、技を励みて、
　　末永く辛棒こそ、真の忍者なり（高松寿嗣）

窪地へと落ちる習いの水なれど、
　　やがては昇るはじめなりける（高松寿嗣）

何もかも君（奇秘＝きび）のためぞと日夜がけ、
　　貫き磨け、正しき技を

からまれて何に一つの勝手なし、
　　身を捨ててこそ浮ぶ瀬もあれ

極意とは己が心の奥にあり。只一筋に覚悟あるのみ
　　（注・心の奥＝識の世界）

ふりあげし太刀の下こそ地獄なれ、ただふみこめや、
　　先は極楽

我が術は、手向えば倒せ、ただ祈れ。
　　手向わざれば、対手せぬ術

柔術の極意は、平和の基礎と知れ。
　　忍めば真の極意なりける

練習は心の構、身の構、
　　鬼も仏も技（和座）にありける

何もかも、皆、自然の為ならば、日夜をかけて、
　　学び磨け

心だに正しかりせば、あやまたず、手も濡らさずに、
　　勝（価値）となるらん

剣をもち、槍をもちても、道一つ、正しき技ぞ、
　　真の術なり

澄む水も、狂える波も、従うて、身をまかせてこそ、
　　浮む瀬もあり

柔術の極意は、平和の基礎と知れ。
　　荒魂をも和らじるなれ

うつものも、うたるるものも、もろともに、
　　唯たわむれの夢と思えば

忍術こそ、真の武人であり、
　　名人達人こそ忍術より生ず

阿字の子に、吽字を生ませ、育てつつ、
　　また立ち帰る、阿字の古里

　これらの歌詞ならぬ武士の花詩花伝は、生命のサウンドによくハモるものである。そして、武芸百首が、ようやく東方から昇伝（招伝）する日がやってきたということである。即ち、私が東方の関東に住んでいたので、高松先生は、私の弟子は東から来ると唄われていたのである。

　古来から、兵器は身を守るもので、やむをえぬ時、これらを神殿から拝授する心得を秘とし、武器は絶対に凶器としては使わぬ心得を第一としたのである。

第二章　槍術の極意

鎗とキリスト

　鎗の矛先を、古代に向けてみよう。別天津神から天沼矛をいただく伊弉諾尊と伊弉冉尊の二人の命が、淤能碁呂嶋を性作（製作）し、日本の国土・大八島が出来上がった。

　マウリ族の鎗の柄は、胎盤を肥として生長した木で作られるという。インドの鎗はカル（石）ムンギール（棒）だ。60年ものの竹の幹を夏に切り、水に叩いて素性のよい形とし、太陽の炎で竹の幹が黄色になるまで焼き、節をとらずに、葉で訓生（燻製）する。次に、ガンジスの河床に眠らせ、起床とともに、棒のてっぺんに孔雀の油の入った瓶を、逆さに挿して立てる。孔雀明王に祈る！　かくして６ヵ月間、藁の護摩の煙が天に登る。カルムンギールは漆黒の輝きを偃月とともに見せる。

　如意なり。孫悟空の耳に隠れて、観音様の命を待ち、ロンギネスの鎗で開眼する。

　盲目の戦士ロンギネス、鎗をもたされ、キリスト様とは知らず、命令でキリストを刺す。鎗からしたたり落ちるキリストの血が、盲目の兵士の眼に降る。すると血塗られた兵士の盲目の眼が開眼して見える要になった。盲目の兵士は、偉大なるキリストの愛に導かれて、キリストの教えに帰依したという。

槍術の伝書

　槍術と書けば、木片の槍、木製の穂先、柄ということになる。鎗と書けば、鉄の柄の鎗ということにもなる。この槍術を、争術と書けば、何やら戦場にて槍で戦っている光景へと、イメージが大きく変化してくる。

　この章では槍術宗家であった高松先生より受け継いだ、槍術の伝書を公開する。写真については、形を一定して覚えることよりも、槍の穂先の石高を計り、鎗形を手話と見て、歴戦を聞いてほしい。

笈之中得二餘論一蓋存二十一於千百一也皆片紙隻言次序不レ論今而不レ輯恐帰一謹録為レ冊号曰二天道自然法一苟讀二此書一明二其意一則武技之妙瞭二然乎目然一子孫其勿レ忽焉惟時保元二歳在二丁丑一秋七月記二義照一
　　　　　　　保元二丁丑七月　　出雲冠者義照

槍術

　槍の種類については、自然の創期から見つめなければなるまい。それは土地土地のもの、木や石や骨や銅や鉄で作られたものなどで分類される。そして鎗と言われる時代などが争案される。手槍、竹槍、長槍、短槍、鉄槍、鎌槍、十字槍等々があるが、鎗を用いる人によって鎗人一如となる。九鬼神流は短槍を用いる。槍技は扞法、四方技、飛鳥抛げ、一突挨法、一擣三當、撥擢、秘槍、天地摧、撥捕扼の九法からなっている。それ槍法に九軌あり。「護攻虚変争精神不動」一致決死なり。この九法の力はよく百敵に対する秘技なり。

　長短無双、長柄の鎗の使い手、切り断たれた槍柄も敵の心中を突く也。

扞法（かんぼう）

右足を一歩退き、槍先を相手方の眼に付ける。一寸腰を落し、石突の方は下り目なり。身体をそのまま突きに出て、一方で引き退き、勢よく右手を右肩の処に上げ、敵の胸部に繰り出す。忽ち素早く引き、再び繰り出す。敵が付け入らんとす。左足を引きて右は石突きにて、敵の左足を払い倒す。

四方技（しほうぎ）

槍の切先を下に向け、右手はわが頭上に。左右の足を二尺程度開き、左足を一歩前進。槍を敵の胸部目差して繰り出す。（ただし槍は繰り出しも早くし、手元に引く時は最も素早きこと）手元に引き、右に開き、再び繰り出し、引くのと同時に、石突きにて敵の左横面に叩き付ける。同時に槍を一転回して左手を放ち、右手の後を握り、左突き。引いて石突き。敵の下段を撥ね上げるなり。

飛鳥抛（ひちょうはく）

この技は槍を中段に敵胸部に付け、突き入りて、忽ち引き退く時は右側に飛び退き、同時に左手を放ちて鋒先で横しばき、手元に引いて再度突き入る。また右横に飛び退き、忽ち左手を放ちて横しばき、手元に引いて突き入る構え。残心。

一突挨（一突挨法）（いっとつあい・ひとつきあいほう）

左側に一寸よるこの一突挨は、槍を持つ両手を頭上よりよく差し上げる構え。ちょうど槍投げのごとく左側によって右足を前進、敵の左横面を左手を放ち廻して、鋒

先で敵の左横面を打ち、体を落し、左足を一歩退き、左突きにて胸を突き、左手を放ち廻して、右突きにて胸を突き、そのまま右足を一歩出して、敵の左足を石突きにて払い倒す。右足を引いて一突とす。

一撞三當
<small>いっちゅうさんとう</small>

体を落し、右足を一歩引くのと同時に突き入り、同時に右足を出して左横面を石突きにてしばき倒し、左手を放ち、槍を廻して左に突き入る。右足を一歩引いて右手を放ち、後の方を持ち、槍を廻して左突き、素早く引いて再び右に突き入る。

撥摧
<small>はっさい</small>

槍を下段にて敵の胸を突き入る。左手を放ち、敵の左足を払い、また左手を放ち、元に帰して突き入る。左手を放ちて左横面をしばき、左手を放ちて突き入る。

秘槍
<small>ひそう</small>

槍を中段に構え、敵の胸に突き入る。そのまま右足を出して体をひねって石突きにて下段を撥ね上げ、右足を引いて再び突き入り、右足を出して石突きにてまた下段を撥ね上げ、右足を引いて坐して、下より敵の剣を巻き上げて突き入る。

天地摧
<small>てんちかく</small>

まず槍先にて突き入り、左足を退いて、石突きにて敵の剣を撥ね上げる。左手を放ち、右手下を持ち、鋒先にて左横をしばき、そのまま後方に飛び退り、右手にて鋒先を一尺程度下りし処をもって、敵の顔面に向けて突き差すように投げを用い、近きは胸部に向けて突き投げる。注意。一方に退くというのは敵に付け入らるる恐れある故なり。敵が付け入らざる時は一歩前進すること。

撥捕扼
<small>はっぽやく</small>

これは我が突き入りし槍を、敵は剣にて左右に撥ねかわせし場合に用いる。まず我が突き入る。敵は剣にて右に撥ねかわす。我は敵の剣の上部を切先にて廻し、小手をからむごとくして撥ね上げ、再び突き入る。敵は左側の剣にてかわす。槍の鋒先を敵は剣の下を小手に掛けて廻し、突き込む。則ち敵が左右に剣にてかわすことはその力が充実しない。ここを附け入りて剣を巻き上げ、巻き下すようにして突き入ることが大事なり。

槍という武器は変化が少ないようであるが、然らず。槍で横なぎ倒すということは、突き伏せんがために、敵の体を崩す、痛みを入れて崩すことであり、ここに技があるのです。然れども、無理が生じてはならぬ。無理勝にて十本捕るより、正しい真妙な技で一本の勝を捕ることを心掛けること。ただ動作を軽快に、柔らかなように見えて素早に使う手を充分滞りなく出来ることを肝要とす。ただし槍は突き入りが大事であり、むやみに突き入れる力が入りすぎて、進退の動作が重苦しくなるようでは付け入られる。剣に付け入られた時は忽ち敗北となる。かくのごときは決して武風の道ではない。力の扱いは何技にても一般に忌み嫌われる。特に槍をもて対立する場合、敵の出方を悟ること、突き入りて手答えと同時に力を入れるなり。鎧槍ならばこそである。

> 心眼で悟りて捕れむ秘剣とて
> いと極楽に利し得るなり

およそ槍術の発達したのは、主として戦国時代なるが、私が継承した数流のうちの九鬼神流は、他流よりも古く秘伝として伝えられたために、広く伝えられなかったらしく、本流より出て㺃神三寳流として天正時代に現われている。

この当時、宝蔵院流、大滝流、富田流、打身流、本心鏡智流、中村流、般津流、木下流、淡雙流、中根流、佐分利流、大島流、一百流、離想流、一旨流、宝蔵院高田流等が現われ、慶長年間には無辺流、本間流、真柄流、建孝流、下石流<small>おろし</small>等が出で、天文年間には四條流、三位一條流、八條流等が出で、永禄年間には虎尾流、鞍馬新流等が出で、承應年間には自得流、大國流等が出で、寛永年間には種田流、大島流、樫原流、京僧流、無辺流、宝蔵院三槍流が出で、元和年間には疋田流、正慶神体夢想流、文禄年間には無辺山本流、一中派本心鏡智流等々、多くの流派が現われている。然れども、現在なお伝えらる流派は、九鬼神流以外二、三派しか残されていない。

さて本流九鬼神流の秘伝とせらるる三呼吸㺃神伝ということが皆伝の秘とせられている。この秘伝の伝説は、初代源家の義家の三代の孫、為義の子、丹波六郎為宗の子、義為の子である義照より出でて、五代出雲冠者義隆までに九つの器の使用の法が完成したのである。

ここで申し上げたいのは筆者（初見）の家系の紋所は一本鷹の羽であり、源義家の流れを汲んでいることである。

　前記の三呼吸とは、この呼吸が気合となって現われ、これを三聲不言という。則ち三つの気合、これを合致せしめて声なく、心に三つを合致せしめて無言の一念となる。これを三聲ということは則ち三つの声であり、一つは勝声の気合。敵に負けたと観念せしめ、再度の攻撃を失わせしむる気合、これを扞技扼（かんぎやく）という。

　二つには、今攻撃に出るという気合。敵が隙を見つけられたと思い、八方に心を乱す故に実力を失う。八方に隙が現われる気合である。

　三つには、敵が技を掛けんとした寸前に、敵の技を前知したぞという虚の気合。敵は悟られたと思い、疑うために隙が出る。これに付け入るから首尾よく勝を制することが出来る。

　最後に三つ合せて不言の気合。敵の技、実力を封じて挫く。これが秘中の秘なり。攻撃に出る扞技扼の実の気合は、ヤー勝声なり。二の抛益槍（はくやくそう）の実の気合であり、攻撃する気合であり、アーの一声である。三の相手の技を知ったという虚の気合はトアーの気合。挨攉幣（やくかくへい）の気合。三の全攻不動の虚実無言の気合ウムー、これらの気合を三つ挫きという。一は相手の気を挫く。二は相手の技を挫く。三は相手の体を挫く。これを合致せしめて不動金縛りとなる。則ち当流に実に三あり、虚に三あり、変化に三あり、合して九なり。これを使う時は鬼神の如しというに随って九鬼神流とは言うなり。故に、武人の器による奇合、軌合、生合と寿（す）。即ちカルミンギールの館のルーツにつらなる。

　男には九つの秘穴あるも女には十の秘穴あり。故に九字を許すとも十字を許すなの禁あり。ここで九鬼神流を久奇神流と聞く。

極意型

一文字

体勢は右斜めとなり、左槍先を下目に、右手を我が頭上に位づける。真一文字に右手を下にさげる。勢いを付け

て突きに出る。忽ち槍を引いて石突きを右廻し、左足を引き敵の左裾を払い、一歩引いて右槍先で右裾払い、突き。

菊水

姿勢は前と同じく右斜め。右手右廻し。渦巻きのように三囲し、即ち槍先を渦巻型として真一文字に敵の足を突く。槍を引いて再び突き、胸部の槍を引くのと身体の一足を引くのと同時。敵が付き入るのを石突きにて、右より左横面を左に引いて突き。

巻蔦

姿勢は左斜め。槍は中段。一、敵の胸板を突きに出る。二、そのまま槍を石突きで敵の右裾払い。三、そのまま後に退く。敵が付き入る。四、右槍を先上に廻して敵の下腹部を突き伏せる。

鬼刺

姿勢は右斜め。中段に構える。一、敵の胸板を突く。二、そのまま一歩引く。槍は手元に一寸引く。三、敵の胸板を突く。四、一歩引く。前と同じく槍は一寸繰り引く。五、忽ち胸に突き行く。六、前と同じく左方斜めに一歩退く。槍は一寸繰り引く。忽ち敵の右足に突き進む。

飛龍

姿勢は左斜め。下段に構える。一、敵の右足に突き入る。右に飛び退く。二、忽ち右槍を先上に振り廻し、胸部に突き入る。左側に飛び退く。三、忽ち槍を上に振り廻し、槍先にて裾払い。突きに入る。そのまま槍を石突き。敵右横面。四、右斜めに退き、石突にて胸を突き入る。

突伏（つきぶせ）

姿勢は右斜め。一、敵の胸部に突き入り、槍先を引くのと身体を一歩引くのと同じ。二、再び下腹部を突き入る。槍を引くのと身体を一歩引くのと同じ。三、敵の胸部に突き入る。槍を引くのと身体を引くのと同じ。四、また突き入る。この技は敵に付き入られないために槍を引き、身体を引くのと同時に突く。即ち突き伏せの型なり。

蔭蝶

姿勢は右斜め。敵の胸部に突き入る。右に横飛び。その時槍を石突きにて敵の左胴払い。二、槍を下段型に振って突き入る。右に横飛び、同時に槍を石突き、敵の左胴を払う。この技は右へ右へと躰を廻し、突いては石突きにて左胴払い。また突技にて、これは敵に手元に付き入られぬために石突きにて胴払い。右に廻る敵の切込みに不便のためなり。

三ツ玉

姿勢は右斜め。上段の構。即ち槍先は敵胸部に当て、右手を我が頭上より上げる。右手を繰り下し、突き。二、敵は槍先で撥ね上げられ、その反動を利用して左手を放ち、右へ廻し敵の左側を足払い。そのまま腹部へ突き入る。

七枚葉

姿勢は右斜め。中段の構。身体を一歩引くと見せて槍先を右へ廻し、敵の左裾を払い、姿勢を一歩引いて槍先を左に回し、敵の右裾払い。これは突きより右に左に払い倒す。七枚返しともいう。葉隠葉乱万象を伝象するものである。

免許皆傳変蝶型

　この変蝶型というのは、ちょうど蝶が舞い遊ぶがごとく、右に左に身体を転じて相手方の虚に付き入るというのが目的で、槍を充分に使うことが出来得る者に於て、この型を練習と共に使うことが出来るのである。

横倒

槍は上段の構にて、突き入ると見せて我が頭上にて右廻しにして敵を近づけず、最後に石突きにて左横面打ち。頭上を左廻しして右横面打ち。これを繰り返すなり。敵の横面を打ちて倒すという異変なり。

龍頭

槍は下段の構にて、右斜めに位捕りして、右足で坐して胸突きに入る。左斜めに体を転じ、槍を右に廻し左裾を払い、同時に左足に坐して敵の胸板に突き入る。この型は敵の斬り込みを防いで片坐立てとなり、ちょうど龍が頭を突き上げるがごとくにて、この突きは相手方が大刀にて撥ねがたい姿勢なり。一説に俵返しとも言う。

巴（ともえ）

槍を上段に構え、頭上で巴のごとく右左に廻し、敵の顔面を打たんとするため、敵は下らざるを得ない。ここに付き入りて、二度三度突き伏せる型なり。

釘抜

この型は槍を上段に構え、右斜めの姿勢から槍を突き撥ねる。即ち釘抜型にして、突いては撥ねる故に、相手は突きを一刀でかわすとも、後の撥ねで小手に気をつけ、そのすきに再び突き上げて撥ねる捨身の槍なり。

嵐

槍を中段に構え、槍先を渦巻きのように右廻し、体を左斜めに転じ、右より左胴（槍先にて横なぐり）、そのまま石突にて左足を一歩出して下段を撥ね上げ、左足を引いて突き伏せ、この突にも槍先を渦巻きのように左廻し。突きの型なり。勝虫トンボ捕りとも言う。

心明

これは槍を中段に、右斜めの姿勢に構える。敵は一刀大上段。敵の身辺に一寸きざみに進む。敵が斬り込めば負けなり。一寸きざみに進む故、敵が最後に斬り込むと同時に、一突きに伏せる。捨身心明ともいう。

瀧落（たきおとし）

この構は右斜めの姿勢。右足を充分に割って、気合と共に遠方の敵に対して槍を空に向けて投げて、突き差す。槍投げは上部より投げる故、瀧落という。この瀧落の場合、槍は七三の割にて、槍先から三分の一の処をもって、右足を出すのと同時に投げること。

横投

この横投は、槍を突き差すというより、倒すという方が適当だろう。即ち我が頭上にて右突きの方を右手にて持って、左手にて真ん中を持って頭上に差し上げる。振りかけた時に足を前後に動かし、呼吸を持つ。左手を放つのと同時に右振りを三、四回して、敵に対し振り投げる。練習後は突き差すことになるが、はじめは横に打ち付けて倒すことになる。

立投

この立投は、近くの敵に対し、右足を後ろに引き、充分に足を割って、右手にて槍の千段巻の五寸下りし処を持って、敵に対し投げるもの。右足を出すのと同時に投げること。

日月

これは槍を持って敵中に飛び込む時に用うる技で、槍の石突き。五寸上を持って横投げの時の呼吸で上部に右廻し、二回、下部に一回を繰り返し、敵をなぎ倒すために用うる練習を充分心用とす。

極意型

極意型は報道されるものにあらず。法道だけを行うにあらず。

闘鎗術（闘争術）すべてにおいて、空間で壁を作らぬ型とすべきである。型とは秘戸型ならずであり、方方＝型宝である。「ほう」は宝の字を生むと見れば、鎗に宝蔵院流や堤宝山流があるごとく、極意の意、自ずから解せるものである。常に一対一の心得にあらず。片方から方方へ、我蝶に変じて飛びたわむれる如し。まさに変兆型を一体化し、空間、宙間、忠貫なる想念に舞うが如き栄誉を見せる。

薙刃術

薙刀、長巻、眉尖刀の世界を能舞台にのせてみよう。「舟弁慶」で、敗勝（将）・平知盛の凪刀が蹴り足、流れ足で海に舞い、熊坂の重い薙鉈が戦場の長範、その丁半の十体を、勇幻に、かつ幽玄に演じてみせる。重厚なる舞台なり。

薙刀、それは長刀、眉尖刀をも意味する。また薙鉈と書けば、闘具としての見方も変わってくる。九鬼神流で言うなれば、薙刀の九鬼が幻妖巨大化して、大鉈、大斧、如意刀と変じ、鉄壁の楯兜を打ち砕く秘閃刀となる。

さてここで、北欧の神話にあるオーデンの十八の極意を得よう。それは敵の剣を無力化し、飛び来る鎗を睨み落し、武友を守り、戦う者を蘇らせ、戦う英雄を讃え和すものなり。

九鬼神流八法秘剣中の薙刃術は、唐の眉尖刀術より現われたるが如しというが、私は唐を闘の眉尖刀と言いた

い。これは同じ武器の如しといえども、眉尖刀は薙刃よりも刃尖が長く、多少違った点があり。よって他流の薙刃術とはその趣きを異にす。敵を充分引き付けることは武器の便となる。相手方を充分引き付けざれば、わが身は捨身となる。ここに体のこなしと強襲の備えが大事なり。則ち勝は謀に於て得らるる。謀事に於て相手方に実がありても虚が生ずる。謀事に於て弱者にても勝を得る。これを虚実の虚という。

戦いに勝たんとばかりあせりなば
破れを生じ敗をとるべし

負けて勝つ後手の先手というものがある。これを悟手の閃手という。

伝説に言う。初代源家の出雲冠者義照は保元元年、関白平忠通に反し、逃れて出雲猪目洞窟に至る。この洞窟に唐より逃がれ来りし鉄杖僧住む。この僧は唐の武将、武の達人なり。よって僧に従うて兵法を学び、眉尖刀術を習得したりという。また一方、義照は洞窟に於て修業、平治の乱に源家敗北と共に逃れて唐に渡り、鉄杖僧に学び、数年後帰朝せりとも伝えられる。その実体は不明なり。ともかく鉄杖僧に学びしことは古記録に残れるなり。また義照は平治の乱に源家に味方して、逃がれて伊賀山中の洞窟に於て唐人より、この眉尖刀を学びしともいう。眉尖刀は切先長く、普通の薙刃と異なる点があり。そのため、体のこなしを最も肝要とす。

ここで大切なことは、この武人が僧侶となって、即ちある時は武人、ある時は僧となる争侶双旅の生活をして、戦乱の虚実を生き抜いた様（左馬）を見ることである。京の町を祇園の薙刀鉾の山車が悪霊を薙義払う。五山に紺碧の三日月が照る。

掬上

この構は右斜めに足を割って腰を落す、横一文字の構なり。相手方の出方による。相手方が一歩先に斬り込み来る時、左足を引いて、薙刃で敵の左脇を下より斬り上げる。相手方が未だ来らざる時は右足を一歩前進して、左脇下より上に斬り上げる。同時に相手方の先手をうって左足を前進し、右脇下より上に斬る。これを数回繰り返すこととなる。

抜倒

この構は八相の構とす。相手方が青眼の時は左足を引い

て、敵の左より左小手を斬り下ろす。敵が大上段の時は右足を前進し、敵の左脇下に斬り込む。小手を返して右裾に斬り返し。次は小手を返して左肩先に斬り込む。一歩引いて元の位置。八相の構なり。

足拂

平一文字の構。敵は一刀を大上段にして斬り込み来る。左手を頭上高く伸ばし、右手の腕を折りまげて受ける。この受け型に於て、敵の一刀を右に流すこととなる。同時に小手を返し、左手を引き、坐して敵の右足を払い、小手を返し、同時に左足を払い、一歩引いて残心。横一文字の構に変化す。

撥倒

青眼に構える。敵の一刀も同じく青眼。我は左に体を転ずる。敵は突き入らんとす。小手を上部に返し、下より上に斬り上げる。即ち敵の小手または刃を撥ね上げることなり。忽ち小手を返し、右肩より首に斬り込み、再び小手を返し、左肩より斬り下げるなり。

繰出

この構は中青眼のこと。敵の大上段に対して、青眼にて左足一歩後ろ、なお退ると見せて左側に身を転じ、小手を返し敵の左胴に斬り込み、忽ち右側に身を転じ、小手を返し右胴に斬り返し、右の如く身体の掛け引きに応じて繰り出すことなり。

前後薙

八相に構える。敵は前後に数人なり。左より右に斬り返し、忽ち右腕の返し方で右に斬り返すこと。早くすることを薙刃振り廻し斬り返しという。かくのごとくして敵中に斬り込むなり。

差違

平一文字の構にて敵の大上段に対し薙刃を横刃として突き、小手を返し、裾払い、再び横刃として突き、小手を返し、裾払い。数回にて敵を倒す。

飛切

これは八相に構え、敵の左胴に斬り込めば、その反動を利用して左に飛び、右胴に斬り込めば右に飛ぶ。即ち飛び違い斬ることなり。

眉尖刀

眉尖刀の術を見たとき、私は人の眉に喩えたことがある。眉は喜怒哀楽心技体の動きを表すものである。唐代の玄宗皇帝は画工に十眉図を作らせたという。日本でも、『源氏物語絵巻』や『平家物語』などを見ると、眉毛を抜いて、白粉で濃化粧をして眉を描いて、心を抽象化させている。鎌倉武士は剛勇を一として、作り眉などと眉作りはしなかったという。

眉は月状を通常描いている。月は変化を表す。眉は月の経路を辿ったのだろう。薙刀は女子が使用する武器へと変わっていく。眉は額の毛が退化して、抜けた後に、その部分だけ残ったもので、人類以外は眉毛がないだろうといわれている。では、何故に人間だけに眉が残ったのだろうか。額に汗したとき、眼に入らないように、横に流れるように、そう残されたものだという。すなわち、武士の涙をはっきり見せる闘魂正義反応汎溢。「望敵倒滔鎖 虐 翻悪絶」の九字がある。

眉尖刀術型

汪振

大きくなるの意。眉尖刀は鐺（こじり）が重く、斬り込みに小手を返しするという事を、忽ちにして行い難し。故に汪振を以て練習する。青眼の構え。大きく廻し、左胴に斬り込み、大きく廻して右脇に斬り込み、左肩より竹割りの如く斬り下す事の練習法なり。

鬲逆

胸を逆切りにせんとするに大きく廻し、右より敵の左胸を逆に斬り下げる。敵は受けては不利なり。体をかわし一歩引く。我も同じに右胸を斬下げるなり。

竹斜

竹を斜めに切る如く、左方よ斬り下す。右足を引いて右肩に竹を斜めに斬る如く斬り下げる。再び左脇を斬り下る。右脇を斬り下る事なり。

波刃

荒波の如く斜めに左右早く数回に斬り下す。

抜刀

抜き手の如しという。石突きを以て左足前に突きを心見

て、忽ち右足前進、左首に斬り廻す。石突きにて右足前進。突きを心見て忽ち左足前進。右首根を斬り廻す事を早く練習す。

曦先
切先の蔭の技。中青眼にてこの技をなす。即ち相手方の小手を下より頭上にすり上げる如き心にて、突きに出る。敵は剣で右に撥ねる。撥ねられて忽ち刃先を上に向け、小手をすり上げる。忽ち転じて右裾払い。

伸刀
切先が伸びる技。これは体を落して足は右足前方、右足後方。体を落す事に於て体だけが一寸後方に。敵は付け入らんとす。忽ち体を前方に出し、右胴より斜めに左肩の方へ斬り上げ、体だけ落して忽ち左肩より斬り下る。

惺刀
悟りより出ずる技。これは相手方の大刀大上段、我は横一文字に構え、敵の斬り込みを待つ。敵は忽ち大刀で斬り込み来る。左足を充分引いて、我は敵が左より斬り込みし刀の鍔元をたたき落す。然る時は敵の小手に斬り込むか、刀の鍔元ならば、敵の刀が折れるか、叩き落すかにあるなり。

魅剣
まどわす虚技。八相の構えで左足前に敵が近づかんとす。敵は一刀中段に構える。然る時は我が左胴は備えなし、すきあり。故に敵は斬り込みやすけれど、敵の構えに心が迷うなり。敵が斬り込み来るも、来らざるも、左裾より斬り上げ、再び体が変ずると同時に、右裾より斬り上げる。斯くの如く繰り返すなり。以上

薙刃術　眉尖刀技　勝虫相伝
九鬼神流八法秘伝中薙刃術は眉尖刀技より現われたるが如し。よって他流の薙刃術とは其の趣きを異にす。相手方を充分引き付ける事は、我が身は捨身となる。ここに体のこなしと強襲を大事と知るべきなり。勝は謀に於て得らるる。謀事に於て相手方に実がありても虚が生ずる。謀事に於て弱者にても勝を得る。これは虚実と言う。

　　　　戦いに勝たんとばかり　あせりなば

　　　　破れを生じ　敗をとるべし
　　武心となれば、魂全一体閃手必勝なり。

伝説
出雲冠者義照、保元元年、関白忠通に反し、逃がれて出雲猪目洞窟に至る。この洞窟に唐より逃がれ来りし鉄杖僧あり。この唐の僧により学ぶ処によって、眉尖刀技を得たりとも、また義照洞窟に於て修行、平治の乱に源家に味方して逃がれ、唐に渡り、これを学び、数年後、帰朝せりとも伝えらる等、その実体は不明なり。眉尖刀は切先長く、そのために普通薙刃と異なる点あるとも、察せらる体のこなしが肝要とせらる。

　さてここで、眉尖刀の刃天棟打ちの威力を伝授するものとして、棟打ちの妙勢を会得する事。

汪振　大きくなる
先右横一文字の構え。鐺にて敵の右足をはね、そのまま鐺を右脇下に切先にて敵の右首に打ち込む。

髙逆　胸を逆棟打撃
前と同じく、切先を今一層大きく廻し、敵の右胸を上の方へ逆打撃。

竹斜　竹を斜めに打つ如く
青眼の構え。左手上を落ちかえて、右側鐺にて敵の大足を払い、また左手に持ちかえて、敵の左肩先より竹を斜めの如く打ち砕く。

波刃　荒波の如く、一文字、左手先に繰返す
抜刀　抜き手の如し。正眼。

曦先　切先の蔭の技。地当正眼。切先を小手に返す技。
伸刀　切先が伸びる技。地当正眼。敵の左脇を返し、右脇返し、左脇。

惺刀
悟りより出ずる技。これは敵が上段にて切り下げ来ると見れば、下よりすくい棟打ち。敵が突胴に来ると見れば、右一筋の上より蓮割り。または左筋上より蓮割り。

魅剣　まどわす虚技。

一文字より上蓮割りの如くして、実は下より打ち砕く。下より砕き上の如くして逆に敵右より落ち砕く。体技を大技とす。

魑魅魍魎 消隠幻実の如し

以上裏型十八本、左右逆と別る。

十手術

人の一生は重荷を背負って坂道を登って行くようなものであると、徳川家康が言っている。ならば、「窪地へと落ちるならいの水なれど、やがては登る始めなりけり」の一苦（一句）をだぶらせてみよう。十字架を背負って坂道を歩いていったイエス・キリスト様に、「そうなのでしょうか、人生は？」と伺ってみよう。答えはやはり、「イエス」とお答え下さった。これ武命坂と言う。

十手術も、術技だけにとらわれず、夢窓国師（1275-1351）が十牛図を夢想しおり、鈴木正三の『盲安杖』の十の徳目を読んで武徳とするとあるが、闘う絵姿、十勇姿闘牛図、火牛図の如し。

武神は祈る。「神より十魂の魂宝をたまわりて、天の曲事、罪汚れをたちどころに消滅せん」と。

十手術というものは

十手術、それは十方折衝の術とも言われているが、それらを略伝の一つとして、略々とした伝證（伝承）の頁を開いていこう。禅の画風も、必要なきものは略し、略しぬいた所に真心の画禅たるを見る。

（一）桐葉　十手術の一つに「桐の一葉」という技があるが、「桐一葉落ちて天下の秋を知る」の言葉で知られる『桐一葉』『杏手鳥古城落月』などの、坪内逍遥の戯曲がそれを見せている。桐の臺は神紋とされている。

（二）落花　十手術の実伝落花を、武士の花、桜、椿、牡丹に見て、その散り様、その決意を美として見よう。そして、次の年にも咲き誇る、その花と会おう。

落花　桜、椿、牡丹、落花養生残月

敵は一刀大上段。我は十手青眼。腰を落し構える。敵が斬り込み来る。敵の一刀を受ける。敵の刀が十手の横

鞘に流れるや、体を左向けの体勢に転じ、右手を、敵の手を巻き込むごとくして、右足を敵の下段に蹴り込んで、刀を逆さに捕るなり。

裏　同じく左技のこと

*

争う者は亡ぶ。和を求めよ。武は正義心にて人格常識の完成に於てあらゆる障害を排する事を得る護身術なるが故に、毎年正月に道場四方に注連縄を張り、文武両神を祭り、左の歌を三度唱え、九字を切って初練習せし事、古伝の教えの通りなり。

「千早ふる神の教えはとこしえに
　　正しき心　身を守るらん」

桐之葉　桐一葉、落ちて天下の秋を知る。（注・O・ヘンリーの「最後の一葉」に描かれた、生き抜く少女の姿が思い出される）。また竜を退治した英雄ジークフリートの、葉隠の急所を思い出していただきたい。

十手術の構えは体構えとなる。即ち、十手を右手後ろに左足前進。十手を全面に突き出し、左足を前進。上段に構え、右足前進。体はいつも落していることなり。

相手方は一刀大上段。我は十手を前方に体を落して位取りす。敵が大上段に斬り込み来る。右斜めに飛び違い、一刀をかわすのと、手元に飛び込む型なり。忽ち、十手にて敵の首を横打ちにする。敵は眼がくらんで倒れるなり。

裏　左技のこと

水鳥　水鳥湖水に遊沈、幽脚に遊ぶ。白鳥伝説の数々を……。

相手方は一刀大上段。左足にて前進。右手の十手は後ろに。腰を落とし、位取りす。この姿勢は鳥の沈むごとくなり。まさに敵が大刀で斬り込まんとする。一歩前に飛び込み、十手にて水月に当て込み、幽脚より、そのとき右足は座し、左先座立ての姿なりといえども、沈勇不動の遊姿なり。

裏　同じく左技のこと。天地人の識を得哢。

五輪砕　仁義礼智信、砕武鬼仏魂

相手方は大上段。十手を前に、青眼の構え。敵の斬り込みに対し、右の体を開いて、忽ち敵の流るる腕の小手を十手にて打ち落とす。飛び込んで十手にて当て込みのこと。

裏　同じく左技のこと。

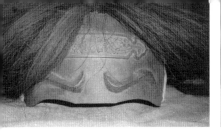

廻捕　円空一閃、十方軌喝で取りをとる

　敵の大上段にて斬り込みに対し、右手で図の受け方を
して、忽ち、刀の刃止に触れるや、その下を体がくぐり
廻り、右足で敵の禁穴を蹴り、刀を打ち落とし、取り押
さえるなり。識得足利折衝なり。

　裏　同じく左技のこと

　とにかく十手術は、十分に体術を心得る者にしてはじ
めて十手術が出来得るものなり。故に、我が手に武器を
持っているという気持にならず、体術によって捕り押え
得るの技なり。

　聖徳太子様が、三宝を重んじ、和を以て貴しとなすと
言われたが、私は和は倭にして、日本を以て貴しとなす
と言う。そこに国造りを見る。

　十手と縄はつきものと言うなれば、一筋縄多縄仏心
十縄の構えなり。結秘なり。

武道体術の妙

　十手術は、武道体術の妙を得たものでないと、桜花、
椿華牡丹の美しきかな、の感動を見ることはできない。

　ここで大切なことは、十手術という、十手の術を教授
しているのではないということだ。十手術というと、読
者は斬りつけてくる大刀を、十手の鉤で捕る、とまず思
うに違いないが、十手にはいろいろの形がある。鉤のな
い十手、要のところで十文字に開く十手や、まろほしと
いうものもあり、これはすいじ貝の魔除けの姿であり、
また鎖あるいは鉄砲あるいは目潰しがしこまれているも
のもある。このように、無限に久風（工夫）された武風
がある、その人間の知恵が隠されている。十二支十干で
ある。

　十手という形を武意識として生かし、またそれと見破
らないといけないのである。　そのほか、鉄扇、鉄刀、
馬手差、隠し武器、日常ここかしこにある十牛図（秘め
たる十義勇図）が画かれた一休の茶碗など、隠さざるも
のが武器に早変わりする暗示がある。

　禅において、悟りは脚下にあり、とよく言われるが、
『奥の細道』のごとく、月日は百代の過客にして、むし
ろ、悟り（武器）はここにも、そこにもあるのである。
刀、槍、薙刀、剣においても、闘っているとき、それら
の武器は斬られたり、折られることがあるが、十手の
フィーリングを悟れば、生悟に一変。棒術、半棒術、挫

術しかり。十手の十をプラスの言霊と解せば、万物術
手の早替わりとなる。

武道研究家からの手紙

　「現代武道に一筆参らせ候」と題し、いまから40年
前、ある教育雑誌に、新田義貞（1301-38）が鎌倉の
稲村ケ崎で海中に太刀を投じ、引き潮に進軍した故事に
ならって、当時のスポーツ化あるいはショー化した武道
の風潮について、一刀一筆を投稿したことがある。いま
では、私の世界の武友たち、それも実戦の経験のある人
たちが、その通り、と答えてくれている。解説的な文章
ではなく、また虚構でもない私の文章が、実戦の死生観
を通り抜けてきた強者に贈る、名曲「引き潮」に乗せた
サウンドとなっているのだ。

　ここで、それを読んでくださった、武芸風俗等の研究
家・綿谷雪氏の手紙を紹介しよう。氏のペンネームは
別に戸伏太兵がある。

　「貴文の趣旨、まったく賛成であります。私は御承知の
ごとく武技には全然アウトサイダーでありますが、いう
ところの現在の武道家の言動には、ホトホトあきれてお
ります。長らく古武道の伝書も読んできましたが、なる
ほど理論は立派でも、一般的にいって仏教家（若干の流
は神道家）の口まねにすぎず、殊に現在、剣禅一致など
は僧侶の大森曹玄氏以外に、じっさいに禅堂に坐った人
があるのでしょうか。理論だけではマンネリズムにすぎ
ないと思います。」

スポーツ化された武道

　スポーツ化された武道に対して、初見さんはどのよう
に見ていらっしゃるのですか、と問われたことがある。
そこで即座に答えた。スポーツ化されている武道の素晴
らしいことはね、人を殺さないってことだよ。と。柳生
の言っている「活人武道」と同じだからね。

　武士の涙、なんて言われるが、泣き虫・直江兼続じゃ
ないけど、オリンピック（五輪の武蔵マーク）で金メダ
ルを旨にして、澄水の涙を見せている。選手たちの太刀

姿（立ち姿）、感動させますね。望敵倒滔鎖 虐 翻悪絶の九字が聞こえてくる。侍の涙、それは悲劇の涙にあらず、幸福に溢れ出る豊穣の涙のことを言うのである。

焚書坑儒のこと

「勝負に成功不成功、強弱柔剛あるべからず。己を空にして、また体に配す」とは、戸隠流三十二代宗家であった戸田真龍軒先生の言葉である。

真の武道家たちは、闘争の道を経て、やがては現世から隠遁したり、俗を離れて僧侶となったり、高野聖にちなんだ聖の道を歩んだりした。かくして戦いの経験者が尋ね来るのだ。若干の兵法者や、武道求道者を導いたという輪廻転生の道を求めて。戸田真龍軒先生は幕末の混乱期に講武所教授の職を辞し、次世を生かした。林芙美子は、名作『放浪記』を残し、森光子はその二千回を越す舞台公演を続けている。我が師、高松先生は神仏の門に入り、熊野修験道の座主にもなられた。闘争の世界から離れて次の世代を生かす。

「真離」的な生涯の生き様がある。我が身を荒波に投じるや、放浪というニュアンスは、新田義貞が稲村ヶ崎で太刀を投じて祈願をしたところ、潮が引き天意に叶った話に似ている。

義生の上にあった主義を遠く見た変遷に、焚書あり。遍戦は消え去り、変戦悸は恐ろしい話に繋がっている。その恐ろしい正義の義正を見据えながら、義生を自然が自然に帰す季があるように、焚書の日を回想しつつ、戦乱という自然の姿、その炎の火伝の書籍を、赤い炎の中に黒字で執筆している。赤と黒である。そこに鳥の巣を見る。

但だしいことの繰り返しは伝承する必要がある。その役割を果たすのは語り部である。そうしていくうちに、闘うというものは無を作る産物として見すえ、闘って生き抜いてきた。「抜かず勝て」という耆六極意を会得できてこそ、正しい生き方を語ることができるのであろう。

ここに掲げた、高松先生からいただいた手紙をそのまま見ていただこう。

剣舞を舞った高松先生

もう四十年も前になるだろうか、七人の弟子を、高松先生がお元気な時に、一度先生に会わせておこうと、橿原の自宅に連れていったことがある。

先生は一人一人の弟子に、掛け軸とした絵を、微笑みながら一巻ずつ手渡された。そして腕に針を刺し、ローソクに火をつけ、美化針棒の神に祈り、橿原道場では剣舞を舞って下さった。ちなみに高松先生は、日本剣舞大会で日本一を受賞されたこともある。若い頃は神戸一の美男と新聞にも書かれたほどなので、歌舞伎の寿海さんから、養子になってくれと言われたことがあったそうだ。高松先生が寿海と武号を名乗られたのも、そんなことがあったからであろう。

その師の接待を大切にして、エンを切ることなく師影を奉じ、一貫できている者は、平成21年、十五段の瀬能英夫、大栗紘一の二人だけであるということを、灯として伝えておこう。なぜ、ここで「師逢和瀬」のまぼろしを書いたかというと、私と一度だけ会って写真を一緒に撮っただけで、私と長年稽古したなどと自己ピーアールする不届き者が、世界のあちこちにいたからである。

空の中に生きていく

武道において大切なのは「常」の化音の一字がたくさんあることを発見することである。常、条、状、情、冗、縄、鎖、丈、城、錠などで、十化音。常から離れて、常のカラを破ってみる、武風守破離。人には超能力が潜んでいる。その正しい超能力に気づきなさい、そして、それらを覆い隠している一般常識から離れなさい、ということである。

例えば「残心の構え」。ふつうは、相手に対して技を極めた後も、そのまま体を崩さずにいることを言うが、残心とは漸心であり、さらに言えば惨心である。すなわち残心の構えとは、敵と戦ってきたことの無惨さ、それを忘れてはならない、という武道の心構えを教え伝えているのである。武道の極意のひとつはここにある。

「幽玄武」と言う。玄は一般に玄妙なる黒色を意味しているが、天の色であり、微妙で深遠なる離でもある。玄とはまた匈奴（漢民族を脅かした遊牧民のフン族）のことでもあった。玄に導かれる源・元の文字から、突発的変事災玄の意味と読み取ることもできるのである。

伝承されなければならぬものが、今や絶えつつある、そう社会では語られている。しかし、自然の中にある、伝承されてきたものは、四季（博識、認識の「識」でも

ある）の変化に耐えて独尊し、生きていくように導かなければならない。そして、戦う者の結果の無惨さを肝に銘ずることである。

生きるための勘覚

2008年の稽古のテーマは「空」、即ち忍法体術をテーマとすることであった。そこで忍法体術についての師伝「己、空となれ」の格言のもとに、消える体術、見えない体術、透明なる体術、見え消えする遁形体術について、こんなふうに語り始める。「体術ってのはね、性感帯にのめり込んで、消える体術なんだな……」と。すると、弟子たちはＹの笑顔を見せる者が多かった。たぶん……なのだろうと想起したようである。私はその体術を見せながら、消えていった。

彼らに語る。「私の筆法では、生勘体と書くが、それは生きるための勘覚を養うという忍法体術なんだな。性感帯という言葉を聞いて、直勘的に笑みを見せた者は、もう忍法体術の罠にはまってしまっていたということになるんだな」と。

そして平成21（2009）年は、空間にもある繋がり、すなわち縄道（定道）と結ぶ武神館道場本部東南の本陣に大黒天（6トン、六根六道）武徳威光を示す灯台として建祭った。

秘剣

剣道とか剣法といって、そこで極意を見つけようとしている人がいるが、私に言わせると、道とか法には極がある。「極まりなきが故に極意とする」という言葉を借りれば、剣道、剣法でもない秘剣、そこにこそ極意があるのである。「秘すれば花」という世阿弥の言葉があるように、秘剣には、底知れぬ極意が秘められているのである。なぜならば非常識とは、虚実に生きる者にとって秘常識であるからだ。

2009年のテーマとして、「縄のごとき秘術」を稽古しているのだが、極意を会得した者に対し、「きやつは一筋縄ではいかぬ」という武士言葉が囁かれるような男になってもらいたいからである。

武道の伝書

武道の伝書には、仏教や神のルーツの一片が記されている。ここで、このルーツの一編を紹介しておこう。これらの書物は、その中から、己が極意の一片として引用され、影の化身として照らされた光である。師の影をふまずの診の先から光る、伝承される畏敬の心なくして、心伝されることはない。

その記憶された一字一字を記事にあらず、生字と見なすことができれば、古と文の記々が奇々として怪奇快読できるものとなる。

神明四維の書

「見上げてごらん」で始まる歌といえば、もちろん坂本九が歌った名曲「上を向いて歩こう」である。アメリカでは「スキヤキ」と改題された。あの歌のごとく、小さな夜空の星たちが、ささやかに、幸せのメロディーをかなでている。ガリレオやコペルニクスも、いま天国で、九ちゃんが口ずさむ、あの歌を聞いているかもしれない。

宇宙についての研究は続けられている。が、いまだに宇宙には96％もの暗黒ゾーンがあり、人間の視力、眼力（勘力）では4％しかわかっていないそうである。忍法には暗黒透視術というものがある。「じゃあ初見忍者、暗黒界が見えるんじゃない？」と問う人がいる。そんな時、「お前の腹黒いのはわかるけどな……」と答えている。

私が師伝された古文書に、「神明四維」と記された文書がある。武道家の心ある者が心眼で読めば、読める活字となるが、心ない者が読めば、長文が迷文、妖文、そして化文として脳にとどまり、心を動かすことがない。

これらは残心の書であり、斬新の書として心が読ませるものであって、天体望遠鏡や電子顕微鏡でも見えぬところに蔵されてある。

これらの書は教科書的に伝承されたものではない。心ある人から人への協花書であり、秘すれば花の散る姿であり、そして次に結実させる化実の書なのである。

宗門と武門

宗門と武門、この二門には、死と生の門、虚実、陰陽、生老病死、表鬼門、裏鬼門、玄武門、青龍門、朱雀

門、白虎門、辰巳門、甲酉門、天門地門、などがある。

　聞歩（文武）両道とよく言われるが、宗門を文、武門を武と聞くとき、宗門と武門の扉が開かれてくる。門外不出、門外漢が文武両道について語るであろう。「宗という字、それ自体、違っているんじゃあないの。宗はそうではないよ。鎗だよ。戦国時代は太刀より鎗の方が勇理（有利）だったものな。奏だよ、夏草や兵どもが夢の跡。草だと。争門だよ。ゲートだよ。走門（スタートライン）だよ。玄武裏門だよ。そしてな、僧門に入っちゃったんだよな。想、思いたくないよな。」破門は波紋となって消えていく。

　黒田節にある、尋ねる人の琴の音か。蒼然たる一定の夢とでも想うか。織田信長を本能寺で弑した明智光秀は、三日天下の天下人、天門から下門の人となってしまい、孟母三遷の夢ならず、賤ケ岳の七本鎗は豊臣秀吉（1537-98）を天下人へと導いたのであった。

　かつて天下を取るため、敵将の首を切るという時代があった。だが今や、生き延びるために部下の首を切るリストラに始まり、闘産倒産、闘倒合わせのカルタを見る。

　映画「モロッコ」のラストシーンに始まり、「マノンレスコー」「マサダの戦い」「トロイのヘレン」、登竜門、「地獄門」「狭き門」を叩く修験者の山越えの唄。禄魂笑浄（六根清浄）を唱えて、五山ならぬ武山を行く。黒澤明監督の「羅生門」で雨宿りをする。

　武の極意を求める者は、極意至上主義であってはならない。芸術至上主義 縄識（常識趣技を会得する）。主にあらず趣とす。趣技となす。完璧ということより、貫璧に作られた武風門と知ることである。

高松先生三十七回忌

　平成20年4月2日は高松先生の三十七回忌でもあり、一悟三十七年を経験した山岡鉄舟（1836-88）の話をしよう。山岡鉄舟の義兄、山岡静山（1829-55）は槍の達人として名をなした人であるが、稽古はすさましく、夜中の2時には起床して、重さ十五斤の槍を千回から五千回、天地十方に振り回し、跳ねる突きを行い、ある時は夕日が沈むのを見て、星月の光や闇、朝日の昇るまで暗黒の闇を切って、虚空を三万回も突いたと言われている。

　静山は、「人に勝とうとするには、技より心、徳を修めることじゃ。心が勝てば、敵は自然に負けをとるもの。本当の勝利とは、技で勝とうとすることではなく、心の徳で、武徳で克というものよ」。

　山岡鉄舟も後年、得意技として得手としたものに、槍の呼吸から学んだ突きの一刀一手がある。山岡鉄舟は鬼鉄と言われるほどの剣豪であった。ある日、師の浅利又七郎義明と立ち会ったときのこと、又七郎の竹刀は朴刀ではなく、又七郎の腕の続きに映り、閃胆は神眼の如くに見えるではないか。鉄舟も又七郎同様、突きの名手であるにもかかわらず、鉄舟は又七郎の突きを逃れることができない。そればかりか、又七郎の突きは、咽喉に触れていないのに、鉄舟はその剣先から出る霊気に打たれ、肝が冷える汗が湧き上がるとともに、足下もおぼつかなくなった。思わず、「まいった！」の一言が、自然に口を衝いて出ていたのである。

　鉄舟は、静山の「人に勝つのは技ではなく、人の徳である」旨の言葉を反省の糧として、江戸から三十里離れた伊豆・三島の龍澤寺の星定和尚の所へ、三年もの間、たびたび歩いて参禅に訪れたという。

　あるとき、鎌倉の名刹・建長寺の願翁から、こう言われた。「敵に驚いたり、恐れるなどという心が残っていて、どうするのじゃ。又七郎殿の剣が心にいまだ止まっているようだったら、生も死も、心に止まっているということじゃ。生死がいまだ念頭（年間）にあるようでは、武士にあるまじき心構えなり。そんな心構えは即座に捨てよ。本来無一物。この悟字（五字）を銘とされることじゃ！」と。

　しかし、なかなか無一物にはなれず、京都・相国寺の獨園和尚、鎌倉・円覚寺の洪川和尚などの門を叩く。はては、京都・天竜寺の滴水和尚の門を叩く。和尚は一喝す。「両刃鉾を交う。避くるも須いず……」と。

　山岡鉄舟が剣の道を辿って37年目の明治13年3月13日、浅利又七郎先生に入門して23年目に、45歳にして、師より夢想剣の極意を許されたのである。鉄舟は東京の谷中から、千葉の野田にある私の曾祖父の家に尋ね来て、「つぶさに道を問う。里にもおもむきあり」の一書を残している。それは昔のことであるが、不思議なことに、浅利又七郎義明の極意の書が現在、私の手元にある。それはおそらく一刀流の達人・浅利又七郎が遺した、現存する唯一の書である。拙著『英文版・日本剣法秘伝』に掲載してある。

　剣禅一如で知られる山岡鉄舟に対して、剣法家・浅利

又七郎は禅は全然やらなかった。だが、浅利又七郎の剣の技倆は抜きんでいた。この二人の武道家の姿のごとく、武道とは頭だけでは駄目であり、頭ばかり働く人は、蝋燭のように、光は放つものの、いつしか消えてしまい、己は蝋体であることに気づかないのである。得意技は徳威技と書くゆえんである。

高松先生の三十七回忌には、大黒天（インドでは最大の戦の神と言われるマハーカーラ）の像を建てることができた。一名、威光武徳大黒天という。

鉄舟の悟りも、三十七年眼であった。

無になれ

「無になれ」を表現するには、無は無限、無心、無尽、無象といったさまざまな意味があることを理解するもよい。

無になれということは、自分自身を隠身遁形させて、心技体の術を、勝負という虹（二字）を空間に放ち、この二字を虹に見せると七色の虹になる。七は凶数というが、七色とすれば、時に危色、奇色であり、生色、すなわち黄色に見せる、またダイオードの八色を見よ、というならば、鮮やかな透明なブルーを見せるのである。読者諸君、おわかりか。発光ダイオードの輝きを。喝。

空間を知りたければ、釈迦十大弟子の一人、解空第一という須菩提に聞いてみな。……同じことを想っているかもしれないよ。

守破離

能の世界において、能を能力というパワーとして、武風の追い風として感じたとき、夢幻能、その幽玄の勘覚は、幽玄を勇元、幕楯なしの能舞台とする。役者にとって、幕がないということは、始めも終りもない、無限の舞台を現しているような、裸になって構えた、武士の楯なしの八方無構えの心意気さえ感じさせる。

幽玄という言葉は、老子や荘子もよく用いた二字トークである。芸談に「守破離」という言葉があるが、これを解くには「十人十色」となるということを知らないと、痴愚なことになってしまう。例えば「守」、これは師の教えを守るという常念のことを言い、「破」は師の教えを守らず、教えを破ること、そして「離」は師から離れること。この守破離を極意とするが……。

離とは宇宙観でもあり、自然観でもある。家康は狸と呼ばれて、天下を取った。破とは石に皮と書いてあるように、忍者は化け石によって遁行する。

さて、私はいまだに師の教えを守っているが、その「守」という、師の教えを守ることで大切なことは、真持っているということである。師の真の要の教えをよく心得ているということである。「破」という一字は、石偏に皮と書く。忍者は化け石というものを作って、この化け石で遁形の術を使っている。その化け石は、離れたところから用いる。即ち「離」である。これは見破られないようにするためである。人類はいま、離とは宇宙衛星からも地球を見ているさま（左馬）を知ることである。また意と識の間をはなし、離をそこに入れてみることも必要である。また集中力を周宙力に変えることも修業である。破は卵のカラを破って孵る生気を言うのである。

北辰一刀流の祖、千葉周作（1793-1856）は「守破離」をこんなふうに書き残している。

「守敗離と云う三要あり。守とは其の流儀の趣旨を守る事。一刀流ならば、下段星眼【筆者注・ここでなぜ千葉周作が星眼と書いたか、ピンと来るようでないといけない。周作は北斗七星を尊敬していたのである】、無念無流なれば平星眼にして、其流の構えを崩さず遣うという。敗とは此の構えに拘泥せず、之を一段破りて修業する事なり。離とは、以上の二條を超越して無念無想の場に至るという。」

言うなれば、敗れても惜しからぬ人との出合いのマナーを記したものである。修羅場は時としては朦朧体の心構え、幽玄の構え、夢想の構えに似せるものがあり、この三構えは三心の構えに通じるものがある。

この三心の構えは地水火風空の「悟爾」で表現させながら四季（識）を超越する。朦朧体で描かれた横山大観（1868-1958）の「生々流転」は、毛利元就（1497-1571）の「三本の矢」ならぬ三本の絵筆、山馬筆ならではの、馬の尻尾につかまる力強さを感じさせる作品である。

周作の言葉からも、離とは超越をも意味することがよくわかる。

ちなみに、歴の音、その音響は離であり、離の音が歴に変わる。その足跡は富久亀足の、兎と亀の一睡の夢の象となって語り継がれている。

無刀捕りの本質

　武道、武芸、それは人をあやめるものにあらず。「非切」を極意として、「剣術とは心の非を斬る事である」と新陰流の神谷傳心斎頼春は唱えていた。名人、達人と言われた武術、武芸兵法者は、仕官、立身、出世という二字のために争う愚かさを了知して、僧侶、隠者、仙人といった、聖（ひじり）への道を選んで、修羅の世界から離れ、ゴーギャンにも似て、現代でいう大切な自然との共生を、真の強生として生きたのである。これこそ本当の生人（私は、聖と生と正を三位一体と解く）であろう。伊藤一刀斎、塚原卜伝、上泉（こういずみ）伊勢守信綱、戸田真龍軒正光、高松寿嗣先生しかりである。自然至極の極意と無刀捕り無闘捕の真理が、単純なる自然勘と合致するからである。

　去る昭和38年10月8日、高松先生からいただいたお便りの、無刀捕りの解説を紹介して、無刀捕りの極意の一端としていただこう。師は次のように述べている。

　「武道は無刀捕りが肝心だと思う。相手方の武器が槍、剣、薙刃、小刀、棒であれ、弓であっても、あるいは手裏剣であっても、この無刀捕りの練習と心得をよくよく研究しておくことである。

　例えば弓を以て矢を射ると一秒間に50メートル、野球のボールを投げると一秒間に45メートル飛ぶとしたならば、相手方が大上段に振りかぶった剣を我が頭に打ち下ろす速度は、それよりはるかに速くて、懐中時計のセコンドがカチという間でしかない。故に、相手方が気合を発すると同時に、体をかわさなければならない。というのも、野球のボールが一秒間に45メートルも飛ぶ場合、20メートルの時間は一秒間の三分の一ほどになる。すなわちその速度は均一ではなく、近いところほど速く、遠いところほど遅いからだ。従って、鉄砲の弾でも、遠く離れていれば、その音を聞いてから体をかわしても遅くはないのである。この心得を以て、体をかわす練習をするとよい。

　次に、刀を伸びきった手先で切ると、弱く、よく切れないため、相手がそのように攻撃してきたときには、無刀捕りで体をかわすと同時に、相手方の手元に飛び込むことである。また自分が十手もしくは小刀を持っている場合でも、必ず無刀捕りの心得によって、体を変じて飛び込む、この練習が大事である。

　また、柔道、柔術、体術にしても、相撲の場合でも、腕を真っ直ぐ前に突き出した場合と、上方に突き上げる

場合とを比べると、腕が上部に行くほど力が弱くなることがわかる。重量挙げでは、両端に鉄の輪の付いた棒を両手で上げるが、胸までは訳もなく上がるが、胸より高く上げるのは容易ではない。

　こうした真理から、割り切って型の教えに当たることが大切である。かような文章が残っている。

　吾祖師曰　實受二封於京土一夙大和民族慕二美風一尊二神道一繼二武備一明倫　生名以藩二屏於国家一国威海外為レ輝　爾来二千六百数十年世　承二遺緒一　沐二浴恩沢一以至二今日一　云々

　ここで一考してほしいのは、武風というと、相手に勝つこと、相手を倒すことのごとく思われがちだが、そうではないということである。相手がどこまでも戦わんとしても、己より先手を打たず、充分相手に先手を取らす。相手が忽ち逃れようとする際には、やむを得ず相手を倒さざるべからず。これには勝身という真理を研究することが肝心である。これぞ武道なのである。

　真理には自然が伴っている。不自然ならば妙を得ない。身体でも己の体温が平素37度ならば、ふだんから、その体温が保たれる程度に着衣する。夜は体温が下がるから、適当な方法を以て、その温度を保つように工夫する。重量挙げにしても、当初三十貫の重量を持てるならば、重さをだんだんに増やしていくうちに、六十貫がなんともなくなるものだ。

　このように真理とは自然なものであり、修業とはそれを自得することである。よくよく研究ありたし」。非切とは秘節と見てもよい。

武の神髄は柔体術にあり

　武というものの神髄は、柔体術にある。この体術については、忍術の技がその妙理の根本を成している。それはなぜか。

　剣は人を斬るものであり、槍は人を突き殺すものである。相手より先に斬ること、突くことが達人の証（あかし）であり、勝利者への道であるという考え方で、武、武道を学んだのでは、邪剣、邪槍となってしまい、断じて最後の勝利は得られない。武の肝心な点は、心の構え、身の構えであり、その武の神髄は忍術の技に体現されているのである。

　ここで、勝利という二字について考えてみよう。それは実は、生理（しょうり）（生きる理）であり、生理（しょうり）の神理とも言う

べきものであろう。この身心一致する構えが、武風の体風（台風）の眼を天授された、玉虎流で言う風天護身の構えと化すのである。時とは反應汎溢風水の座を好む龍神と化す里（境）なのである。

フランスの生理学者シャルル・ルシエの一言を付け加えておこう。「人類はホモ・サピエンス（賢い人間）からホモ・スツルツス（愚かな人間）に名を変えるべきではないだろうか」、……それは良寛が言う大愚だよ。愚ならば滅び、大愚ならば道が開ける。

「位取りは平等」、武心和の教えはここにあり

武道修業の段階には、初伝、あるいは基本八法、三心の型、中伝、奥伝、免許、そして皆伝とあるが、平等の二字を「兵闘」と転換したとき、それらいずれの段階においても、極意が潜んでいるということである。共通と見てもよい。

こんな話がある。信じられないことであろうが、忍術秘伝書『万川集海』の語り部の話として聞いていただこう。あるとき、「それでは、五段の昇段テストをやりましょう」ということになった。日本語がわからない一人の女性がすっくと進み出て、審査を受けた。見事、合格。思わず、彼女の表には微笑が浮かんだ。ところが、間もなく判明したことによると、彼女は五級の審査を受けたつもりだったのである。

初級者が五段の試験に合格する、いったいこれはどうしたことであろうか。しかし、彼女が合格した事実は厳として存在している。武神館では、四段まで修業した者でないと、五段の試験を受ける資格がない。それは誰でも承知している。しかし彼女は、このことを知らない国から初めて武神館に来訪したのだった。

師匠の高松先生がよく言われたものだ。「武道をやる人も、やらない人も、立派な人は立派なのやで」と。まさに詞韻波羅密大光明である。このとき、次の八字が私の脳裏に閃いた。試金石腹満大光明だ。そう、士、すなわち武士は、腹ができてないといけないのである。さすれば、腹の虫が蝶に変じて、極意を見せてくれるのである。

「腹が備わっている人」とか、「武士の腹芸」という言葉があるように、「以心伝心」「心念意力」「心念威力」「武徳威光」の四力（死力）を尽くせという、一点察知する位取りの境地を見るのである。

虚実転換法

極意とは、地球が軌道を廻っているような自然体で生きているものだ。まず我々は、その地球の中で生きていると思ってみよう。戦傷で生死の境にあるとき、師伝には、万変不驚とか不動心という口伝がある。そこで虚実転換法という、死線を越える自然について答えよう。

武道を修業して一貫したところで、「万化驚かず」の不動心を会得したとき、自然と一致した現象が起きる。というよりも、起こすことができるのである。つまり不動心の場合は、一般に、「心技体が動くものではない。その構えは鉄壁なものであって、どんな敵に対しても動じぬものだ」と早合点してしまうものであるが、地球は軌道ならぬ鬼道を歩いているのである。我座すとも地道の大道を歩いているということである。

コペルニクスの地動説を語らん。そこに、朝に祈り、夕べに感謝する、士道の礼に体する構えの日々の作法を会得するのである。心臓が動いて生きているように、地球も生きている。だからこそ命があるのである。極意と共に生きる心構えが大切である。

自然は人間を、ある時は厳しく、ある時はやさしく諭し、育て生かしてくれている。それをぶちこわすかのように、心なき無人兵器やクローン人間が人類を脅かす時代となっている。今こそ正しい人間の心の魂が大切になっている。

そこで三心の型は、これらの敵の攻撃的心を三振させる決意と知ることである。

映画の極意とは

黒澤明監督（1910-98）は、80歳にしてアカデミー特別賞を受賞した。その席上で語る。「僕は映画のことはわからない……」と。ボクシングのノックアウトパンチや、野球のホームランも、等しく、自分でわからないときに出るものである。黒澤作品の「七人の侍」「蜘蛛巣城」「椿三十郎」「影武者」「乱」等の中に、三途の川を渡る武士の映姿を見てとるのも一興であろう。

小津安二郎監督（1903-63）は言う。「映画の終りは始まりなんだ」と。ルネ・クレール監督の「巴里の屋根の下」のイントロの映像は煙突と街並の屋根が印象的だが、小津安二郎監督の「東京物語」も、東京の屋根と煙突のシーンで始まる。「巴里の屋根の下」は1930年の作、「東京物語」は1953年の作というが、共に時差を

忘れさせる。名作には時咲がある。小津作品の「晩春」「彼岸花」「麦秋」「浮草」「秋刀魚の味」等を、時差をおいて何回か見るが、そのたびに、しまり（締まり、始まり）があることに感動する。そこに笠智衆さんの残心な武士の姿を見るからである。

ビリー・ワイルダー監督は言う。「完全なる人間はいない」と。私もその通りだと思う。武風は、いつもドラマを雲に乗せて運んでくる。

ゲーテが会得したこと

黒澤明監督が「映画のことはわからない」と言ったということを本で知ったが、ゲーテはなんと言うだろう。ファウスト博士は、哲学、法学、医学、科学を学んでも、自分は真理について何も知らないと嘆いていた。そこで、魔法を使って何かを会得しようとしたが、うまく行かない。そこで自殺をして他界を見るしかないだろう、と思い始めていた。

その姿をじっと見つめていた悪魔のメフィストフェレスが「よし、ファウストを悪魔道に導いてやろう。さすれば……」と主に許しを請うたところ、主は「お前の好きなようにせい」と言われた。そこで、ファウストはメフィストの誘惑のままに生きることになった。恋愛、破局、恋愛。まさに小津安二郎監督が言った、「映画の終わりは始まり」である。ファウストの、生成、発展、創造、その一貫の姿に、己の魂を見るがごとしという、主の言霊が聞こえてくる。ハッピーバースデイ誕生だ。「七生報国」だ。

生成化育、進歩発展を求めて努力する人間には、神の救いの手が、「007」のゴールドフィンガーならぬ五本の指の願い、地水火風空のラロンド五輪に見えてくる。○を孔とも解してみよう。007は、二つの孔である両眼と、七つの孔を合わせて、孔が九つということになる。もう一つの孔の発見が、くの一、九の一女性ということになる。ホールインワン。いま地球上に007のような偉大なる男が生まれるよう、私はかく書き加えたのである。

仏教風にいえば、極楽往生には、九つの段階、すなわち九品あって品人なり、行雲流水に導く阿弥陀九字と言う。

虎倒流の極意

虎倒流に「神心神眼」という悟りへの一定がある。これは「肝心要」とも転換できるが、この転換は天観（天の眼）と見てもよいだろう。

さて、その眼の玉の視点、その注心（中心）である神心神眼について、三世紀の錬金術師ヘルメス・メトリスメギストは言うに違いない。「至る所に中心のある、円周のない円」が眼に映る、と。極意の姿は、哲学者・中村雄二郎の言う「共通感覚論」とオーバーラップされてくる。

人間が武風一貫した、その経験が、その実場のとき、仮象の映姿を生じ、化象した遁形の術のままに転形する。名人はその天象転生のままに浮遊しているのである。

高松先生、夢で悟る

伝書の中に、よく夢で悟るという話がある。次に、夢の中の蝶をめぐる、高松先生から伺った手記伝、口伝を紹介しよう。

拙著『英文版・武道体術』の一頁に、猫が蝶を一心に見つめている絵がある。そこに「一心之を貫く」の書がある。ちなみに、蝶は平家の武将の家紋でもある。

昔々……、高松先生が清国にいらっしゃったときの話である。この一書が手元にある。

「私が26歳のとき、清国にて、前皇帝の叔父に当たる連宗明という大人が私のことをたいへん可愛がりまして、日本の武の達人であると非常に自慢をされたのです。すると、600人あまりが私に教えを乞うようになり、毎夜稽古をつけました。そのうち、丸太の六尺棒の両端に三十貫の石をつけて、それを毎朝百回振り回すという、山東省の力自慢の者が、連さんあてに試合を申し込んできました。張子龍という少林寺派の拳法の達人です。

二度断ったのですが、また申し込んできました。今度は断ることもできそうにありません。

ある夜、夢を見ました。赤鬼が鉄棒をもって小蝶を打たんとしています。小蝶は笑い笑い、八方に体をかわす。赤鬼はとうとうグタグタに疲れて倒れてしまいました。目が覚めて、私は悟りました。これだ、これが極意だ、と考え、連さんに、いつでも試合を致します、と申し上げたのです。

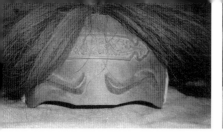

私は26歳、体重20貫。彼は体重37貫、六尺二寸、32歳とのことでした。

6月のことでした。二十畳敷の道場にて、古礼に則り、試合が始まりました。彼が飛ぶこと、天地左右二間余り、私も同じくらい飛びました。やがて彼は一撃の下に私を倒さんと考え、私もまた両手さえ彼に近づければ、極意によって一撃の下に倒せると思い、互いに入り乱れました。彼が飛び来たれば、我は左右に体を転じ、彼の隙に我飛び込めば、彼は高く飛び上がる。こうして一時間余り。彼は額に汗を流し、一方、真夏に60人の門人に教え続けても、一滴の汗も流さなかった私は、このときも汗は出ませんでした。

ついに連さんが割って入り、試合は引き分けました。そして連さんの仲介で、二人は兄弟分となりました。やがて、彼は私のためならば、百里の道を飛んできたものです。

人間と下等動物を比較すれば、まず第一に、人間は笑うことができます。人間は怒らず、目をむかず、やむをえぬときは死は万変であり、不驚でしょう。第二に、下等動物は笑うことはできません。牙をならし、眼を怒らせ、死にものぐるいで飛びかかるが、もう駄目だと思ったら、恥もなく鳴いたりするでしょう。

下等動物は豪放です。まして人間である忍者は豪放かつ沈勇でなければならないのです。」

蒙古の虎、高松先生と猫

いま私は、世界にたくさんの立派な武友があり、武風に吹かれて幸福な日々を送っている。去る日、こんなお便りを、高松先生から頂いたものである。

▼昭和37年11月7日の便り
「初見氏は武道家として最も勝れた点がある。人間は、精神の勝れた者を真の達人と言う。」(筆者注・精神とは正心、生心、精心とも書ける)

▼昭和36年12月12日
「昨11日、テレビに映っているのを拝見しました。上出来でした。人間は度胸です。そう、過日、門弟の一人と話しました。私がいささかでも教えた者の数は過去数千人と言っても誤りではないだろうが、初見氏ほどの度胸のある者は一人もない。度胸があり、技も

何もできるのである。私は少しの度胸があったため、数十度の試合に、また真剣の場にて、一度も負けをとらなかったのだと思います。」

蒙古の虎と謳われた頃の高松先生を知る人が、数十年ぶりに高松先生と会われたとき、次のように言った。「高松はん、まあ久しぶりやな。やあ、驚きました。なんやら蒙古の虎と言われたお人が、猫になりよったな!」と言う。高松先生は笑って答える。「そや、猫になりまったな。猫になるとよろしいおますな。女子(おなご)の膝の上にのって、ぬくうおます(温かい)で、よう眠れますねん。日光・東照宮の眠り猫やな……」と。

アメリカの作家ジョン・スタインベックは言う。「天才とは、蝶を追っていつのまにか山頂に登っている少年である」と。

首売り女

織田信長(1534-82)は、敵将の頭蓋骨を盃にして、勝利に酔ったと言う。人類は勝利の首(しるし)として、敗者の首や肉体の一部を切り取って、勲證(勲章)として、それを誇りとしたものである。

関ケ原の戦いの前、信州上田の城主、真田昌幸の城攻めの際に、徳川秀忠の家来の武士たちが一番槍を競った、上田七本槍の話がある。戦いが終わり、勇者七人、そのうち六名が敵の首をもって、その勇姿を誇っていた。

「御子神典膳(みこがみてんぜん)(後の小野次郎右衛門忠明)殿、おぬしは剣の道に秀でていると聞いたが、このたびの合戦では首一つ持参しておらぬではないか、のう」と、六名。

御子神典膳が答えて言う。「修羅場の中で、一人一人の首を打ち掻く暇などございませんぞ、のう。手前は六名の者を打ち取っておりますぞ。その首の耳の下に、手前が打ち取った印がのう、鮮やかな傷跡として残してある故、ご安心あれ」。

戦場の夢の跡を、首を拾って商う女がいた。鎧や兜の優れたものを着けた武士の死骸の首を斬りとって、髪を整え、よく洗い、傷を縫い、酒壺に漬け込んでおき、武士の縁者が探しに来たら、金子(きんす)に代えていたと言う。

戦闘の残酷さは浮世絵師、月岡芳年(1839-92)が描き出している。

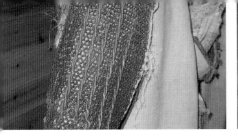

第四章　心技体

心技体

　実戦のほとんどなくなった江戸時代ですら、外部の者が道場の稽古場をのぞいただけで、痛めつけられたり、あるいは殺されかねない事態が生じたものである。悪人が万一にも技を悪用するならば危険であると考え、悪人への防禦態勢をとったのである。武道は殺人技にあらず。人を生かす術と見ることのできぬ者に対しての戒めであった。

　常識から離れた人物は奇人にあらず。生人である。それを貴人と言う。

　武道においては、長年の実戦の中で積み重ねられた、戦いのための心技体は、口伝として、その経験者が、伝授するにふさわしい人物のみに口頭で伝えたものである。そして、そうした必要なもの、大切なものを文章で記し、伝書として渡したのである。

　近頃私は、その心技体という三つのものを統べる、「才能」と「魂」と「器」が大切であると説いている。

　昔は本当に会得した武道を伝達する機関はなかったと言ってもよいだろう。そのために、客観的に武道を解説することができず、いうなれば空想の世界から作り上げた譚や芸能によって武道の常識を作り上げてしまった。というよりも、大多数の人たちがそれらを確信してしまったのである。

　最近では、一般に暴力はよくないものとされ、暴力を遠ざけて、暴力を否定する傾向が強い。そんな時代に於いて、武道を間違って暴力と見なし、悪と思いこむ人たちが少なくない。武道は過去に於いて誤解され、現在はさらにまた誤解されている。ダブルの誤解が、そこに悟怪できぬ現世における愚かさがある。

　昔、悪党（悪い奴。強い者という意味もある）と言われた地侍たちが武力によって領国を持つようになり、やがて天下をとろうとするほどの力を持つに至った。そうした中で人々は、一家の平和を切実に求めていたのである。動物は群れを作り、生き抜くものだ。

　映画俳優などにしても、最初の頃は悪役を演じていたものの、名をなしてからは悪役から脱して、名優となった者は少なくない。黒澤明監督の「酔いどれ天使」で闇市のやくざを演じた三船敏郎しかり。同じく黒澤映画の「生きる」の名演技で知られる志村喬しかり。映画デビュー作は悪役だった。ジャック・パランス、アンソニー・クイン、ジェームス・キャグニー等々を思い浮かべれば、このことは肯けるに違いない。

　哲学者ジョルジュ・ソレルが、無抵抗の人ガンジーに向かって、「あらゆる革命は、暴力によってなしとげられる」と語ったならば、ガンジーはなんと答えたであろうか。

稽古は精神的な病から戦士を守る

　一人の武友が、こう私に語りかけた。――

　いったい、何人のいわゆる武道家戦士が、命を奪うのは病的な行為だということを理解しているのだろうかと思います。先生はいつも、武道は命を「守る」ものだとおっしゃってきました。ハンフリー教授もそうでした。それはまさしく真実だと思います。私は武神館の、他とは異なる稽古方法と、ハンフリー教授の哲学を合わせたものが、人が人を殺すという病的な行為の解毒剤になることを学びました。

　これはとても重要なことです。私はなぜわれわれが、他のスポーツ武道やペーパー武道と違った稽古をしているのか、ようやく少し理解することができました。

　戦士は、命を守るために殺さなければなりません。稽古は、命を奪うことによって受ける精神的な病から、戦士を守ってくれると思います。私はこのことを、やっとこの歳になって悟りましたが、この重要なことを若い人たちに伝えていけると思います。心から感謝しております。

あそびと実戦

　私は初めての外遊の時代から、プレイという言葉を使った。武道の本質を知らせるための一段階としての行為である。遊びのない暴力には悲劇があるからだ。その行動は交動化して、私を指して、キュートボーイと呼んだ。

　犬や猫など動物の子の様子を見ればよくわかることだが、人間の子供たちが遊び戯れる行為は、成人してからの、闘うため、生きるため、食うための、実戦「遊び」稽古である。親離れしてからは、その子供の頃のプレイの思い出が、実戦のときにオーバーラップされて、成長するとともに、遊びの恐ろしさを自覚してくるものである。

柳生新陰流の達人とされる柳生宗矩が無刀捕りを演じたという文章を読んだら、闘いを避ける無刀捕りである、と勘じなければならない。無刀捕りの真義とは「生命をおびやかす武器を捕る、それを察知する能力が必要であるということだ」とわかってくるはずだ。故に、人を稽古中でも傷つけることがないように、袋竹刀を用いたのである。そこで、無刀捕りを無闘捕りと書けば、この理はより明瞭におわかりになると思う。

ここで、遊びを知る者は人生の至宝にありという、孔子の一言が聞こえてくる。

武芸を通して、演武で武道を語り、表現するには、今まで以上に演技演出に力を注ぐ必要がある。それも伝承のひとつの姿である。武芸十八般ならずとも歌舞伎十八番に恥じぬ、名優の位として名優たらんとする者の演武が必要とされるのである。

ある女性画家の言葉

90歳の女性画家が言う。「絵とは描き上げるごとに、捨てるものである、と私は思っている」と。

稽古においても、それと同じことが言えるに違いない。私は、毎日のように弟子たちに稽古をつけているが、二度と同じ稽古をしたことがない。また、その稽古の場では、これまで覚え込んだ常識と非常識、その双方をすっぱりと忘れ去りなさい、とも言っている。忘却されることにより、心技五体の新陳代謝を旺盛にして、武風一貫できる健康体を維持するには不可欠のものだ。

そうすることによって、武道と人生の極意の唄「山川の末に流るる橡殻も　身を捨ててこそ浮ぶ瀬もあれ」の語韻が響き、体内を活性化するのである。

師恩に報いる

鴨長明（1155–1216）の随筆『方丈記』の冒頭「ゆく河の流れは絶えずして、しかももとの水にあらず。よどみに浮かぶうたかたは、かつ消え、かつ結びて、久しくとどまりたる例なし」は名文として知られている。私はその冒頭の句に対応させて、「来る雲の流れも絶えずして」と言いたい。龍は雲を呼ぶからである。

琳派を代表する尾形光琳（1658–1716）の名作「風神雷神図屏風」の詞韻は、俵屋宗達の傑作「風神雷神図屏風」から流れる風雲と、その伝雷の稲妻によって写し出されたものである。そして、その映像が絵となって琳派の流れが生まれたのだが、以心伝心ならぬ「絵心伝心」されるその姿は、武道の道を継承する様にも似た、武雲武運たる光景が描けるのである。

高松寿嗣先生が少年の頃、師の戸田真龍軒先生の伝書を何回も師命により書き写したと、私が春日和に聞いたことがある。そして高松先生は、話の最後に「初見はんにこれで全部伝えたによってな、師恩に報いることができました」と言われたのである。恩は音なり。それからの私は、詩吟を毎日口ずさんだものである。

慈言を遠く聞く78歳の今、私が今日あるのは、恩賜師の師恩と、そしてまた弟子の子恩のおかげであり、そこに「師・我・弟子」という縦の柱と「父・我・母」という横の柱とで十字を見せる四恩がある。

牛の画伯

牛の絵を描き続けた日本画家の奥村土牛画伯（1889–1990）は高松寿嗣先生と同じ丑年に生まれた方で、八十路を越されたとき、次の言葉を残している。「これからも初心忘れず、拙くとも生きた絵を描きたい。難しいことではあるが、それが念願であり、生き甲斐だと思っている。芸術に完成はあり得ないが、要はどこまで大きく未完成で終わるかである。余命は少ないが、一日一日を大切に精進したい」（随想『牛の歩み』）と。

また、世阿弥（1363？–1443）の「八十歳にして初心に帰る」という一言が、同調した詞韻となって導く。

私は土牛画伯のこの一節に大いに共感している。私はいろいろの型で武芸を表現しているが、高松先生もきっと四つの胃（意）をもつ牛の歩みで、私に武芸を伝授してくださったものであろう。牛が歩む牛歩は、「義勇歩」を示す。

画の好きな高松先生があるとき、「わてはな、井戸の中に一人入っていても、絵を描いているときが楽しおます」と語った。煙草の煙は雲魂にあり。そこにある高松先生の微笑は、神々の古里の古道を歩まれる姿として、私の前から消えることはない。「要は、どこまで未完成で生きていけるかということが人としての味わいなんでしょうな、魅力というものはな」。そう、師は語りかけるのだ。そのいさぎよさが武士の美学でもある。

霊峰富士の絵で知られる横山大観（1868–1958）画

伯は、「絵というものは、山水を描いても、花鳥を描いても、宇宙が描けなかったら、芸術とは言えないよ」と、天霊地気の秘を語る。

土牛先生は曲がったことは心から憎み、正しいことを常に行うよう心掛け、慈父のごとくやさしく人に接したという。高松先生の言われた、武人の心、花精竹性のごとしであった。

武道の極意を得ようとする人は多いが、それを武道の中だけで見つけようと思っても、ピントがあってこないものである。ではどうしてピントを合わせるのか、と問われれば、次の如くお答えしよう。

それは、武芸者としての神心、神眼のナビゲーターを備えて、武士道を駆けることである。武芸道と武士道、その二道を虚実として、転換ならぬ転勘を養ったところにこそ、極意へ、そしてその象があるからである。プラトンが言う理想の国家芸術追放論や、アイ・ウェイウェイさんがデザインした「鳥の巣」スタジアムに見られるごとく、時代ごとに極意があるよう（要）に……。

桜は桜、梅は梅と言うが、本当だろうか

人間には個性という象がある。従って、子供を教育するにも、「個性を伸ばす教育が必要だ」と叫ばれる。まことに、ごもっともな意見であって、どんな子供にも、その独自の存在を特質づける個性がある。桜は桜、梅は梅、太郎は太郎、花子は花子、みな個性をもっているから、その個性を生かすように、といわれる。

媒材に合わせる、媒材なりに生かす。それが自然律である。

しかしながら、花を見て、また松の緑を見て、みな個性であると一様に思うのはいかがなものであろうか。同じ松の木であっても、枝振りの良いものもあれば、良くないものもある。たしかにそれは共に個性といえるが、私は取り柄のある個性は伸ばしていくのもよろしいが、かっこの悪い松の個性は、剪定と習慣づけによって直るのだから、改めていくのが本当だと思う。良い個性は伸ばし、悪い個性は矯正するのが本当の姿だ。盆栽を見れば、そのことがよくわかる。

その昔、宗門と武門の道を通り抜けたというならば、それは表鬼門から裏鬼門を駆け抜けるナビゲーターを見る思いがする。

武道はスポーツにあらず。だが、武道をスポーツと見なす傾向も少なくはない。

今、教育は学力や個性を競う「競育」になってしまっている。そんな環境では、子供たちは人間らしく成長しない。武風の一例を上げれば、ゼロ歳から6歳までは、健康に生きる期間、6歳から12歳まではしつけの時期、13歳から18歳までは戦乱に通じる時期と見なす。これらの時期を「武競争」で健全にすごしてこそ、武芸十八般と同格の道が開けてくるものである。
「義は武の徳で、武芸の根本、軍法射御兵法は芸で、武徳の枝葉とされると翁は言う」（中江藤樹の『翁問答』より）

宗教は衆境の先達先道を行きて、その道をナビゲーターで見る。道の近くに道場があり、武道への道はどこにあるのですか、と聞く。ここですか。師答えて曰く、「五十畳が古式に則った道場なり」と。「悟十生の道場なり！」と。ここで鬼も十八、番茶も出花、さくらんぼの甘さと、梅の酸っぱさ、甘酸っぱい初恋の味に触れて、思わず「若いのう」と翁が言う、『武道初心集』の姿が見えてこないだろうか。

十牛図

私は友からいただいた、底部には円相が、胴には十牛図が描かれている抹茶茶碗を愛用している。妙心寺派管長であった山田無文老師（1900-88）の作品である。十牛図とは禅の修行と悟りの段階を十図の牛の絵に表したものである。武道では修行者の段位があり、一般に初段から十段までとしているが、そうした段位もこれにつながっている。お茶をすすりながら、十年一昔の話を語り合う喜びを味わうのもよかろう。茶道と武道、そして禅を結ぶ円相と、一からゼロに通じる十の段階に思いを巡らすのは楽しい。

十牛図に画かれた陶器で茶を一服、その静寂の茶（差）は戦国の戦場での闘気を養う茶禅一如の瞬間であった。

武道は文化であり、かつまた芸術である。かといって文化芸術が優位とはいかない。武道を学ぶ者が強いとか弱いということばかりにとらわれていると、その人生ははかないもので終わってしまう。

まず十という字を分析してほしい。10は1と0である。ゼロはすべてであり、そして一はゼロのつながるゼロの象。すなわち万物とは一のつながりに他ならない。そこで和尚が語った、「あなたはあなたです。私は私で

す」の、釈迦の「天上天下唯我独尊」の虚実の風韻、「転浄転我勇雅独尊」が聞こえてくるのである。

強弱も柔剛も、ともに虚実、明暗、陰陽の世界のものである。「強弱柔剛あるべからず、故に此の心を離れ、空の一字を悟り」とあるのは、己を空にしてこそ、円明なるインスピレーションが生まれてくることを述べているのである。故に私は、空間においた姿を「アイアムユーフォー」と言っていたのである。

正義という一字がよく使われる。だが、この正義を分析してみると、

一、一見して常識的であっても、じつのところ常識的でない正義と言われる象。

二、非常識と常識がぶつかりあっている正義の象。

三、非常識と非常識がぶつかりあっている正義だという象。

この三つがあることに気がつく。常識で理解できる正義は、一つの象ではないということだ。三つの象を見てみることである。

オクターブの秘音

オクターブ、それはCDEFGABCの八音の世界にある、両端のCの音を同時に奏でたときに発する美音である。この八音は、仏教で言う八正道であり、武道で言う基本八法でもあろう。CとCの間には、DEFGABの六音が黙視している。この六音は、地獄、餓鬼、畜生、修羅、人間、天の迷界があり、布施、持戒、忍辱、精進、禅定と、人が修業すべき六波羅蜜との六音と共に浄化されていく。

オクターブ、すなわちCとCとの同音。これは師弟の姿であり、武友の姿なのでもあろう。死してなお同行二人は、四国を巡礼する。オクターブの秘音が極意の音を知らせてくれると武芸者が言う。

悟り、これはCとCで結ばれた韻が時を知らせる。はじめに基本八法というスタートの扉が開かれる。続いて八法秘剣の幕が開かれる。名曲がオクターブで奏でられたとき、三心の型がキャロル・リードの「第三の男」の名曲へと一変する。

鏡と曲玉と剣から成る三種の神器ならぬ三種の人技は、肉食と草食と霞を食う。それを戦国時代における男食と断食と霞の法と見てとることもできる。これを三心の型で解いてみるのも一興であろう。

武道の種

大泥棒・石川五右衛門の辞世の句は「石川や浜の真砂は尽きるとも、世に盗人の種は尽きまじ」とされている。私が弟子を取り始めた頃は、弟子に教えるというより、自分自身の自己学修のようなものであった。そして50年、何万粒という種を世界に撒き、210本の木が育った。「権兵衛が種まきゃカラスがほじくる」、そんな唄を聞きながら、カラスでなく、人間が種を食っている姿も見ることがあった。

そこで武道の信化（進化）論を一言。種は撒かれたまま眠ってしまうことがある。そしていつまでも眠っていられるものもいれば、夢の中で食われるものや、発芽できず腐ってしまうものある。動物の熊太郎君も冬眠する。蛇も蛙も、我が家で40数年飼育している亀7匹も、冬が来ると眠っている。

今も鳥が、私の撒いた種を食っている。しかし、今でも私は、鳥を追い払うことなく眺めている。自然律を見たからである。その鳥は、食った種を糞とともにへり出す。その糞の中から、新芽を出して生長している木気の姿も見るからである。

武風一貫の風が吹いてくると、木々が騒ぐ。大木の年輪には極意を会得した印が残されている。

宮本武蔵がたけぞうと言われた若き日、松の大木に吊され、沢庵に諭されている。夕日が落ちる頃、鳥が松の木のてっぺんに止まって、アホー、アホーと騒いでいる。お杉ばばあが、怒りのまなこでたけぞうを見上げている、お杉花粉症——こんな回想が、異説となって愛読されている。

私の武道十五段、年輪と共に太く成長する150本の友木（勇気）が、いまの時代、オゾン層を抜ける強い光を守る影を作っていてくれる。鳥も大木の陰に止まっている。その木はなぜ松かといえば、人間は「待つ」という、忍耐と努力の時代を夢中に過ごすことがあるからだ、耐えがたきを耐えた時に発見した極意の数々がそこにある、と私は言いたい。

テレビで放映してから20年、このたびDVD化した「世界忍者ジライヤ」のワンシーン。山地哲山の「邪悪な欲望を捨てろ、毒斎！」の一喝に、毒斎の子分の烏天狗たちは「そうでやんす！」とへこたれる。

トスカニーニと観客

イタリアの指揮者トスカニーニ（1867-1957）さんは、音楽は聴くものだとおっしゃる。ならば私は、「五線譜に伝書を書きましょう」と言おう。そして、「トスカニーニさんは、指揮をなさっているときは、観客に背を向けている。私には、演奏者は味方であり、観客は後ろから攻めてくる敵のように見えますね」と。

「五段のテストのとき、武神館では十五段の極くらいに達した者が、五段を受けようと覚悟を決めた者を、自分の前に背中向きに座らせ、十五段の者が後方より武念を発し、と言いましょうか、影の気合とも言うのですが、一刀を斬り下ろす。それをかわした者が昇段を許されるのです。これは識の世界の指揮武曲です。

私の場合ですか、この老体でありながら、たえず高松先生の影が、私の存在する命体につながり、高松先生の影が葉隠れとなり、一休の日陰を作ってくれる。そんな日々が幸運の道を示してくれて、何か高松先生に護られているという安心感が、そこにはあるのです。高松先生という大樹の下でいまペンを進めている。トスカーニさんは何よりも影（聴衆）の感動を求めました。私も影の力で生きています。

三尺下がって師の影を踏まず、という格言（鶴言）も、そこにはあるのです。

変想術と変争術

哲学者で女性を哲学的に論書（諸）した者は三名しかいないという。ショーペンハウエルの『女について』、ボーヴォワールの書いた『第二の性』（では、第一の性は？　第三の性は？　とも聞きたくなる）、そしてジンメルが『女性文化史』を著している。

男女の差について、SとかMではなく、平常心で、かつ暴力的にいうならば、肉体的には男性が七、女性が三、精神的には、あるいは神経的には、男性が三で、女性が七という、一般的な哲学で男女は生きている。

七対三といえば、忍者が変装するときには、七方三法型というものを用いている。このことは、変装という字を変えて、変想術、あるいは変争術と解けば、うなずけるであろう。

戦の仏を三面の姿で表す場合がある。例えば阿修羅像、摩利支天、大黒天像である。大黒天の顔の側面というか、左右に弁財天、毘沙門天があり、この三体が一体

となって、護身像としてつくられている。

いま私は、極意の表現の三法として、絵で表現してみたり、写真で表現ひようとしたり、写真に合わせて字を変体させて感じてもらう、そんな手法でいきたいと思っている。そこで漫画を万画とし、それを逆にすると、我慢となる。そう、我慢こそが万画を描くうえでの、多得る（耐える）力となるのだ。

武道の極意書

宮本武蔵が武道の極意書として『五輪書』をしたためているが、地水火風空の五つの巻物に記された文字をいくら読んでも、極意はつかめないものである。仏教でも、地水火風空の五つに識を加えて、説いている。

宮本武蔵の識の時代の遺作の絵や不動明王像などを見ていると、武蔵が求めていた極意の文字が、空間の世界、識の世界に写し出されてくる。文字、活字よりも、イメージ（意目異示）の方角へ寄り揃う。活字、すなわち決まり事や勝字ばかり求めていると、「虚実」が、虚の一字、あるいは実の一字だけとなってしまい、終着駅に一人たたずむことになってしまうが、識は超越の世界に向けて指揮をしてくれるからである。

山本常朝の「武士道とは死ぬことと見つけたり」の言葉については、すでに触れたが、人間は識を忍ぶ死悸（死期）を自覚することは大切なことである。巨象は、死悸を知ると、象の群れから離れて、死に場所に赴くという。巨は「大きな」、象は「カタチ」と読むように、それは死という瞬間（旬間）における巨匠巨人の姿と理解できる。

そこで宮本武蔵の『五輪書』と、井原西鶴（1642-93）の『日本永代蔵』や『世間胸算用』の三冊を、たまには武芸書と見てみるのもよいものである。西鶴は俳諧師であり、浮世草子の作者でもある町人だが、彼の作風には、武士の才覚（西鶴）に通じるものがある。戦乱の世も平和な日々も、乱世と見て、いつも死生のはざまに生きているんだということをたまには両眼で見てみることである。

九死に一生と万が一

「九死に一生」という言葉があるが、武士道の心構えにおいて、玉が散る玉砕という十死の音からは闘士を連想

する。それを闘う武士と解く。すなわち闘詩には「九字を許すも十字を許さず」の掟が秘められている。闘うことを許さずの深（信）意があるのである。『八犬伝』の八つの玉が光る。

　十年一昔、万死に値するという諺の中に、九死に一生、万が一の門をくぐり抜けた闘士の残した極意も消える。

　独眼竜の武道家が、「やよう、おぬしは、八百万を透視する眼力をおもちか」と問えば、世界の宗門（宗教）、哲門（哲学）、思門（思想）、教門（教育）の四門が閉門されて玄武、青龍、朱雀、白虎の門が死門から幸運の門へ変わるものじゃ、と謎の風水師がささやく……。明路も迷路も暗夜行路が生門に導く。フラッシュ、ストロボ、シャッター、稲妻、土門拳が切る。

　八百万の門を自在に稲妻の如く閃くままに行く、門を開閉する閃道者（先道者）に問わねばなるまい。すると、「奇門を行く閃道者を武芸者とでもいおうぞい」と独眼竜の免許皆伝の武道家に答えるであろう。「一番鎗じゃ！」

波のこと

　口絵に「那須与一・なぎのかちどき」の絵を掲げた。イギリス人建築家ジョサイア・コンドルの師として知られる日本画家の河鍋暁斎、その跡を継いだ暁雲による絵である。那須与一が波間で平家の軍船の的を射落とす光景が描かれているが、私は渚の描写のあまりにも見事なことに圧倒された。波にはなぎ倒す、肝心要の意味がある。

　那須与一のこの射法は、的を射抜いたのではなく、扇の要、平家軍の要を意抜き、源氏を勝利に導くものであった。

武道家と禅師

　武道家が禅師の導きによって悟る話は少なくない。

　剣禅一如のみならず、武禅一如、茶禅一如、芸禅一如、悪善一如という言葉もある。私は一如を一助とも書いている。じつは剣禅一助のほうが正しいのである。武道家は、禅師の言葉を全部鵜呑みにするのではなく、一つの助けにするようでなければいけない。

　さて、「禅」の一字を分解してみると、「単」に「示

す」ということから、胆（たん、きも）を示すと思えばよい。沢庵和尚（1573-1646）は『玲瓏集』に、こんなことを書き残している。

　「この世において最も重要なことは、欲と生と義である。しかし、欲っていうものは生命を保つためにするのじゃから、欲より命の方が位が上なのじゃな。だがな、義ってものはな、ときとしては、義のためには命は惜しんではな、そんな腰抜けではあきまへんのや。義のためには、命なんちゅうものは捨てんとあかんこともあるのや。人間、この世に生まれてきたのも、目的はそれやで…そやかて命を軽んじてはあきまへん。…本当の義を重んずる本当の欲、すなわち宝の欲を大切にするんやで……」

　沢庵和尚は権門に道を説いたが、自分から権門をくぐろうとはしなかった。沢庵は臨済宗の僧で、紫衣事件で幕府と抗争して出羽に配流されたが、後に許された。沢庵は、俳諧、茶に通じた人で、代表作に『不動智神妙録』がある。

　また、仁王禅、にらみ禅と言われた鈴木正三（1579-1655）という禅僧が書いた『盲安杖』がある。正三は徳川家康に仕えて、関ケ原の役や大阪夏の陣で戦功を立てた武者であったが、元和六年に出家した。徳川家の浄土真宗の寺を多く建てて、自分の奉ずる曹洞宗の寺一つを建てているが、彼はそれにとらわれず、無宗派的な行動をとっていた。正三には、「身を思うこころぞ身をば苦しむる　身を思わねば身こそやすけれ」の禅風が吹いていた。

　以下は『盲安杖』に説かれた処世の信条十ヵ条である。

　　生死を知って楽しみがある。
　　おのれを顧みて、おのれを知る
　　物事に他の心に至るべきこと
　　信あって患者を励むべきこと
　　分限を見わけて、その性々を知るべきこと
　　住するところを離れて、徳あること
　　おのれを忘れて、おのれを守るべきこと
　　立ち上がりて、ひとり慎むべきこと
　　心をほろぼして、心をそだつべきこと
　　小利を捨てて、大利に至るべきこと

　夢窓国師は『夢中問答』のなかで戦争の罪悪について強調している。民衆のためになる徳行を説きながら、死者の霊を弔うため、諸国に安国寺利生塔を建てて、天龍

寺の開山となった。

　さて私事となるが、豊岡村に、高松先生の碑、ならびに私が継承した九流派の供養塔、武神館道場の供養塔を「献設」、平成20年に開山供養を行っている。

大僧正位　白龍寿宗

厄年と鬼門は躍年と生門と思え

　弟子の一人が、「今年は厄年なので、初詣に行ってきました。先生の護摩札も頂いてきました」と新年の挨拶にやってきた。「いやあ、ありがとう！」、その心がうれしい。厄年とは人生に於いて、厄（苦しみ、災い、災難、生死に繋がる現象）にあう恐れが多いから、忌み慎まねばならないとされている年で、男性は25、42、60歳で、女性は19と33歳だといわれ、その大厄の前後の年を前厄、後厄と言って、恐れ、用心している。そこで厄払いと言って、神仏に祈って厄を祓い落して除けるということを祈願するのである。

　私の42歳の男の大厄の年には、高松先生がお亡くなりになっている。その頃の私は、厄年ってあるんだな、とただそれだけを考えていたのだが、78歳になった現在、私の42歳の大厄年は、高松先生と一体となれた躍年なんだ、と訳せるようになっている。

　言うなれば厄年の災難、苦しみ、悲しみ、それを忍耐することによって、厄が薬と化して、良薬となるのだ。厄年とは、人生で人の器を大きくする、悟る場でもあるのである。麻雀でも、ヤクがつくと、「イーハンついた、リャンハンついた、スーハンついて満貫あがり」などと言うものだ。

　厄年と同じように、多くの人が気にするものに鬼門がある。丑寅（北東）の方角のことで、忌む方角と見なされている。京都でも江戸でも街造りに当たっては、この方角に鬼門よけの寺社が建てられたと言われている。だが、鬼門とは生門である、と言う度胸が明日の生命の門となるのである。

虚実現象の変化

　「アモ一寸の玉虫」と呪文を唱えて、蜂を握って捕ると、蜂は針を使うことをやめるという。サソリを口の中に入れて口を結ぶと、サソリも毒針を使わないで生死（静止）するという。極意の裏技を示す自然奇然があ

る。まさにファーブルの『昆虫奇』である。

　これは大自然の、不動心の教えにもつながると思ってもよいだろう。アモとは天照大神のことをいうと、古文書には記されている。玉虫、スカラブは不死虫とアフリカでは喩えられている。アフリカ戦線で活躍したＳＡＳのジョー・ボーン少佐より贈られた不死虫を、私は大切にしている。昆虫ならず塊虫である。

　「虫も殺さぬようなヤツが、とんでもないことをした」という話を耳にすることがあるが、最近、働き蜂が消える蜂群崩壊症候群が世界に広がり、果物や野菜の生産が低下しているという。

　「代自然」は世々変わる。その変化の中で生き続けられる肝心要も会得させるためにも、この変化のテーマは毎年変化させることが大切と思い、私は一年ごとに九年間、そして九流派の極意とすることについての伝承を教え、次には九流派の空間について一年、次には空間につながる縄の意図について指導した。即ち状態（縄体）術の武風自然論となっている。さて、その次は、と問われれば、禄魂笑浄と答えよう。

性と暴力の自然体とは

　暴力は見え隠れして生きる魔物である。用兵、備兵、要兵と、時は変える。武器を使う時、匠は見せる武器と、見せない武器とマジックする。映画監督のビリー・ワイルダーは、巧みに小道具を使い分けて、見事な映像を演出した。小津安二郎監督も、演出に際して、小道具を出演者の一人として登場させ、品格を醸し出している。

　男だけの兵士の部隊では、強姦しようとする輩が出てくる恐れもあるので、アフリカのリベリアに駐屯する女性だけの部隊は、男性だけの部隊よりも評価されている。がしかし、と言えば、うなずく人もあるだろう。

　凡人には本能の流れは、意のままにならないものである、そう思うことは分別がないからだと思ってみるがよい。すると、内因外因から生じる悪い事柄や、不安だと思い込んでいる小心が吹っ飛び、消えていくものである。

　戦国の武将・山中鹿之助は「我に七難八苦を与え給え」と三日天下の戦雲に光る三日月に祈ったという。そこに山中鹿之助の武士の時代が見え隠れして、月岡芳年の「月百姿」の幕末を見る。「和をもって貴しとなす」

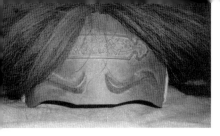

と聖徳太子が言う。私にはそれが「倭（日本）をもって貴しとなす」防人（さきもり）への語りにも聞こえてくる。

機械と人間

ラ・メトリは『人間機械論』において、人間はきわめて複雑な機械であり、自らゼンマイを巻く機械であり、経験を積んだ機械であり、素直に立っている機械であるなどと発表している、デカルトの「動物機械論」にも同意している。

現在私には、ロボット化されていく武道や、無人兵器を用いだした、いまの人類に対し、生物奇怪論に立って、王道を極めていかなければ、恐ろしい時代に突入していくのではないかと思われてならない。

そんな機会の時である。時の三針が知らせる。時分秒の三心の型、それは三心に組み込まれている。地水火風空の五大は、十五段の道を一貫させる。それを伝書に書き込ませるためには、カタカナ、ひらがな、漢字で表現する。そして、その裏書きには、古き神代文字、ひふみよと始まる出雲文字、と、あいうえおで始まる倭文字、等々。ワープロ、コンピュータといった機械では自覚透視できないのが人間である。

漢字は一字音によって八変化する。上代には、武士を防人、護り人、と言っていたということを見逃してはならない。天武天皇は、八色（やくさ）姓（のかばね）という八つの姓を制定した。

今は亡き強者たち

寿命の輝きを無量に見せて、西方浄土にある極楽浄土へと導いてくださる阿弥陀様という御仏がいらっしゃるそうな。そうそう、今考えると、生まれ育った土地から見ると、西方奈良に住まわれた高松先生のお宅へ、武道の極意を求めて、汽車に乗った私は、27歳の青年になるまで、無明の路を走り続けていた。27歳のある日、阿弥陀如来が高松先生に化身して私を来迎してくださったのであろう。お迎えをいただいた私は、それが私の死出の旅路とも思わず、七難八苦六道の路をがむしゃらに歩いていたのですね。高松先生の慈顔慈魂のおかげで、今があります。

経を見るに、王が出家して法蔵と名乗り、比丘修行者となり、武風一貫した武風修行者となり、無量の智慧と

慈悲の心を会得し、法蔵四十八手を本願として、西方浄土、極楽をお作りになった阿弥陀様のお話があるが、いま考えると、27歳のとき、私は武士道とは死ぬことと見つけたというより、27歳にて死に、誕生したのだと思います。そう考えると、私はいま50歳ということになります

「虎倒流骨法術・極意の書」に書き残されている仏心、悟心、一念の三文字にも、こうした経路はうかがえる。

私の武友の弟子たちや友人が、癌を告知され、死ぬことを見つけ知りながら、身を忍び、心を忍び、識を忍んで、ともに浄土へ旅立った。その姿を見つめる私の瞼に浮かんでくる彼らの姿は、なぜか円空仏のように微笑を浮かべている。田中洋さん、佐川巌さん、東浦さん、ボニー・マルムストロムさん、ビング・フォードさん、グレン・モリスさん、デック・セベランスさん、アラン・コリンさん、ブッティ・ジョンソンさん……etc。

私は彼らに答えている。「武士道は土貫（しぬ）ことと見つけたり」をお先にと極意を得た君たちは、本当の強者（つわもの）でしたね、武士だったんだ、侍だよ、と。映画「おくりびと」の納棺士のように、彼らの武量（無量）なる寿命を祈り、その死の門出（かどで）を生涯胸に秘め、讃える日々である。

極意の木

源氏の守り神が鎌倉の弁天にあり。
平家の守り神が厳島弁天にあり。
それは、源平の盛衰の守護神とされている。
大黒天はインドでは最高の必勝の守護神とされている。武神館本部コミュニティセンター前に立つ大黒天像は、6トンの重量があり、武徳の金箔の文字が輝いている。
ゴータマ・シッダルタは29歳で出家。菩提樹の下で大悟し、仏陀と化し、釈迦牟尼となる。その日こそ12月8日だったという。そして相手の能力に応じて、教えを説いて歩いて80歳。
高松先生の碑のかたわらに、菩提樹の木を一本植えた。私も80歳を迎える日々を、葉陰で待つことにした。
武神館の2009年のテーマは、才能、魂、器である。これは相手の能力、弟子の能力に応じての、私の教え体（たい）オーラをスポットライトとして心技体を見せる、慈悲、辞秘（じひ）に近づく年なのである。

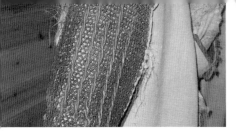

宇宙戦艦ノア出発

　私が九流派を継承し、それからの52年、七つの海の船旅も、彼岸に到らずとはいえ、ようやく悲願を成就した思いがする。高松先生が最初に許伝された言霊、今様の要神眼と思える「初見はんをわての愛門人として、ようきばりなさい！」の一言がいま語りかけられているような気がしてならない。

　ある日、私に子供がいない、できないと思われたのか、奥様がお茶を運んでくださった折り、高松先生は「初見はん、自分の子がおまへんでもな、縁がありまったらな！　人の子でも誰でも、子は愛情やさかいな！」と言われた。奥様も、「そやさかいな、初見はん、自分の子でのうても、お父はんのおっしゃるように、愛情さかいな！」と言葉を添えた。あのときのサウンドが今も耳に聴こえてくる。

　私の世界漫遊の船出の時も、世界の人たちに武道を知ってもらえばよい、と一人一人の武友たちに愛を第一として尋ね回ったのである。それは武道を知ってもらえばよいという愛だったのかもしれない。そして八つ目の海があることを知った今、アニメ「宇宙戦艦ヤマト」ならぬ「宇宙戦艦ノア」に乗ることに決めた。六十年前にスチールギターで爪弾いた「ハーバーライト♪」、今日はウクレレで奏でよう。

　私が高松先生から継承した九流派の先輩たちの供養塔は、闘詩の魂生の輝きを見せる灯台となり、武神館道場の供養塔は、武道家の心をひたすら貫いた武生（無償）の魂の光を放ち続けている。

　これらはマーシャルアーツを通して、武友と武友の永遠の愛を示す光とするためである。人間のつくったシステムは次々と崩壊している。その中でいま、地球を救う宇宙戦艦ノア号が出発する。シャンパンが爆音とともに八つの海に出航する。

　なぜか小津安二郎監督の秀作映画『秋刀魚の味』のサウンドに流れていた軍艦マーチが、老いの心に青春を甦らせて聞こえてくる。

　ノアの箱船には、武道の極意書、宮本武蔵の『五輪書』ならず、「武風はうつる日々に豹変する化け物である」と武神が記す『五臨の書』、すなわち剣、太刀、銃。刀、核、その五臨である臨兵闘者開陣烈在前方の奇魂を綴った一巻が載せられている。

Drawing by Hideo Shinoda ／絵・篠田英男

（英文版）武道の極意
The Essence of Budo

2011 年 3 月 29 日　第 1 刷発行

著　者　初見良昭

発行者　廣田浩二

発行所　講談社インターナショナル株式会社
　　　　〒112-8652　東京都文京区音羽 1-17-14
　　　　電話　03-3944-6493（編集部）
　　　　　　　03-3944-6492（マーケティング部・業務部）
　　　　ホームページ　www.kodansha-intl.com

印刷・製本所　大日本印刷株式会社

落丁本、乱丁本は購入書店名を明記のうえ、講談社インターナショナル業務部宛にお送りください。送料小社負担にてお取替えいたします。なお、この本についてのお問い合わせは、編集部宛にお願いいたします。本書の無断複写（コピー）は著作権法上での例外を除き、禁じられています。定価はカバーに表示してあります。

© 初見良昭 2011

本書のコピー、スキャン、デジタル化等の無断複製は著作権法上での例外を除き禁じられています。本書を代行業者等の第三者に依頼してスキャンやデジタル化することはたとえ個人や家庭内の利用でも著作権法違反です。

Printed in Japan
ISBN 978-4-7700-3107-5